READING JOHN KEATS

John Keats (1795–1821), one of the best-loved poets of the Romantic period, is ever alive to words, discovering his purposes as he reads – not only books but also the world around him. Leading Keats scholar Susan J. Wolfson explores the breadth of his works, including his longest ever poem *Endymion*; subsequent romances, *Isabella* (a Boccaccio tale with a proto-Marxian edge admired by George Bernard Shaw), the passionate *Eve of St. Agnes*, and knotty *Lamia*; intricate sonnets and innovative odes; the unfinished *Hyperion* project (Keats's existential rethinking of epic agony); and late lyrics involved with Fanny Brawne, the bright (sometimes dark) star of his last years. Illustrated with manuscript pages, title-pages, and portraits, *Reading John Keats* investigates the brilliant complexities of Keats's imagination and his genius in wordplay, uncovering surprises and new delights, and encouraging renewed respect for the power of Keats's thinking and the subtle turns of his writing.

SUSAN J. WOLFSON, Professor of English at Princeton University, is widely published in the fields of English Romanticism and poetic theory, including Keats-inspired sonnets in *Literary Imagination* (2010) and her books: *The Romantics and Their Contemporaries* (co-edited with Peter Manning, 2010), *Romantic Interactions: Social Being and the Turns of Literary Action* (2010), *Borderlines: The Shiftings of Gender in British Romanticism* (2006), *John Keats, A Longman Cultural Edition* (2006), *The Cambridge Companion to John Keats* (2001), and *Formal Charges: The Shaping of Poetry in British Romanticism* (1997).

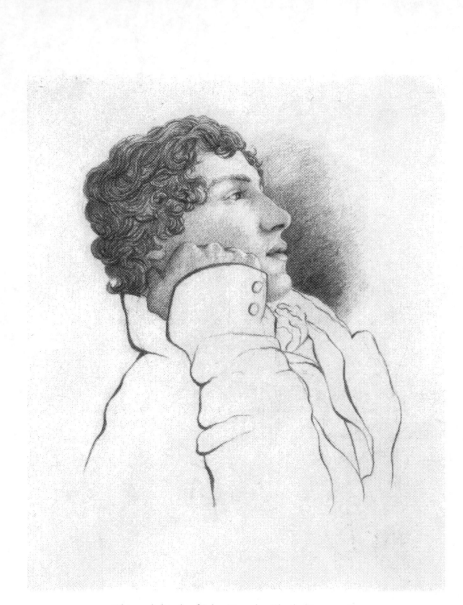

Charcoal sketch of John Keats by Charles Brown, 1819.
© National Portrait Gallery, London. Not published until the twentieth century, Charles
Brown's sketch of Keats in 1819 renders a handsome "young poet," big-fisted,
contemplative, self-possessed, the pose conscious of Richard Westall's famous profile of
Lord Byron (1813, after the overnight success of *Childe Harold's Pilgrimage*).

READING JOHN KEATS

SUSAN J. WOLFSON

CAMBRIDGE
UNIVERSITY PRESS

CAMBRIDGE
UNIVERSITY PRESS

University Printing House, Cambridge CB2 8BS, United Kingdom

One Liberty Plaza, 20th Floor, New York, NY 10006, USA

477 Williamstown Road, Port Melbourne, VIC 3207, Australia

314-321, 3rd Floor, Plot 3, Splendor Forum, Jasola District Centre, New Delhi - 110025, India

79 Anson Road, #06-04/06, Singapore 079906

Cambridge University Press is part of the University of Cambridge.

It furthers the University's mission by disseminating knowledge in the pursuit of education, learning and research at the highest international levels of excellence.

www.cambridge.org
Information on this title: www.cambridge.org/9780521732796

© Susan J. Wolfson 2015

First published 2015

A catalogue record for this publication is available from the British Library

Library of Congress Cataloging in Publication data
Wolfson, Susan J., 1948– author.
Reading John Keats / Susan J. Wolfson.
pages cm
Includes bibliographical references and index.
ISBN 978-0-521-51341-8 (hardback)
1. Keats, John, 1795–1821 – Criticism and interpretation. 1. Title.
pr4837.w654 2015
821'.7 – dc23 2014046184

ISBN 978-0-521-51341-8 Hardback
ISBN 978-0-521-73279-6 Paperback

for Jack Stillinger
my Keats teacher before he knew it and ever since

Contents

Figures

Preface

"The poetry of earth is never dead," wrote Keats in the dead of winter.[1] Let's say the same about the poetry of John Keats (1795–1821). It flourishes in edition after edition, on the walls of libraries and reading rooms, in book titles and popular songs, and in phrases we all know: "A thing of beauty is a joy for ever"; "tender is the night"; "alien corn"; "Beauty is truth; truth Beauty"; "season of mists and mellow fruitfulness"; "fanatics have their dreams." What if this talented young man had had the means to attend a university? He would have been a star student: vigorously underlining and annotating, eager to talk about his reading, rereading constantly, and probably petitioning for an interdisciplinary program in literature, philosophy, and medicine. Keats was a voracious reader, lived in books he said, had read *Hamlet* forty times (from his ease of reference, it's clear he had much of Shakespeare by heart). His letters bristle with his reading, not only in reports but in their very metaphors, figured as books, passages, and reading itself ("dark Passages"; the heart as a "horn-book"). He began writing poetry in his teens, with *Imitation of Spenser* (he read the entire *Faerie Queene*, a feat few professors today may claim); one of his first publications was a sonnet written after an all-nighter with George Chapman's 1616 translation of Homer's *Iliad* and *Odyssey*. To firm up his vocation, he sat down to reread Shakespeare's fiercest tragedy, *King Lear* – and wrote a sonnet on this event, too. Keats's poetry often pivots on events of reading – by turns, passionate, careful, interpretive, skeptical. Great literature, Keats knew, is intellectual vigor with aesthetic complexity, and it always rewards concentrated reading.

Keats-the-reader is also a critical rereader, and the lively density of his own poetry repays such attention. In *Reading John Keats* I attend to the actions of Keats's language and to how these activate our reading. *Reading John Keats* provokes us to reflect on what it is to read, fail to read, misread, reread, read better. Keats's favorite term for this energetic concentration is "intensity." He works out his most important thoughts and passions in the formings of language, in sentences, phrases, words, even syllables and letters. At these sites meanings accumulate, bear down, dovetail, and radiate anew. The Keats-archive includes his letters, a cache of correspondence serious and playful, thoughtful and reflective, full of affection for his brothers, sister, and his friends, his excitement about what he's been reading, his feel for solitude as well as society, his candor and intimacy, his views of the world, and his ironizing self-regard. The letters are often as well written as his poetry. Here Keats also found a medium for speculative thinking and critical formulations that are now part of our vocabulary – most famous of all, "negative capability."

Keats would be gratified by his fame today as a "poet's poet." Yet this emerged in no burst of éclat, but rather from a life of struggles and aspirations, and quite soon over – a career spanning little more than half a decade. When Keats proposed to his brother, "I think I shall be among the English poets after my death," he wasn't boasting, but braving a battery of bad reviews.[2] It would take a couple of decades even to glimpse the fame that is secure today. And it would take a couple of generations for decisive vindication. At the start of a "Lecture on the English Renaissance" (9 January 1882), Oscar Wilde declared that "it is in Keats that one discerns the beginning of the artistic renaissance of England. He was the forerunner of the pre-Raphaelite school, and so of the great romantic movement."[3] Wilde had already extended the line beyond this nineteenth-century arc. "It is a noble privilege to count oneself of the same race as Keats or Shakespeare," he had said in 1877.[4]

The pairing was getting credit. Matthew Arnold placed Keats "in the school of Shakspeare" in his "perfect treasure-house of graceful and felicitous words and images . . . vivid and picturesque turns of expression, by which the object is made to flash upon the eyes of the mind, and which thrill the reader with a sudden delight."[5] In 1884 Arnold's nephew introduced his edition of Keats by hailing the "phenomenon" of

> work produced in the brief twenty-six years of a young man's life, but which nevertheless has at its best reached a point of perfection which compels one critic to say that its author "is with Shakspere," and another great master of our tongue to confess that "I have come to that pass of admiration for him, that I dare not read him, so discontented he makes me with my own work."[6]

In 1883 Poet Laureate Tennyson gave Keats's "among" an upgrade: "He would have been among the very greatest of us if he had lived. There is something of the innermost soul of poetry in almost everything he ever wrote." He was willing to say (more than once) that Keats "promised securely more than any English poet since Milton."[7]

Such currency, such fame, was no lock in Keats's lifetime, when the most influential reviews ridiculed a "vulgar Cockney poetaster" reveling in "the most incongruous ideas in the most uncouth language."[8] This was partly political crossfire, and partly a reaction to the nexus in Keats's poetry of sensual intensity, poetic extravagance, and skeptical, ironic modernity. Some contemporaries (poets J. H. Reynolds and Leigh Hunt, painter B. R. Haydon, publisher John Taylor) were sure of his genius, and poet Shelley was warmly (if a bit patronizingly) supportive. Yet England's two leading poets, William Wordsworth and Lord Byron, though seeing some spark, were mostly cool to cruel. Wordsworth, flattered as he was by an early sonnet praising him as one of the age's great spirits, was terse when he met Keats and didn't even look into the 1817 *Poems* Keats sent to him, warmly inscribed "To W. Wordsworth, with the Author's sincere Reverence." Byron disliked "all the fantastic fopperies of his style," teased Shelley about the dreamy idioms and sensual gushing, fumed at the "depreciation of Pope," believed the fable of his collapse from fatal reviews, and ridiculed "Johnny Keats" for all these faults.[9] The tide of opinion did begin to shift in 1820 with Keats's last, best volume (including *Hyperion*, which Byron did like, and *Ode to a Nightingale*, *Ode on a Grecian Urn*, *Ode on Melancholy*, *To Autumn*); but even this brilliant publication was remaindered within a few years.

A poetic vocation was scarcely an open call to Keats. Wordsworth, Coleridge, Byron, Shelley: they all had university educations and connections (Cambridge and Oxford); Felicia Hemans, Keats's near contemporary, was home-schooled by a devoted mother and her early efforts at poetry were encouraged by family and friends. While Keats did enjoy a liberal education at the progressive Enfield school, with a generous mentor and friend in the headmaster's son, he had no formal study in literature, and this whole world came to an abrupt end in 1811 when his grandmother died (his parents already no more). His legal guardian yanked him out of school and apprenticed him to an apothecary (general medical practitioner), training followed by study at Guy's Hospital in London. Always the good student, Keats ably earned his apothecary's license, but his passion was poetry – reading and talking about it, and soon writing it. When he came of age in October 1816, he gambled on the vocation, dismaying his guardian but certain that this was "the deed / That my own soul has to itself decreed." "O for ten years, that I may overwhelm / Myself in poesy" was the petition of the capstone poem in his first volume.[10]

The deed proved exceedingly short: 1814–20. In his lifetime, Keats published just fifty-four poems, forty-five in his books, the rest in the periodicals (five of those forty-five also in this media). Usually work before age twenty-five would be classed as "juvenilia" or "early." Compare Keats to some of the English poets among whom he hoped to be counted. At twenty-four Chaucer and Spenser had yet to write anything, Shakespeare was known only (if at all) by a few early works, and Wordsworth had two slender volumes of descriptive poetry (thirty-four and fifty-seven pages respectively), known today mostly by specialists (*Lyrical Ballads* came at age twenty-eight). The first publication of Victorian sage Thomas Carlyle, born just weeks after Keats and surviving him by six decades, came in 1824, on the cusp of thirty, and it was a translation (Goethe's *Wilhelm Meister*). "Books of poetry by young writers are usually promissory notes that are never met," quipped Wilde, but added that now and then "one comes across a volume that is so far above the average that one can hardly resist the fascinating temptation of recklessly prophesying a fine future for the author."[11] Though he meant W. B. Yeats's *Wanderings of Oisin*, at age twenty-four, it's an apt review of Keats's 1820 volume, published before he turned twenty-four. A fine future for Keats was never to be, but it's tempting to speculate. What if he had had Carlyle's full span (or Yeats's mere seventy-three years)? Would he have stayed with poetry, having hit his stride in 1819? Would he have followed his aspiration in drama and become a modern Shakespeare? With his sharp ear for conversation and wry regard of friends and acquaintances, would he have turned novelist? His letters suggest this skill, as well as a talent for personal essays, in company with Charles Lamb and William Hazlitt, who made their names in this genre. Or (Keats considered this) would his political passions have joined him with Leigh Hunt and William Hazlitt (political progressives and anti-monarchists) as a journalist for the liberal press?

The fascination of guesses testifies to what Keats did accomplish in a short life: in effect, a major "career" on a range of challenges, from the sonnet, the ballad, the ode, doggerel, songs, a romance epic, Miltonic epic, a dream-vision. All those now famous odes published in 1820, *The Eve of St. Agnes*, the sonnets on Chapman's Homer and "Bright Star," are now at the core of the movement we call English Romanticism, at the core of English poetry itself. Elizabeth Barrett Browning gave this tribute in 1856 to Keats's "strong excepted soul":

> the man who never stepped
> In gradual progress like another man,

> But, turning grandly on his central self,
> Ensphered himself in twenty perfect years
> And died, not young, – (the life of a long life
> Distilled to a mere drop, falling like a tear
> Upon the world's cold cheek to make it burn
> For ever;)   (*Aurora Leigh* Book I)

Though shortening the life by more years yet, her sense of a long life distilled into a burning drop is fair biography, beautifully figured in the sphered typography of parentheses.

"Reading John Keats" gives a verb for our attention and a definitive adjective for this poet. *Reading John Keats* is for everyone with interest in Keats's creative temper and practical art. Here is a poet eager for challenges and productive conflicts, capable of witty self-regard and serious self-consciousness, and ever alive to words. You'll see Keats discovering his purposes within and against literary traditions, within and against his modern times. Featuring the best-known poetry, I take a few turns to some fascinating lesser-knowns (except by professionals): *Endymion: A Poetic Romance* (his longest poem ever), *Isabella; or, The Pot of Basil* (a Boccaccio-tale with a proto-Marxian edge that G. B. Shaw admired), *Hyperion* (an existential reforming of Milton's epic of mortality), *The Fall of Hyperion* (a revision, with an acute focus on a poet's capability), and some late lyrics occupied with Fanny Brawne, the bright (sometimes dark) star of his last years. While Keats's poetry requires no decoding from biography, it's clear that Keats's life leverages meaning into his poems. The most arresting passages of his letters can feel like poetry. I've been reading, writing about, and teaching Keats for decades, but my every return brings surprises, new delights, new respect for the power of his thinking and the complexities of his writing. What Keats said to a friend about reading Shakespeare – each time there is something "rather new . . . notwithstand^g that we read the same Play forty times – for instance, the following . . . never struck me so forcibly as at present" (*K* 49) – I'm happy to say of Keats (even in rereading for this book), and to relay to you.

SUSAN J. WOLFSON

Acknowledgments

My happy debts are to generations of editors (especially Jack Stillinger on the poetry and Hyder E. Rollins on the letters), scholars, biographers, and critical interpreters – many of these items listed in "Further reading." Garrett Stewart's work on *Lamia* is so woven into my own that citations are hopeless; I refer to his groundbreaking essay for my debts and your pleasure. Citations of critical studies in my chapters are (of necessity in the Press's series genre) selectively brief, incommensurate with the wealth of interpretations and the range of approaches that Keats's writing has drawn, for which see (selectively here, too) the "Further reading." My career of publications on Keats and the Romantic era (several times with Cambridge) is reflected throughout and noted in "Further reading."

I've had great resources at Princeton University Library, especially its rare books and manuscripts, and all kinds of practical support in the Department of English. I'm especially grateful to Kevin Mensch for generous technical expertise, moral support, and friendship, too. AnnaLee Pauls, librarian at Special Collections is a model of extraordinary efficiency, good humor, and generosity. The open-access, on-line Keats Collection, Houghton Library, Harvard University, is free, fascinating, invaluable. Leslie Morris is a resource unto herself, and Mary Haegert is a model of efficiency and positive capability.

I thank Linda Bree for inviting, encouraging, and advising this project. Garrett Stewart's extraordinary level of friendship and attention is inestimable. Christopher Rovee's scrupulous review was characteristically generous and acute. And always Ron Levao.

SJW
Princeton, New Jersey, 2014

Note on the texts

Keats's poetry: the lifetime publications that Keats supervised, supplemented by his manuscripts; otherwise, Jack Stillinger's unrivalled edition (*P*) or my selected (*K*). Keats's titles are in italics; for poems he did not title, I follow the tradition of using the first words, in quotation: e.g., "I stood tip-toe"; "When I have fears." Line numbers for *Endymion* follow the 1818 publication; other numberings are my additions. I follow the first publications in styling of Keats's subtitles: Book I, Book II, Book III; Part I, Part II; Canto I, Canto II, when I refer to these units in the body of my discussion. When my purpose is just a parenthetical location in a text, I forgo the clutter of roman numerals and use arabic numerals for Book, Part, or Canto, followed by line number(s). For instance a quotation from *Hyperion* would be identified (2.380). For stanza-references for *Isabella* and *The Eve of St. Agnes*, and for sonnets in *1817* identified by roman numerals (e.g. Sonnet IX), I follow Keats's style and use roman numerals.

For letters, I transcribe the most legible autograph manuscripts in Harvard's Keats collection; otherwise, I use print sources, as indicated. I retain Keats's idiosyncratic punctuation, style, and spelling (e.g., but not alone, "camelion"). I don't interpolate in brackets apparently dropped letters (*s*, *i*, *l*, and especially *r*); my study of the manuscripts convinces me that Keats used a bold down-stroke as shorthand for two letters. I give him this benefit.

Quotations of Shakespeare and references to Keats's markings are based on his copy of *The Dramatic Works of William Shakespeare*, 7 vols. (London: Chiswick Press, 1814), in the Harvard Keats collection: *EC8 K2262 Zz814s. Quotations of *Paradise Lost* follow, whenever possible, Beth Lau's expert edition of Keats's 1808 text, which he marked up in 1818–19.

Abbreviations

1817	*Poems*. London: C. & J. Ollier, 1817
1820	*Lamia, Isabella, The Eve of St. Agnes, and Other Poems*. London: Taylor & Hessey, 1820
1848	Richard Monckton Milnes (Lord Houghton), *Life, Letters, and Literary Remains of John Keats*. 2 vols. London: Edward Moxon, 1848
&c [in a citation]	and other publishers or booksellers
&c [in a title]	and other poems
BLJ	*Byron's Letters & Journals*, ed. Leslie A. Marchand. Cambridge, MA: Harvard University Press, 1973–82
CCK	*The Cambridge Companion to John Keats*, ed. Susan J. Wolfson. Cambridge University Press, 2001
FQ	Edmund Spenser, *The Faerie Queene*
HK	Houghton Library John Keats Collection, Harvard University, Cambridge, MA http://www.hcl.harvard.edu/libraries/houghton/collections/modern/keats. Citations are to series 1 (Keats's letters) or series 2 (Keats's manuscripts), then letter number. For example: HK1.18.62 indicates: series 1, letter 18, page 62. References are often followed by a reference to published editions, *K* or *L*
K	*John Keats, A Longman Cultural Edition*, ed. Susan J. Wolfson. New York: Pearson, 2006
KC	*The Keats Circle: Letters and Papers*, ed. Hyder E. Rollins, 2 vols. Cambridge, MA: Harvard University Press, 1965
L	*The Letters of John Keats, 1814–1821*, ed. Hyder E. Rollins. 2 vols. Cambridge, MA: Harvard

	University Press, 1958. I often elide canceled text <marked by Rollins with angled brackets>. When I show a cancellation, I use ~~strike-through~~.
Lau	Beth Lau, *Keats's Paradise Lost*. Gainesville: University Press of Florida, 1998
Lemprière	*Bibliotheca Classica; or A Classical Dictionary*. 1788; 4th edition, London: T. Cadell Jun. and W. Davies, 1801. Entries herein are unpaged, alphabetical.
OED	*Oxford English Dictionary* (also consulted for all Keats-coinages)
P	*The Poems of John Keats*, ed. Jack Stillinger. Cambridge, MA: Harvard University Press, 1978
PL	*Paradise Lost*
1808:	*Paradise Lost: A New Edition. Adorned with Beautiful Plates.* 2 vols. Edinburgh, 1808 (the one Keats underlined and annotated)

CHAPTER I

Life and times

To be a Poet, a poet among Men

"O Poesy! for thee I grasp my pen / That am not yet a glorious denizen / Of thy wide heaven" – so pledged John Keats, ardently, energetically, as he hazarded a vocation.[1] It was a good time to be a poet. By the nineteenth century, English poetry was a celebrated heritage and ready for modern inspirations. Everyone was reading it, talking about it, even imagining poets as the voice of England. "Great spirits now on earth are sojourning," Keats began a sonnet after visiting Benjamin Robert Haydon's art-studio in November 1816. Haydon's epic canvases (and epic self-confidence) fired Keats with a sense of a cultural momentum, inspiring a sonnet:

> These, these will give the World another Heart
> And other Pulses — hear ye not the hum
> Of mighty workings? — — — — — — — —
> Listen awhile ye Nations and be dumb!²

Haydon suggested the expressive dash, and he promised to send the sonnet to Wordsworth himself. Thrilled at the prospect, Keats wrote out a fresh draft (Haydon cadged it, sending a copy to Wordsworth). Wordsworth wrote back on 20 January 1817, jesting that the praises did not allow him and Haydon to be "deemed judges altogether impartial," still thought it "vigorously conceived and well expressed," especially the conclusion – all in all "good promise" in "young Keats."³ Keats was over the moon. At Haydon's studio, he had recited lines lovingly memorized from Wordsworth's *Excursion*, about the "expansive and animating principle" of the old mythologies (IV.846–82), a passage that Haydon's friend Hazlitt had praised (in these terms) in a review for *The Examiner*.⁴ Keats had Wordsworth's 1815 *Poems* with him during his medical studies at Guy's Hospital. When he met Wordsworth (who visited London early in 1818), he eagerly recited the "Hymn to Pan" from *Endymion* Book I to him. A "very pretty piece of Paganism," said Wordsworth. Haydon thought this "unfeeling," but

Wordsworth had more than once expressed a feeling for Paganism.⁵ In the sonnet that begins "The world is too much with us" (1807 *Poems*) Wordsworth yearns for nurture in a Pagan creed of a nature vital with spirits, and the passage in *The Excursion* speculates more fully on what it was like to live in such a world. Wordsworth kept his eye on Keats after this meeting, even writing to Haydon in January 1820 (congratulating him on his painting *Christ's Entry into Jerusalem*, where Haydon had put him in the crowd, just below Keats): "How is Keates, he is a youth of promise too great for the sorry company he keeps" (i.e. Hunt, Hazlitt, and maybe Shelley).⁶

It was altogether a good time to be a poet. Publishers in London and Edinburgh had growing lists and paid popular poets well; regional publishers were taking risks; circulating libraries were multiplying; monthly magazines were welcoming. A career was possible. Robert Bloomfield's *Farmer's Boy* (1800) sold 25,000 copies in two years, prompting an advance in 1804 of more than £4,000 for another collection. Walter Scott made a fortune in poetry: in 1810 *The Lady of the Lake* sold over 20,000 copies (priced upscale, at two guineas, no less). *Childe Harold's Pilgrimage*, a "Romance" wandering with theatrical world-weariness, propelled Lord Byron to overnight fame in March 1812; in February 1814, his pirate-romance, *The Corsair*, sold 10,000 hot off the press, 20,000 within a fortnight.⁷ Notwithstanding Byron's titled Lordship and his respect for eighteenth-century poets and poetics, the new poetry was eclectic and democratic, untethered from traditions of rhyme and meter, no longer the preserve of the elite or university culture. In 1818 Hazlitt, who also offered public lectures, introduced his series on English poetry (attended by Keats and everyone in London, it seems) by hailing a general franchise:

> Many people suppose that poetry is something to be found only in books, contained in lines of ten syllables, with like endings: but wherever there is a sense of beauty, or power, or harmony, as in the motion of a wave of the sea, in the growth of a flower that "spreads its sweet leaves to the air, and dedicates its beauty to the sun," — *there* is poetry in its birth.⁸

Keats could dream. "Hazlitt's depth of taste," he said, was a thing to "rejoice at."⁹

Keats could also rejoice at the liberal wit of Hazlitt's mapping eighteenth-century poetics as an *ancien régime* primed for a revolution of "something new and original":

> Our poetical literature had towards the close of the last century, degenerated into the most trite, insipid, and mechanical of all things, in the hands of the followers of Pope and the old French school of poetry. It wanted something

to stir it up, and it found that something in the principles and events of the French revolution . . . The change in the belles-lettres was as complete, and to many persons as startling, as the change in politics, with which it went hand in hand. There was a mighty ferment in the heads of statesmen and poets . . . all was to be natural and new. Nothing that was established was to be tolerated . . . rhyme was looked upon as a relic of the feudal system, and regular metre was abolished along with regular government.[10]

While this was satiric hyperbole, it caught the revolutionary spirit of the 1790s for poets in 1818. How pleased Keats must have been to see *Endymion* advertised on the volume's back-page of "Books just published," third in a list dated "May 1, 1818." His first volume (1817) had been noticed for a style "vivacious, smart, witty, changeful, sparkling, and learned, – full of bright points and flashy expressions that strike and even seem to please by a sudden boldness of novelty."[11] One novelty Keats enjoyed was the "romance couplet." The neoclassic couplet was a symmetry of meter, syntax, and rhyme: "True ease in writing comes from art, not chance, / As those move easiest who have learn'd to dance" (so Pope's *Essay on Criticism* [1717] advised). The romance couplet was a liberal confection, flaunting varied meters, "feminine" rhymes (on an unstressed syllable), and enjambment (syntax "striding over" a line-end). You can see all this in Keats's "I'd wander / In happy silence, like the clear meander / Through its lone vales" (*Sleep and Poetry*, 73–75) – with a nice mimesis in wandering and meandering.

Hazlitt's satire of the new poetry as a wing of the French Revolution did not come out of left field. Or it did. He was jesting at the late-Toryism of "the present poet-laureat and the authors of the Lyrical Ballads" (*Lectures*, 320): Southey, Coleridge, and Wordsworth, former champions of the Revolution in 1789 and now post-Waterloo monarchists. France's revolution became a bloody civil war by 1792; Britain and France declared war in 1793, and soon after, Britain's security became the alert for suppressing civil liberties, hunting out treason, raising taxes, and relentlessly drafting young men into dangerous military service. Keats's generation grew up in the catastrophes and retrenchments of a long war. Even after its emergence as premier world-power after Waterloo (1815), Britain fortified itself with new controls and repressions, its conservative institutions policing anything that looked like opposition, even in arts and letters.

Hazlitt's poetry-politics was more than stand-up wit. It was a barometer of the prevailing review-culture. *Lyrical Ballads* was published anonymously in 1798 because of Coleridge's toxic reputation in political activism. Beyond this stigma, any poetry dignifying the grievances of commoners, peasants, shepherds, convicts, and children could be thought subversive of social

privileges and hierarchal stability.[12] On any scent of suspicion, political
or literary, the conservative press rained down abuse. A prime target in
Keats's day was Leigh Hunt, fearless editor of the liberal opposition weekly,
The Examiner, published by his brother John, both of them fined and
jailed for anti-government agitation. Also abused (just in print) was Hunt's
friend Shelley: scion of the aristocracy, disciple of anarchist-philosopher
William Godwin, expelled from Oxford for his pamphlet *The Necessity of
Atheism* (a critique of the un-Christian Church of England), with fresh
notoriety from *Queen Mab*, a poem that denounced "Kingcraft" and
"Priestcraft."

In this political climate Keats debuted. Hunt's *Examiner* hosted his
first publication, in May 1816.[13] Then in the 1 December issue, an essay
by Hunt introduced "Young Poets," the generation breaking away from
the eighteenth-century regime: Shelley (whose first volume under his own
name, *Alastor &c*, had appeared in January and needed a boost); J. H.
Reynolds, a publishing poet since 1812 (to whom Haydon had also shown
Keats's "Great Spirits"); and the newest and youngest – "His name is JOHN
KEATS." Hunt printed entire "On First Looking Into Chapman's Homer."[14]
It was only Keats's second publication, and a hearty cheer for the *Poems* due
in March 1817 from publishers in Hunt's circle. Hunt fanned the promise
with two more sonnets in February issues. Yet Hunt's wing was also a
lightning-rod, and Keats was singed. The first reviews of *Poems* (beyond
Hunt's circle) were uneven, and the most consequential ones came in 1818,
in the wake of *Endymion* (Keats's major bid). The assailants were high-
profile: a newcomer out to make a name with a bite, *Blackwood's Edinburgh
Magazine*, and the elder establishment *Quarterly Review*, published by John
Murray, prime player in London's literary world (Byron, his star author)
and Tory ally of Church and Crown.[15]

Keats's too happy paganism was interpreted politically, as a coded rebuke
to established religion. (John Hunt put an excerpt of "Hymn to Pan" in
The Yellow Dwarf, a brief-lived weekly of oppositional journalism.[16]) *Blackwood's* branded the counter-cultural insurgency "Cockney," a cover-term
for political opposition, heresy, lower-class vulgarity, unmanliness, immaturity, poetic license, and moral licentiousness. In the launch of a series, in
October 1817, reviewer "Z" had arraigned Leigh Hunt as headmaster of the
"Cockney School of Poetry" and the "Cockney School of Politics," citing
his protégé in a snarky epigraph promising more on

> HUNT, and KEATS,
> The Muses' son of promise, and of what feats
> He yet may do.[17]   (2:38)

The Muses' son of promise was pared to Hunt's scion of promise. Meanly paired, meanly rhymed, Keats registered the forecast. Writing to his friend Benjamin Bailey with a rueful punning on "*End*inburgh," he pressed "Magazine" into a military arsenal:

> There has been a flaming attack upon Hunt in the Endinburgh Magazine— I never read any thing so virulent... These Philipics are to come out in Numbers—calld 'the Cockney School of Poetry' There has been but one Number published—that on Hunt to which they have prefixed a Motto... Hunt and Keats in large Letters—I have no doubt that the second Number was intended for me. (3 November 1817; *K* 67)

Keats braced himself, while a challenge to Z for a duel of honor was sent to *Blackwood's* from *The Examiner's* publisher. Z blew this off, but Keats felt that were Z to serve him such "abuse," he would have to "call him to an account – if... we might possibly meet" (*K* 68). In June 1818 he replayed the November-jest to Bailey: "the Endinburgh Magasine in another blow up against Hunt calls me 'the amiable Mister Keats'" (HK1.31.109).

He had to wait for "Cockney School IV," September 1818 (dated "August") for the aim of attack, now also naming "the Cockney School of Politics, as well as the Cockney School of Poetry" in the indictment (3:524). Z had a fresh arrow for his quiver from an unwitting Bailey, who, when he met Z that summer, hoped to endear him with the story of Keats's dedication to poetry amid his medical apprenticeship. Bailey was mortified to see it turned to satire. Keats was not only assailed as a proxy for Hunt but ridiculed for his aspirations, with contempt for manifold deficiencies: a no-count apothecary's apprentice, no title, no university degree, no family connections. If not the politics, Keats's "vulgar" style remained a focus in other reviews, and the "Cockney" brand held: loose poetics, erotic indulgences, pretentious classical allusions, and aspiration of parity with the great men of poetry, Chaucer, Spenser, Shakespeare, Milton, even Wordsworth.

No less than the gatekeeping were the diminutions regularly applied to "Johnny Keats." He was acutely conscious of his small stature, and the way it could signify of unmanliness – this was one of the implications of the slur "Cockney." Keats was a beautiful boy, and a good looking young man, with large animated eyes, a great head of curly chestnut hair, and physically vigorous (until he began to fail from tuberculosis). But he was short, and so cartoonable: "Mr John Keats five foot hight," he ironized himself ruefully in that letter to Bailey in the summer of 1818 (*L* 1:342). "You see what it is to be under six foot and not a lord," he grumbled early in 1819 on hearing himself described as "quite the little Poet," implying

Lord Byron's exemption (*L* 2:61; Byron had a half a foot on him). One of the first descriptions he gave of Fanny Brawne is that "she is about my height" (*L* 2:13), a self-measuring in more than inches.

The biggest flash in December 1816, however, was not Hunt's parade of "Young Poets." It was that under-six-foot celebrity lord – more particularly, Murray's white-hot sale of Byron's *Childe Harold's Pilgrimage*, Canto III (electric sequel to the fame-maker of 1812). Hunt paused in this very essay for a remark of "delight" at Byron's "real feeling for numbers" (meters) inspired by "Nature" rather than rule-books (*Examiner* 761). Canto III sold about 7,000 copies right out the gate – and Byron wasn't even resident in England. A jealous Wordsworth took pains with friends to explain why the "nature" he described in *Tintern Abbey* was more authentic than his Lordship's Alpine operatics (*MY* 2:385). But he could weather the rivalry on the ground of an established career: two volumes in 1793, four editions of *Lyrical Ballads* (1798–1805), a two-volume *Poems* in 1807, *The Excursion* in 1814, and in 1815, a new romance, and a two-volume collected *Poems*. *Lyrical Ballads* may have seemed insurgent in 1802, but by 1818 Z could praise both "illustrious Lord" Byron and Wordsworth's "dignified purity," "noble compositions," and "patriarchal simplicity," to wield as a cudgel against Keats and Hunt.[18]

A further drag on Keats's aspiration to "man of letters" was his genre-set: not manly epic, tragedy, or edgy satire, but sonnets, lyrics, album verse, picturesque fancies, dreamy musings, and a dream-charged Romance, *Endymion*. Well into 1819 he was pegging redemption on the credit of a tragedy: "My name with the literary fashionables is vulgar – I am a weaver boy to them – A Tragedy would lift me out of this mess," he sighs to his brother and sister-in-law (*L* 2:186). No help to his mess was a new gender for the lighter genres, "female poetry." Although Hazlitt's lectures gave this poetry short, ungentle shrift, it was out there, far and wide. Charlotte Smith's most successful venture, from the 1780s into eight editions by 1800, was *Elegiac Sonnets*. Keats's Regency contemporary, "poetess" Felicia Hemans, was an international celebrity by 1818 – under Murray's imprint, no less. Keats, sensitive to the gender borders, could in some tempers camp it up, or launch extravagances too sensual to be "feminine" – all those luscious nymphs and burning lads in *Poems* and the patent lovemaking in *Endymion*. But it's telling that his poetry also, repeatedly (in *Endymion*, too), figures female powers as perils to young-manly self-possession: goddesses seductive and stern, enchanters alluring and fugitive, suspect modes, such as "Romance" and "Fancy," marked feminine. About actual women, Keats's letters show him by turns adoring, sympathetic, defensive, or hostile (especially about their claims as readers, writers, and arbiters). Surging with poetic genius, adolescent uncertainty, social anxiety, and cultural prejudice, Keats is a case study in gender-edginess.

His famous master-simile for human life as a progress through a "Mansion of Many Apartments" has a legible gender-track into manly maturity. Keats lays this out for Reynolds in a letter of 3 May 1818. We begin in an "infant or thoughtless Chamber"; then, "imperceptibly impelled by the awakening of [the] thinking principle," we move into "the Chamber of Maiden-Thought," a virginal feminine. Full of "pleasant wonders" and "delight," this stage can't last, and as thinking matures and sharpens, it mans up. Among the effects that thought "is father of," says Keats, is a sharpened "vision into the heart and nature of Man – of convincing ones nerves" that the world is not full of delight but "Misery and Heartbreak, Pain, Sickness and oppression" (*K* 129–30). In this morphing from Maiden to Man, women remain creatures of simplicity, or, if not, look like shams. About their exercise of literary judgment, especially over matters of literary taste, Keats clubs with the guys, sneering at "Women, who having taken a snack or Luncheon of Literary scraps, set themselves up for towers of Babel in Languages Sapphos in Poetry" at the cost of "real feminine Modesty" (*K* 59). Writing a bitter sonnet "on Fame" (1819, not for publication) Keats satirizes fame-seeking as the courtship of a heartless girl, a promiscuous flirt. The "generallity of women," he writes in October 1818 just after he met the love of his life, Fanny Brawne, strike him "as children to whom I would rather give a Sugar Plum than my time," and no inducement to matrimony.[19] Looking back in 1841, his friend, manly social and sexual adventurer Charles Brown, thought that this remark sounded a lot like Byron (*KC* 2:79). "He says he does not want ladies to read his poetry: that he writes for men," Richard Woodhouse reported of Keats in September 1819 to his publisher, John Taylor, who was distressed that Keats seemed to be truckling in verse that "can only be read by Men" (*L* 2:163, 2:182).

Wanting to make his mark among literate, urbane men, Keats needed an ambitious genre-credential. No sooner did *Poems* appear in spring 1817 than he set *Endymion* as a "test, a trial of my Powers."[20] "I have asked myself so often why I should be a Poet more than other Men," he told Hunt as writing was underway, and gave eager answer: "What a thing to be in the Mouth of Fame" (May 1817; *K* 50). The real test and trial would not be so much writing *Endymion*, however, but weathering those first reviews. Hot on the heels of Z, *The Quarterly* twisted its barb: not that this poet lacks "powers of language, rays of fancy, and gleams of genius – he has all these," it granted, winding up to a snide query if "Mr. Keats . . . be his real name, for we almost doubt that any man in his senses would put his real name to such a rhapsody." Here were rhymes, diction, and meters as ludicrous as its fantasy, all hallmarking a "disciple of the new school of what has been somewhere called Cockney poetry."[21] This was disingenuous; *The Quarterly* reviewer heard the call of *Blackwood's*, and liked the unmanly slur of "Cockney." "Damn them who could act in so cruel a way to a young man of undoubted Genius" for "imputed political Opinions," fumed the publisher of *Endymion*, John Taylor, to another young talent he was encouraging, the rural poet John Clare.[22]

For his part, Keats assured Taylor's business partner, J. A. Hessey, "My own domestic criticism has given me pain without comparison beyond what Blackwood or the Quarterly could possibly inflict" and moreover, "no external praise can give me such a glow as my own solitary reperception & ratification of what is fine" (8 October 1818; *K* 206–7). He devised the word *reperception* for this accounting – a nice invention, in line with Keats's neo-Shakespearean genius for devising words to become part of the English language.

Becoming Keats

John Keats (b. 31 October 1795) was the eldest of four children, their father the proprietor of a suburban London livery-stable, owned by his wife's father. The siblings were George (b. 1797), Tom (b. 1799), and Fanny (b. 1803). Though not gentry, the family was able to send the boys to a progressive boarding school, Enfield Academy, Keats entering at age eight. But in April 1804 (Keats not yet nine), Mr. Keats died from injuries in a riding accident, and two months later, Mrs. Keats sent the children to her mother, quickly remarried, then disappeared from this second husband. Her affection for John was as doting as it was erratic, and he was devastated.

Enfield became a remedial home. Unlike many schools, it did not countenance corporal punishment or the terrors of hazing and bullying. The headmaster fostered a family culture, with progressive, interactive pedagogy, a care for arts, and a climate of civil and religious liberty. He subscribed to *The Examiner*, which Keats began reading, heroizing Hunt well before he met him. The headmaster's son and assistant, Charles Cowden Clarke, was a generous mentor – one of many older men (Clarke was eight years senior) with a fraternal affection and lifelong support for beautiful, brilliant, engaging, endearing Keats. Everyone loved him (recalled Clarke) "for his terrier courage . . . his high-mindedness . . . his generosity."

Keats was an insatiable reader, burning through every book in the library, with a passion for poetry, mythology, history, and the classics. To encourage adventures beyond assignments, the headmaster gave a prize for "the greatest quantity" and

> such was Keats's indefatigable energy for the last two or three successive half-years . . . he took the first prize by a considerable distance. He was at work before the first school-hour began, and that was at seven o'clock; almost all the intervening times of recreation were so devoted; and during the afternoon holidays, when all were at play, he would be in the school – almost the only one – at his Latin or French translation and so unconscious and regardless was he of the consequences of so close and persevering an application, that he never would have taken the necessary exercise had he not been sometimes driven out for the purpose by one of the masters.[23]

Keats won one prize for translating the first book of Virgil's *Aeneid*. He also loved Ovid's *Metamorphoses*, Milton's *Paradise Lost*, Virgil's *Eclogues*, Lemprière's *Classical Dictionary*, and especially Spenser's *Faerie Queene*. Clarke was astonished that when he lent Keats the first volume, he went through it "as a young horse would through a spring meadow – ramping!" (126). Reading was a world in which to lose himself: "In Spenser's fairy land he was enchanted, breathed in a new world, and became another being," recalled Brown; Keats "was entirely absorbed" when he read.[24]

Four long years after she had vanished, Keats's mother returned, racked with consumption. Barely into his teens, Keats managed her care and watched her die when he was fourteen. His grief was intense and prolonged, at times driving him to nook up under the headmaster's desk. The emotional turbulence – deep love, abandonment, wounded grievance – would infuse his poetry with refuges and retreats, and haunt it with rapturously desired, inconstant women, iconic in the title *La belle dame sans merci*. There was further distress the next year, 1811, when the guardians appointed by his grandmother pulled fourteen-year-old Keats out of school and apprenticed him to a surgeon in the village of Edmonton – his life for the next five years. The loss of his mother had been partly assuaged by the secondary caring family at Enfield, and now this was extinguished, too.

Clarke had introduced him to art and music, contemporary literature and theater. Keats kept up the friendship, kept reading, kept translating the *Aeneid*. In October 1815 he began studies at Guy's Hospital in south London, with lectures by leading scientists and physicians alternating with a grim world of physical distress, pain, and sad mortality. In March 1816 he became a dresser to the surgeons, ever more intimate with the mortal body. From the squalor of London and Guy's horrific operating theaters, Enfield and the country seemed like paradise lost. That summer, always the adept student, and proficient in Latin, Keats aced a newly rigorous apothecary licensing exam. The next stage in his career would have been surgical training.

But his heart was in poetry – reading it, writing it, dreaming of being "a poet." Along with his school-days' enthusiasms, he was now reading Shakespeare, Chatterton, and the contemporaries, Hunt, Wordsworth, and Byron, even glancing at Katherine Phillips (seventeenth-century Anglo-Welsh poet) and his near contemporary poet Mary Tighe (who wrote an epic in Spenserian stanzas on Psyche – and so close to Keats's bone). Responsive to beauty, curious about the world, alive to sensations, Keats had begun writing poems at age nineteen, during his apprenticeship. His first, 1814, was *Imitation of Spenser*, a jewel in skillfully crafted Spenserian stanzas. By 1815, amid medical studies in London, he was affecting "the poet" (recalled a fellow-student) "á lá Byron" (*sic*), disdaining neckwear for a casual collar and ribbon, and occasionally sporting a moustache (*KC* 2:211). By 1816, encouraged by Clarke, he was writing in earnest: sonnets and lyrics, verse-epistles (to a friend, a mentor, and a brother), prospective pieces, romance sketches, and longer ventures of local description, mythological fancies, poetic aspirations. Clarke introduced him to Hunt and his dynamic circle of writers and artists. At legal adulthood on 31 October, cheered by friends and brothers, Keats gave up medicine for a gamble on poetry, innocently confident of a safety-net from his grandmother's estate: £9,000 had been settled on the Keats children. But his guardian and the courts kept the bequest tied up for years, until after Keats's death even. The brothers could have managed comfortably on the interest alone. Each child at age twenty-one would have had at least £3,000; invested at the usual return of 5 per cent, the annual income of £150 would have been comfortable in itself, and pooled, enough to secure modest independence from necessary employment. In May 1817, George, always more business-minded and aggressive in inquiry, informed John that "Money Troubles are to follow us up for some time to come perhaps for always." In 1818 he decided to emigrate, with his new wife, to the US frontier state of Kentucky in search of a living, and this is where he spent the rest of his life.[25]

Through Hunt, Keats soon met Haydon, who introduced him to the rough, grand sculpture-fragments known as the Elgin Marbles. These had been rescued/exported/pirated/plundered (depending on whom you ask): the removal of these sculptures from the Parthenon in Athens to Great Britain was a national controversy, and Haydon was a passionate

champion of their artistic value and of the importance of England's acqui-
sition of them, at great national expense in a time of national starvation.
Keats was stunned no less by the power of what he imagined the originals
must have looked like, than by the decay of this grandeur across a millennium or more. He wrote two sonnets focusing on his reaction, which
Haydon published. Haydon was at work on an epic painting *Christ's Triumphal Entry into Jerusalem*, and in honor to those whom he admired, he
put their faces among the crowd: Keats appears along with Wordsworth,
Hazlitt, and Voltaire. Through Haydon, Keats met "young poet" Reynolds
(a year older) – playful, good-natured, a comrade in vocation.

The were all frequent guests at Hunt's, a convivial suburban hub,
through which circulated Hazlitt, William Godwin, the Shelleys (Percy
and Mary), and the Lambs (Charles and Mary). It was amid this stimu-
lating society of artists, intellectuals, and progressive political thinkers, that
Keats assembled his first volume, happy for the imprint of the Ollier brothers, a firm with Hunt, Hazlitt, and Shelley on its list (Shelley may have paid
for some advertisements). *Poems* appeared in March 1817, with a dedicatory
sonnet to Hunt. The volume was something of an apprentice portfolio,
thirty-one displays of skill and versatility in several genres: Spenserian stanzas, several odes, songs, lyrics, personal verse epistles, album verses, romance
fragments, and twenty sonnets (a few previewed by *The Examiner*). It was
also coterie spin on favorite poets, political and mythological themes, with
a program for modern poetry – especially the way classical mythology
and Spenserian romance could be outfitted for a contemporary urbane
readership.

The concluding piece was a long poem-essay of vocational dedication,
Sleep and Poetry. For the occasion Keats indulged a brisk, Hunt-tuned satire
of eighteenth-century poetics. Haydon hailed the "flash of lightening that
will sound men from their occupations, and keep them trembling for the
crash of thunder that <u>will</u> follow." But Hunt, recognizing an "impatient,
and as it may be thought by some, irreverend assault," forecast a storm.[26]
Byron was soon muttering to Murray about the insult to Pope's school, and
Murray's *Quarterly* geared up. Z turned Keats's call to arms to travesty, with
italics: this "long strain of foaming abuse" issues from "ignorant unsettled
pretenders," "flimsy striplings" unequal to Pope's merits "or those of any
other *men of power*." Reynolds tried to buck Keats up, rebranding the slam
as a merit-badge: "so much of endeavour cannot be directed to nothing.
Men do not set their muscles, and strain their sinews to break a straw."[27]
The Olliers, dismayed by these slams and booksellers' complaints, quietly
jettisoned Keats.

Taylor, unfazed by the partisan attacks and ever on the lookout for new talent, promptly signed up Keats's next venture. His list reflects his acuity: Hazlitt, Clare, Lamb, Coleridge, Thomas De Quincey, Walter Landor, Thomas Hood, and soon the progressive *London Magazine*. Keats's entrée would be *Endymion*. Eager to acquit this confidence and to prove his promise, Keats dedicated himself to the work, taking leave in March 1817 of London, and more painfully, of his brothers, to sequester on the Isle of Wight – only to find himself in a solitude less romantic than lonely, his writing going nowhere. He departed for Margate, a resort on the southeast coast, where sickly Tom came to join him. He was still frustrated: "the Cliff of Poesy Towers above me," he sighed to his friend of heroic scale, Haydon – but added, in a heartbeat, that when Tom reads him some of "Pope's Homer," the lines "seem like Mice to mine." And so, "I read and write about eight hours a day," in alternating hope, anxiety, ambition, and confidence: sometimes harkening to "The Trumpet of Fame," sometimes worrying of "self delusion," sometimes in "a horrid Morbidity of Temperament" – as if amid the corpses at Guy's.[28] But he kept at it.

When he returned to London, Reynolds introduced him to Brown, a playwright, and to Oxford theology student Bailey, another eager reader of poetry. Both took to Keats. Bailey invited him to Oxford, and Keats arrived in September. They read and talked about Milton and Wordsworth, and Keats plugged away at *Endymion*, finishing Book III while confiding (again) his exhaustion to Haydon, and wondering, with cheering wordplay, if he should just begin a "new Romance which I have in my eye for next summer."[29] Back in London in October, he completed Book IV in November. As he reviewed page proofs, he was going to plays, excited by Edmund Kean's acting (he wrote a review for *The Champion*), and attending Hazlitt's lectures on Shakespeare. Yet by the time *Endymion* appeared, in April 1818, Keats knew he had outgrown it. As a "Prologue" to new work (*L*1:264) he took a summer walking-tour with ever energetic and amusing Brown, wending from the Lake District of Wordsworth, to Ireland and appalling poverty, to the Hebrides, Scotland and Burns country. He needed, too, a vacation from Tom's suffering and the shock of losing George, newly married and off to America for opportunity. When he returned, it was clear that Tom was dying, and not easefully.

Keats set his next project as an epic, *Hyperion*, about the birth of poetic power, embodied by the sun-god Hyperion's successor, Apollo, god of medicine, knowledge, and poetry: his symbolic ideal. As he was caring for Tom, he wrote pages of dazzling, haunting poetry – some of the best blank verse since *Paradise Lost*, and more: a radical rethinking of epic purpose for the modern era, one without a Miltonic theology of good and evil, of moral fault and punishment. It was a hard project, not only for this existentialism but also because of its core fable: Hyperion, knowing that all his brothers have fallen into mortality, feels his doom. It was an agony to which any grand argument about historical necessity, original sin, or dynastic destiny seemed horribly inadequate. When Tom died early in December, Keats couldn't go on. Bereft of brothers, he embraced brother-friends, especially Brown, who invited him to live with him. In inspirations that sometimes felt like fever, Keats blazed across 1819: *The Eve of St. Agnes*, *La belle dame*, all those brilliant odes, *Lamia*, two forays into drama, even a return to *Hyperion* to reframe it in a modern (or belated) dream-vision involving a severe inquest, and test of imaginative sympathy, on the purposes of poetry in the modern world. And though never meant for publication, there was also a swirl of verse vexed by, enchanted by, his helpless love for vivacious Fanny Brawne.

When Keats sighed to Taylor about his aspirations in drama, "If God should spare me," this was no casual idiom (*K* 279). He had tried to assure himself back in November 1817 that Tom's illness was not his own fate,[30] but coughs and a sore throat distressed him throughout 1819. Then in January 1820 everything fell apart. Gripped with bad cold, he started spitting blood, two massive pulmonary hemorrhages in one night. With his medical training and his intimate nursing of his mother and Tom, he read his "death-warrant" (*KC* 2:74). During a few better days, he helped prepare his "last trial," the 1820 volume. This came out in July, and Keats read favorable reviews before sailing for Italy in September. The hope for health in the warm south came with a severe cost: removal far from Fanny and all his friends, save a young artist, Joseph Severn, who bravely accompanied him, knowing in his heart what was in store. After a rough voyage, the last indignity was a quarantine, from fear of typhoid, for over a week in the Bay of Naples. Released on Keats's twenty-sixth birthday, 31 October, the two headed for Rome. Although Keats survived until the end of February, he had "an habitual feeling of my real life having past, and that I am leading a posthumous existence" (*K* 432).

The fable of a sensitive boy slain by hostile reviews, retailed in Shelley's *Adonais*, was rehearsed through the nineteenth century as if documentary truth. Shelley was certain (writing to none other than Ollier, 8 June 1821) that "the brutal attack in the *Quarterly Review* excited the disease by which he perished"[31] – a rumor that Byron was quick to credit, caricature, and circulate. But this poignant (then ludicrous) fable was Shelley's polemic, and at odds with Keats's resilience amid disappointment. Keats is the poet who

could declare, in May 1819, "I must choose between despair and Energy –
I choose the latter" (*K* 256). In his last known letter – the one of
30 November 1820 to Brown describing a sensation of posthumous
existence – he wrote half-ruefully, half-comically about its contradiction
to a prized aesthetic value: "the knowledge of contrast, feeling for light
and shade, all that information (primitive sense) necessary for a poem are
great enemies to the recovery of the stomach." And "at my worst, even in
quarantine," he assures Brown, he is still in the game, having "summoned
up more puns, in a sort of desperation, in one week than in any year of
my life." His closing sentence renders a characteristic, wryly theatrical,
self-regard: "I always made an awkward bow" (*K* 432–33).

Keats's bearings: pro and con, "dark Passages," camelion poetics, negative capability

In the age of new poetry, Wordsworth crankily defended his principles
in serial Prefaces, Essays and Appendices; Shelley polished Prefaces and
drafted a long, philosophical *Defence of Poetry*; Byron issued crisp public
letters defending his tastes and wrote editorial Prefaces; Hunt tirelessly
published essays, reviews, and books of literary criticism; and Coleridge
positively flourished in *Biographia Literaria; or Biographical Sketches of
My Literary Life and Opinions* (1817), now canonical in English literary
criticism.

Keats never published, let alone drafted, any position papers. His résumé
as critic was a theater review and a literary review, both unsigned, and a
self-criticizing Preface to *Endymion*. Even for his last, best volume (1820),
he had no "intention . . . to have a Preface" (*L* 2:276). His thinking about
poets, poetry, and poetic practice gets worked out, ad hoc, in conversations
and correspondence with family, friends, and publishers – and in the poems
themselves, in figurings of their own poetics. While Keats's letters ripple
with great formulations and insights, he didn't deliberate any of these into
gems to "brood and peacock over" (*K* 99), coining the second verb to
cartoon Wordsworth's didacticism to Reynolds. It was all lively thinking
in the moment.

Back in London in November 1817, and still at *Endymion*, he exchanged
letters with Bailey about the practice of poetry versus philosophical argument. When the theology student confessed a "momentary start" at Keats's
advocacy for "the authenticity of the Imagination," Keats volleyed back:

> I am certain of nothing but of the holiness of the Heart's affections and
> the truth of Imagination—What the imagination seizes as Beauty must be

truth—whether it existed before or not—for I have the same Idea of all our Passions as of Love they are all in their sublime, creative of essential Beauty . . . The Imagination may be compared to Adam's dream—he awoke and found it truth. I am the more zealous in this affair, because I have never yet been able to perceive how any thing can be known for truth by consequitive reasoning. (22 November 1817; *K* 69)

Blending *consequent* into *consecutive*, Keats invented another needed word, one he'd use again to describe his publisher in 1818, John Taylor, as a "consequitive Man" (*K* 93–94). If the discipline of the "Philosopher" meant "putting aside numerous objections," Keats always wanted to entertain these. Yet he kept weighing liberties against liabilities: was it better to "delight in Sensation" or "hunger . . . after Truth" (*K* 70), to be Keats or Bailey? Speculating in the moment and in turns of conversation, this long letter feels like a prose-poem; how apt that some of it is cast in proto-poetic lines.[32] Keats is surely playing poetic relay when he answers Bailey's *momentary start* with a report that "nothing startles me beyond the Moment," or writes of one moment: "The *setting* Sun will always *set me* to rights." The wordplay pricks key questions. Can poetry abide in moments of sensation, or ought it build a philosophy? Is Imagination true seeing, or is this only for Adam in Paradise?[33] Keats was not after secure answers so much as the energy of thinking, testing, and intensifying ideas. "Let us now begin a regular question and answer – a little pro and con" he proposes, with playful fraternal affection, to his sister Fanny (*L* 1:153).

He subjected his most important contemporary, Wordsworth, to such volley, assaying an undeniably irritating egotism against an undeniably powerful modernity. In the 1800 Preface to *Lyrical Ballads* Wordsworth advocated a poetry of "feeling" (even a "spontaneous overflow of powerful feelings"): "the feeling therein developed gives importance to the action and situation, and not the action and situation to the feeling." He pressed the "fluxes and refluxes of the mind" into a structuring principle, a musculature, for poetry.[34] Fourteen years on, in the Prospectus to *The Excursion*, he trumped Milton on this score, writing in epic iambic pentameter to announce the mind as his terrain. If Milton conceived a cosmos of "Chaos" and the "darkest pit of lowest Erebus," Wordsworth would contend that nothing

> *can breed such fear and awe*
> *As fall upon us often when we look*
> *Into our Minds, into the Mind of Man,*
> *My haunt, and the main region of my Song.*[35]

Loving this plunge into "epic passions," Keats saw it as heart-knowledge, too: Wordsworth "martyrs himself to the human heart, the main region of his song—" (*K* 129). Wordsworth would soon be arguing (also in italics) that the primary "business of poetry" is to "treat of things not as they *are*, but as they *appear*; not as they exist in themselves, but as they *seem* to exist to the *senses*, and to the *passions*."[36] It was this deliberately "internal" register that led Hazlitt to call him "the most original poet now living." In his first lecture on English poetry Hazlitt defined "Poetry" as "the language of the imagination and the passions," and Wordsworth was its exemplar: "he furnishes it from his own mind, and is his own subject."[37] This was Keats's poetic syntax, too: senses, imagination, passion, feelings, and the heroism of the mind in action.

On 3 May 1818, Keats is thinking about Wordsworth's *Tintern Abbey* when he explains to Reynolds why he has kept his medical books: "an extensive knowledge is needful to thinking people – it takes away the heat and fever; and helps, by widening speculation, to ease the Burden of the Mystery" (*K* 127), this last phrase mindful of Wordsworth's gratitude for

> that blessed mood,
> In which the burthen of the mystery,
> In which the heavy and the weary weight
> Of all this unintelligible world
> Is lighten'd.   (*Tintern Abbey* 38–42)

Keats frequently talked of these lines, recalled Bailey (*KC* 2:275). In the letter to Reynolds, he talks of them again, but with a difference: easing the burden, he comes to think, is not Wordsworth's genius; it's his knowledge of, feeling for the burden. The deep pulse of the lines above is everything between *blessed mood* and *Is lighten'd*: thirty syllables of contradiction that weigh the verse with achingly immediate sensation. Not every poet can pace *unintelligible* into iambic pentameter. Wordsworth could, tuned to the somber chord of *mystery, heavy, weary*. Of a line in *Paradise Lost* Keats was struck by how "the sound is unaccountably expressive of the description."[38] I think he took the measure here, too.

Giving *Tintern Abbey* a pro and con with Milton's intent in *Paradise Lost* to justify the ways of God to man, especially the penalty of mortality, Keats argues for Wordsworth's deeper power. In that extended figure of thinking-life as a "Mansion of Many Apartments" (*K* 129–30) he locates Wordsworth's maturity of "vision into the heart and nature of Man." Even as the syntax of *Lines* aims at *lighten'd*, Keats reads its route through prepositions – *In which, In which, Of all* – as the nerve core of Wordsworth's genius in poetry's "dark Passages":

> We see not the ballance of good and evil. We are in a Mist. We are now in that state—We feel the "burden of the Mystery," To this Point was Wordsworth come, as far as I can conceive when he wrote 'Tintern Abbey' and it seems to me that his Genius is explorative of those dark Passages ... in sofar as he can, more than we, make discoveries, and shed a light in them—Here I must think Wordsworth is deeper than Milton. (*K* 130)

Milton's "Philosophy," fixed to "resting places and seeming sure points in reasoning," Keats proposes, "did not think into the human heart, as Wordsworth has done" (*K* 130–31) – his language echoing Wordsworth's Prospectus (with the nice prepositioning *think into*, instead of *think about*) mingled with Hazlitt's admiration of Lear's "irregular starts of imagination, suddenly wrenched from all its accustomed holds and resting-places in the soul." Keats underlined these last words in *Characters of Shakespear's Plays* (1817).[39] To write this way (Shakespeare, Wordsworth, Hazlitt too) was heroic genius to Keats, and personally felt. As he was writing this notion out for Reynolds, Tom had been spitting blood.

Could Wordsworth's subjective power be disentangled from his penchant for exercising the didactic "whims of an Egotist" (*K* 99)? Keats looked to Shakespeare's talent for "fine things said unintentionally, in the intensity of working out conceits" (*K* 72) – that is, poetic figures (how finely Keats relays an authorial *unintentionally* into a poet's aesthetic *intensity*). He compared "the wordsworthian or egotistical sublime" (another great coinage) to "the poetical Character" of no necessary reference to the author, "the camelion Poet."[40] Shakespeare's works, even in first-person sonnets, he calls "Allegory" (*K* 240). "Allegory" is, in root sense, "speaking as another"; how apt for Richard Woodhouse to remember Keats reading his own poetry "after he has composed & written it down" and being "struck" that the words "seemed the prod^n of another person than his own" (*KC* 1:129). Even that subjective hallmark, a lyric "I," might be another.

"Isabella is what I should call were I a reviewer 'A weak-sided Poem,'" Keats confides to Reynolds, playing a reviewer "I" against the narrating "I." In "my dramatic capacity I enter fully into the feeling: but in Propria Persona I should be apt to quiz it myself."[41] Keats's "self" in this sentence is a character of full feeling, a reviewer, a self-critic, a self-quizzer. "Propria Persona" too is a role, a persona.[42] We can see this dramatizing reflex in an intimately confessional letter to Bailey, 18 July 1818: "I am certain I have not a right feeling towards Women," he confesses and explicates, and then shrugs off with a shift to a persona: "after all I do think better of Womankind than to suppose they care whether Mister John Keats five feet hight likes them or not" (K 192). This is a pained self-scrutiny in a world where poetry and manliness were not conspicuous synonyms, but it is lodged in, maybe enabled by, the self as a character.

This reflex of self-distancing is deliberated in Keats's remarks on "the poetical Character." To write in a mode of "no self," "no Identity," is to enjoy creative liberty, to "have as much delight in conceiving an Iago as an Imogen."[43] Keats could surmise such a "camelion Poet" even in passages of Milton, when he conceived what it's like to be the fallen and still proud archangel Satan hiding his spiritual essence for a night in a lowly serpent's body:

> Whose spirit does not ache at the smothering and confinement – the unwilling stillness—the "waiting close"? Whose head is not dizzy at the prosiable speculations of Satan in the serpent prison—no passage of poetry ever can give a greater pain of suffocation.[44]

Compare this largeness of imagination to the narrow, virtuous pedagogy of Milton's epic narrator: "the Enemie of Mankind, enclos'd / In Serpent, Inmate bad" (PL 9.494–95). Keats senses the camelion-Milton in the poet who could convey the pathos of defeated Satan's survey of "The dismal situation waste and wild," beholding "sights of woe, / Regions of sorrow, doleful shades, where peace / And rest can never dwell; hope never comes / That comes to all" (PL 1.60, 64–67). This is Keats's underlining, with another marginal remark: "One of the most mysterious of semi-speculations is . . . that of one Mind's imagining into another."[45] Mind? Keats could "conceive of a billiard ball" from the inside (said Woodhouse) "that it may have a sense of delight from its own roundness, smoothness volubility . . . & the rapidity of its motion" (L 1:389).

This liberal speculation distills for Keats, in the midst of a disquisition with a friend, the (now famous) aesthetic principle, "negative capability": a receptivity to "uncertainties, mysteries, doubts, without any irritable reaching after fact and reason" (K 78). Keats writes this out to his brothers in December 1817, and it would remain an intellectual and poetic throughline. You see it in February 1818 in his satire of Wordsworth's eagerness to "bully his reader into a certain philosophy" of "palpable design" (K 99); or in May 1818, in his disdain of Milton's sure points and resting-places in reasoning; or in September 1819, in irritation at a dear friend's sense of "personal identity" as necessarily having "made up his Mind about every thing." "The only means of strengthening one's intellect," counters Keats, "is to make up ones mind about nothing—to let the mind be a thoroughfare for all thoughts. Not a select party" (*L* 2:213).

In this open, dialectical temper, Keats reads everything. He couldn't absorb Raphael's sketches until he saw "something done in quite an opposite spirit" (*L* 2:19). He's generous to friends this way, too. About a quarrel raging between Haydon and Reynolds, he sighs, "they are both in the right & both in the wrong" (*L* 1:205). It was equanimity with poetic dividend. "Though a quarrel in the Streets is a thing to be hated, the energies displayed in it are fine": "the very thing in which consists poetry." Keats could think of himself as such a spectacle: "By a superior being our reasoning may take the same tone – though erroneous they may be fine." Leaving no tone unturned, Keats quarrels with himself about his love of quarreling, thinking off and on that these poetic energies were "not so fine a thing as philosophy" (*K* 243) – not the dogma but the moral exertion. The most unsettled sentences in that letter to Bailey in November 1817 come near its end, when Keats says that he tends to react to news of "a Misfortune having befalled another" with a shrug, "Well it cannot be helped. – he will have the leisure of trying the resources of his spirit." Then, hearing himself sounding "cold," he claims this is no "heartlessness but abstraction"; then he reviews himself in abstraction: "I begin to suspect myself and the genuiness of my feelings" as "a few barren Tragedy-tears." Then he tacks to nearer news, weighed with genuine feeling: " – My brother Tom is much improved" (*K* 71).

Error, quarrel, speculation, and among the most inescapable of sensations, mortality: this is the heart and mind of Keats's creative energy, soon and late. And all the time as a poet.

CHAPTER 2

Conceiving early poems, and Poems

First looking

Keats seems wired to write poetry in discovery, turning themes, allusions, and formal traditions (stanzas, couplets, meters) into workouts with what he's been reading, has in his head, feels on his pulses. At the same time, he was acutely sensitive to the cultural warfare and social gate-keeping impinging on his vocational passion. Here he was in the summer of 1816, without parents but with good friends, counselors, and sponsors; without a university education and connections, but qualified for a career as a general medical practitioner. In October, he passed his apothecaries examination. But he cast his lot with poetry, wanting to join this company of men. This was the month he wrote his first really great poem, spurred by a transformative event of reading a man's vigorous epic, his sonnet, *On First Looking into Chapman's Homer.*

Clarke had on loan a gorgeous 1616 folio edition of George Chapman's late sixteenth-century translation, and was eager to share it with Keats. They stayed up all night with it.[1] Their excitement played off the eighteenth-century gold standard, Alexander Pope's Homer, which Clarke also laid out, for comparisons. Here's one passage – Pope's Odysseus, tempest-tossed and shipwrecked, staggering towards land:

> fainting as he touch'd the shore,
> He dropp'd his sinewy arms; his knees no more
> Perform'd their office, or his weight upheld;
> His swoln heart heav'd; his bloated body swell'd;
> From mouth and nose the briny torrent ran;
> And lost in lassitude lay all the man,
> Deprived of voice, of motion, and of breath,
> The soul scarce waking in the arms of death.
>
> (*Odyssey* V.580–87)

You can see Pope's technical precision: strong masculine rhymes, mostly regular iambs with measured medial pauses, the syntax fit to the line. Only "no more / Perform'd" runs over, with a nice pause at the end of 581 to suggest not just weak but destroyed knees. Clarke (who thought line 581 just silly) then showed Keats Chapman's Homer:

> Then forth he came, his both knees falt'ring, both
> His strong hands hanging down, and all with froth
> His cheeks and nostrils flowing, voice and breath
> Spent to all use, and down he sank to death.
> *The sea had soak'd his heart through*; all his veins
> His toils had rack'd t' a labouring woman's pains.
> Dead-weary was he.   (V.608–14; Clarke's italics)

With relentless rhythmic stresses against the iambic pentameter grid, Chapman's syntax runs through four lines before stopping, its rhyme pulses rather than pauses in the momentum. While the first sentence stops for *death*, it scarcely halts the intensifying collapse. Compare Pope's "From **mouth** and **nose** the **bri**ny **tor**rent **ran**" to Chapman's "The **sea** had **soak'd** his **heart through**" – a line that had Keats exclaiming (said Clarke). Such dynamism thrilled Keats into "one of his delighted stares."

Reading Chapman, Keats comes to life as a poet. He felt its pulse as he paced the miles back home, and as soon as he arrived, he sat down to write out a sonnet, marking its rhymes and quatrains. As you can see on this draft (Fig. 1), he got it pretty much in one shot, revising just a syllable, *low* to *deep* (6), for the better chord with *demesne*. He ended the last two lines each with a long dash, as if to figure a wonder expanding into the blank, silent space beyond. Blotting the page, he messengered it over to Clarke, who found it on his breakfast-table. Clarke showed it to Hunt, who was "unhesitating and prompt" in "admiration" (*Recollections*, 132), and decided to publish it in his "Young Poets" essay (*Examiner*, 1 December) with this happy prologue:

> we do not hesitate to pronounce excellent, especially the first six lines. The word *swims* is complete; and the conclusion is equally powerful and quiet: –

ON FIRST LOOKING INTO CHAPMAN'S HOMER.

> Much have I travel'd in the realms of Gold,
>   And many goodly states and Kingdoms seen;
> Round many western Islands have I been,
>   Which Bards in fealty to Apollo hold.
> But of one wide expanse had I been told,
>   That deep-brow'd Homer ruled as his demesne;
>   Yet could I never judge what men could mean
> Till I heard CHAPMAN speak out loud and bold,
> Then felt I like some watcher of the skies,
>   When a new planet swims into his ken;

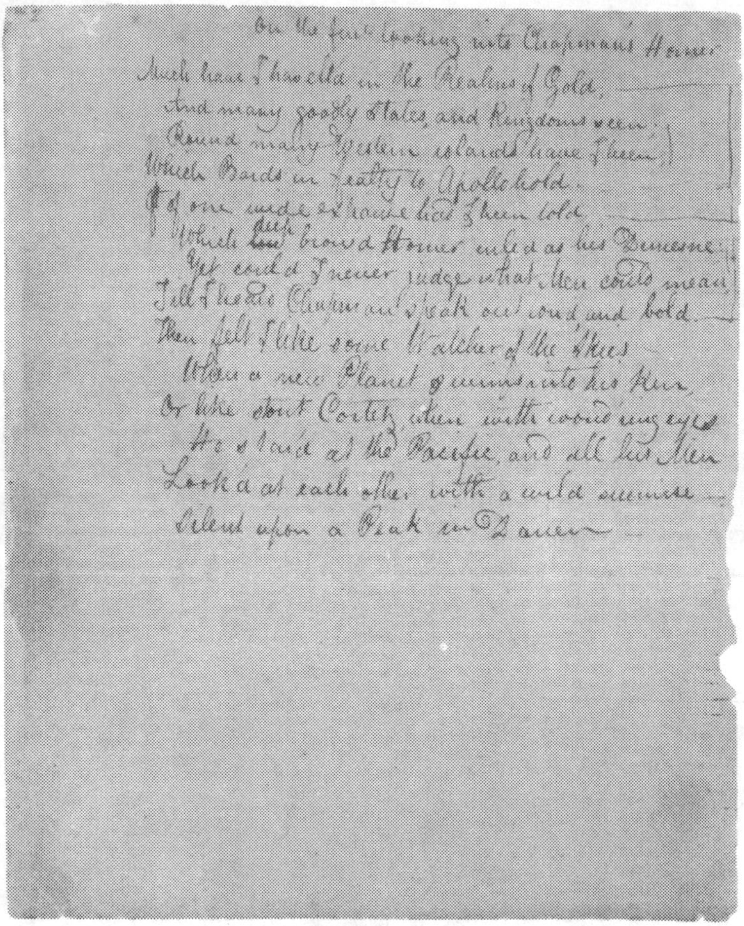

Fig. 1 "On the first looking into Chapman's Homer." Houghton Library, Harvard University, MS Keats 2.4. Keats's first draft, October 1816. Note his marking out the quatrains.

> Or like stout CORTEZ, when with eagle eyes
>   He stared at the Pacific, – and all his men
> Looked at each other with a wild surmise,—
>   Silent, upon a peak in Darien.
>
> *Oct.* 1816   JOHN KEATS.

Keats had one more revision, sharpening Cortez's "wond'ring eyes" into far-seeing "eagle eyes." Its powerfully quiet conclusion notwithstanding, the sonnet rings its words from the very start: "Much have I travell'd in the Realms of Gold." The four initial syllables strike the iambic code into dramatic stress, with chimes of *have/trav-* and *vell'd/Gold*. So too, at naming the poets, Keats beats the stresses: **deep-brow'd Hom**er; **I heard Chapman speak out loud** and **bold**. The sonnet formation deftly structures the drama: a survey of what has been "seen" (first quatrain); a turn to Homer in Chapman (second quatrain); a volta-pivot at line 9 into affective similes of visual discovery (sestet), first to astronomer William Herschel finding Uranus in 1781, then to Chapman's nearer historical company, Cortez arriving at the Pacific. Alert to the figurative use of blank page-space, Keats sets the vast *skies* at the end of line 9 and the staring *eyes* at the end of 11, following this with a fleeting double-grammar in 12. The line unit "He stared at the Pacific, – and all his men" sets the men and the Pacific in the conquistador's stare. Line 13 shifts the grammar to make them all lookers in a relay of rapture at the expanse before them. With *surmise* marked by a comma-pause and then a dash into the page-space, Keats gives *all his men* (another run of three stresses) just a faint rhyme with *Darien* (a falling dactyl) for that quiet, yet still resonant, close.

Taking another look at the sonnet for *Poems*, Keats decided that "Yet could I never judge what men could mean" was "bald, and too simply wondering" (Clarke, 130) and reworked it into a trope of inspiration: "Yet did I never breathe its pure serene" (Sonnet XI). He was tapping an older sense of *serene*, an expanse of calm, clear sky: the "pure serene" of Coleridge's *Hymn before Sunrise, in the Vale of Chamouni* (72) or Byron's "the blue deep's serene: –" (also with a suggestive dash).[2] In Keats's ear, too, is a line in Pope's *Iliad*: "When not a Breath disturbs the deep Serene" (8.689). Keats reverses this no-breath into inspiration, the in-breathing of reading Chapman (*spiritus* is Latin *wind* and *spirit*). His sonnet's reading "I" is a "camelion Poet" (two years before Keats coined this term), "in for – and feeling" what it was "like" to be Herschel looking into the night sky and seeing Uranus, or "like" Cortez, first looking into the Pacific.[3] Herschel and Cortez are at once figurative company and remembered reading. At Enfield Keats had received as a prize John Bonnycastle's *Introduction to Astronomy* (1787), with an account of Herschel's discovery, and he read William Robertson's *History of America* on the conquistadors in Panama.[4] The Keats-brotherhood extends to Clarke, and more broadly, the fraternity of modern poets, looking back to Chapman and forward into the unwritten serene of nineteenth-century possibility. Severn would recall "the almost flamelike intensity of Keats's eager glances when he was keenly excited or interested . . . Those falcon-eyes" – as if he were among these men.[5]

Hunt's introduction of Keats to readers of *The Examiner* with this sonnet was prescient: it's now Keats's most famous one. Noting that this young poet "has not yet published any things except in a newspaper" (that sonnet *To Solitude* back in May), Hunt mentions that he has seen (from Clarke) a manuscript of poems that "fairly surprised us with the truth of their ambition, and ardent grappling" – in effect, a kenning of Keats, with a hint of rhyming company in the way *surprise*d echoes in Keats's ocean-beholders' all-absorbing *surmise*.

Bookending his *Poems* (1817): excursion and dedication

Poems, Keats's debut at age twenty-one, is at once a vocational and a sociable volume, honoring friends and fellow-poets, particularly Hunt's school and its patrons: Homer, Petrarch, Chaucer, Spenser, Shakespeare, Milton. On the title-page (Fig. 2) is a profile of laurel-wreathed Spenser (looking Shakespearean) with this verse:

> "What more felicity can fall to creature,
> Than to enjoy delight with liberty?"
> *Fate of the Butterfly.*—SPENSER.

This honor to a poetics of frisky delight also glances at the risky politics of liberty. In *Fate*, the butterfly is destined for a spider's trap. For his liberty-themed *Examiner* articles "libeling" the Prince Regent, Hunt had been dealt a steep fine of £500 and a two-year prison sentence. He retaliated with a temper of delight, embowering his cell with wallpaper, rugs, furniture, piano, plants, and books, as he continued to edit *The Examiner* and receive visits from Lamb, Byron, Thomas Moore, Jeremy Bentham, and Lord Brougham. Sonnet III in *Poems* is *Written on the Day that Mr. Leigh Hunt Left Prison*.

The last poem Keats drafted for *Poems* is a dedicatory sonnet, "To Leigh Hunt, Esq.," placed right at the front. Its theme is Hunt as muse of "delights," but an epigraph on page 1 –

> "Places of nestling green for Poets made."
> STORY OF RIMINI.

– is more than delight; it's also code. In such a nestling place, Paulo and Francesca, throbbing with illicit passion and reading of Lancelot and Guinevere, give in: "The world was all forgot, the struggle o'er, / Desperate the joy. – That day they read no more."[6] It was Hunt's sympathy for an adulteress caught in loveless marriage by the machinations of fathers that riled Z into his first paper on "The Cockney School." Keats was waving the flag, branded with nestling green.

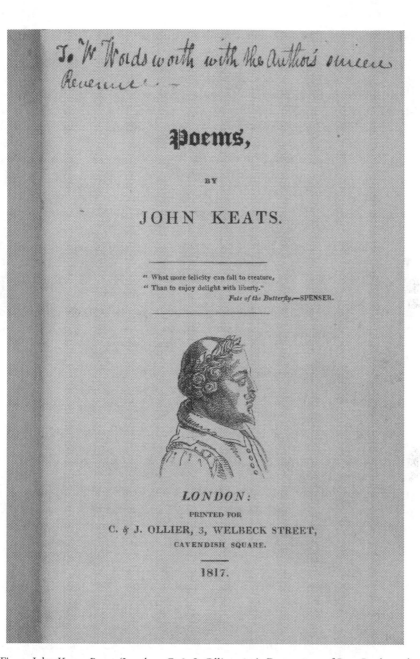

To Wr Wordsworth with the author's sincere Reverence:—

Poems,

BY

JOHN KEATS.

" What more felicity can fall to creature,
" Than to enjoy delight with liberty."
Fate of the Butterfly.—SPENSER.

LONDON:
PRINTED FOR
C. & J. OLLIER, 3, WELBECK STREET,
CAVENDISH SQUARE.

1817.

Fig. 2 John Keats, *Poems* (London: C. & J. Ollier, 1817). Department of Rare Books and Special Collections, Princeton University Library. Keats inscribed the volume and sent it to Wordsworth. The page-design bespeaks "poetry": fancy-lettered title, epigram from Spenser, profile of a Poet Laureate: part Spenser (unofficially England's first Poet Laureate), part Shakespeare. The volume appeared in economical octavo, 3 March 1817, priced 6 shillings. The Olliers, P. B. Shelley's publishers, were part of Leigh Hunt's circle. Keats sent this copy to Wordsworth in the Lake District, with this inscription. He never replied, and left most of the pages uncut (Lowell, *John Keats*, 1:126).

The volume's first poem (untitled, "I stood tip-toe") and its last, *Sleep and Poetry*, are its two most ambitious works (at 242 and 404 lines, respectively), each an extravagance of romance couplets, some played across stanzas even, in rhythms of pleasure and passion, feminine rhymes (*wandering/pondering*), and flagrant enjambments, some for a half-dozen lines: in sum, a full-court press of avant-garde "Cockney poetry."[7] Both poems also involve serious purposes. "I stood tip-toe" wends from picturesque fancies to meditations on the origin of mythologies in human desire and their ever-fresh idiom for modern poetry. *Sleep and Poetry* renders a manifesto for modern poetry and announces its poet's career-goals and principles.

Keats's provisional as well as prospective sense of his occasions comes out in postures of winning wit alongside of, or intermixed with, his visionary fervors. The poet who greets readers with four happy beats, "I stood tip-toe on a little hill" cartoons the redundant elevation for his survey.[8] A "wide wand'ring for the greediest eye" is both the optics and poetry, playing into a light self-parody that catches the syllable *ring* for meta-poetics:

> Here are sweet peas, on tip-toe for a flight:
> With wings of gentle flush o'er delicate white,
> And taper fingers catching at all things,
> To bind them all about with tiny rings.
>
> (57–60)

The tip-toe poet mirrors his flight-readiness, catching all things in rings of verse. The first verse paragraph ends, "So I straightway began to pluck a posey / Of luxuries bright, milky, soft and rosy" (27–28): posey-gathering plays, cross-lingually, on *anthology* (Greek *anthologia*: flower-gather) and anagrams a pun on the literary medium at hand, *poesy*. Another parody unfolds as Keats measures a flow of grass-blades across a stream:

> Why, you might read two sonnets, ere they reach
> To where the hurrying freshnesses aye preach
> A natural sermon o'er their pebbly beds   (69–71)

The opening twenty-eight-line stanza takes the time of "two sonnets" to read, and "natural sermon" is a conspicuously literary flourish, echoing Shakespeare's Duke Senior, his ear to "books in the running brooks, / Sermons in stones" (*As You Like It* 2.1). Wordplay is a reflex in Keats's letters and a social recreation he enjoyed (especially with a partner like Charles Lamb). It is also, intensively, a poetics of language as an ever surprising field of semantic formations. Reading John Keats is always to encounter John Keats reading.

"I stood tip-toe" is witty fun with poetry-making, but it's also on course, by this activated potential, to a sustained, wild surmise in "Shapes from the invisible world, unearthly singing . . . Full in the speculation of the stars" (181–92). This is the mythogenesis of the "sweet tale" of Cynthia and Endymion, a goddess and her formerly mortal, now divine lover. Keats first titled this poem *Endymion* (before reserving the name for his new venture). The poem that his tip-toe poet yearns to tell, and does, is of a divine nuptial night, after an evening "so bright, and clear," its breezes "ethereal, and pure," as to "cure / The languid sick" and waken every tongue into "poesy" (208–36) as shared social transformation. Only Keats, with a love of poetry and an intimacy with mortal sickness, could have put the generative union just this way. He ends with a pause, but not without another one of his long dashes into possibility:

> Was there a Poet born?—but now no more,
> My wand'ring spirit must no further soar.– –
>
> (241–42)

The categorical capital P is pregnant: a Poet might have been born from these nuptials; a poet might have been born in imagining this; and the latest birth may be John Keats, reanimating the old myth for modern poetry. The stake is as present as it is prospective. Does that dash soar? or does it suspend?

This is not the last time Keats will conjure a Latin ghost of *errancy* and *error* in wandering; it becomes a default setting. It already undulates in "the fair paradise of Nature's light" (126) as the first poets' inspiration. After Milton, any writing of *paradise* cannot but evoke *lost*, and Keats pretends nothing more than fantasy in a poetry that "Charms us at once away from all our troubles: / So that we feel uplifted from the world" (138–39). Even if not on the immediate horizon, some compromise is surely in the air when "the soul is lost in pleasant smotherings" (132), the hiss of *s* (in all but two words) issuing seduction.

"Was there a Poet born?" gets answered, in effect, by the rest of *Poems*, especially its manifesto, *Sleep and Poetry*, heralded with a singular internal title-page (97). Composed in Hunt's library, it is a homage to Hunt's school of modern mythology, poetic luxury, and liberal politics. Yet amid the ardent declaration of goals and principles, Keats involves other moods and modes that "a Poet" might take. If vocation is his passion, it's not yet a secure claim, and he hedges with over-stylized affectation:

> O Poesy! for thee I hold my pen
> That am not yet a glorious denizen
> Of thy wide heaven—Should I rather kneel . . . ?
>
> (47–49)

This poet is sensitive, too, to his proximity to the culture of female commonplace-books:

> a bowery nook
> Will be elysium—an eternal book
> Whence I may copy many a lovely saying
> About the leaves, and flowers—about the playing
> Of nymphs in woods, and fountains   (63–67)

Twice-tolled, *about* (66) indicates both objects for poetry and its sites, all very Fragonard: artsy, decorative, and coyly girlish. Keats's safety-clause is the plan for more heroic efforts:

> Then the events of this wide world I'd seize
> Like a strong giant, and my spirit teaze
> Till at its shoulders it should proudly see
> Wings to find out an immortality.   (81–84)

Yet all this big talk – wide, strong and giant – still seems boyish heroics: life as "the reading of an ever-changing tale" about maidens and school-boys "Riding the springy branches of an elm" (91–95). This is an occasion propelled by aesthetic choices rather than life choices.[9]

The poetry zigzags on provisionals, conditionals, subjunctives: *if, may, could, would.* Strong gestures typically waver. Keats boldly splits the rhyme for riding that *elm* (95), starting a new paragraph on the master-plan of vocation:

> O for ten years, that I may overwhelm
> Myself in poesy   (96–97)

This enjambment relays to a rhymed *realm* in the next sentence, first stop on Keats's grand map:

> First the realm I'll pass
> Of Flora, and old Pan: sleep in the grass,
> Feed upon apples red, and strawberries,
> And choose each pleasure that my fancy sees . . .
>
> (101–04)

Yet the stage-managing of a supposedly passing fancy looks a bit as if it might pick and choose forever. Those giant shoulders (82–83) get eclipsed by nymphs with "shoulders white" (107). The syllabus, "A lovely tale of human life we'll read" (110), aims toward this finale. They will

> entice me on, and on
> Through almond blossoms and rich cinnamon;
> Till in the bosom of a leafy world
> We rest in silence, like two gems upcurl'd
> In the recesses of a pearly shell.　　(117–21)

The sonic lure of *on, and on-almond-and-cinnamon* is poetry's enticement to this pearly recess of dead-end of infantine perfection. The poet who would sign "rest in silence" is no Prince Hamlet; he's happy to lose the name of action in this jeweled arrest.

　　Taking a beat with a stanza break, Keats wrestles poet and poem into a fresh start, again splitting a couplet for this turn from the pearly shell:

> And can I ever bid these joys farewell?
> Yes, I must pass them for a nobler life,
> Where I may find the agonies, the strife
> Of human hearts　　(122–25)

Yet in saying "*these* joys" (as opposed to *those*) the farewell is incomplete, and Keats's icon of nobler life, a charioteer, still seems a bit pearly, even in the spell of high intelligence:

> The charioteer with wond'rous gesture talks
> To the trees and mountains; and there soon appear
> Shapes of delight, of mystery, and fear　　(136–38)

This looks like invocational power, if the conjunctive *and* is taken to imply (*post hoc ergo propter hoc*) that the Shapes are an embodied consequence. But *appear* may indicate only a wond'rous fancy. Woodhouse marked these lines with nice qualification: "Personification of the Epic poet, when the enthusiasm of inspiration is upon him."[10] And when Keats gives the Epic poet an entourage of girls, girls, "girls / Dancing their sleek hair into tangled curls" (149–50), the nymphs are back, those *curls* even recalling those "up*curl*'d" gems of the pre-noble recess. If it was a no-brainer for Z to dismiss such poetry as "very pretty raving" from "a boy of pretty abilities," it's telling that even Amy Lowell, a sympathetic biographer angry at the reviewer-bullies, could blush for Keats's "manhood" here as "mere vision": "Was ever a more unsatisfactory statement of intention put into words?"[11] Loving these lines, apparently, Keats didn't cancel them, just (again) shifted gears, with a vow, at the end of the next paragraph, to "keep alive / The thought of that same chariot, and the strange / Journey it went" (160–62).

The line that ends *strange* is part of yet another couplet split across a stanza break, a formalism that Keats keeps foregrounding for new purposes born from habitual affections. This one heralds the launch of those Huntian polemics, Keats's bait for some immediate strife:

> Is there so small a range
> In the present strength of manhood, that the high
> Imagination cannot freely fly
> As she was wont of old?   (162–65)

The question previews "a scism / Nurtured by foppery and barbarism" that has consigned Pegasus to "rocking horse" meters of "dismal soul'd" instructors (181–87):

> closely wed
> To musty laws lined out with wretched rule
> And compass vile: so that ye taught a school
> Of dolts to smooth, inlay, and clip, and fit,
> Till, like the certain wands of Jacob's wit,
> Their verses tallied   (194–99)

Keats's satire of these "thousand handicraftsmen" in "the mask / Of Poesy" (200–01) was a cheer for the Hunt-school.

The battling critic is not Keats's only role for audition in this venture. His next turn is to try out a chivalric pose, disdaining "strength alone" in devotion to a "poesy" of

> might half slumb'ring on its own right arm.
> The very archings of her eye-lids charm
> A thousand willing agents to obey,
> And still she governs with the mildest sway.
> (237–40)

Such poesy is divine, a human comfort, and obliquely poetical-political, a new mode of government, an image of a world in which "they shall be accounted poet kings / Who simply tell the most heart-easing things" (267–68). Keats could have ended here, with a teasing of mature development seeded in "simply" and "heart-easing." He seems, even, to have thought about this, dropping the line down for the poem's only single-line stanza,[12] as if in provisional farewell:

> O may these joys be ripe before I die.
> (269)

Yet this hope of ripeness is not all.

And so another couplet splits for a new stanza, to resume the reviewer-baiting:

> Will not some say that I presumptuously
> Have spoken? that from hastening disgrace
> 'Twere far better to hide my foolish face?
> That whining boyhood should with reverence bow
> Ere the dread thunderbolt could reach me ?
>
> (270–74)

Keats drives his defense against such charges into an extreme, with the heroics and mock-heroics so indistinguishable as to seem synonymous – an ode and a parody at once:

> Ah! rather let me like a madman run
> Over some precipice; let the hot sun
> Melt my Dedalian wings, and drive me down
> Convuls'd and headlong!   (301–04)

The lines run a poetic excess of meta-enjambment with *run* and *down*, as the sentence hurtles into flagrant anti-Augustan couplets, even hazarding *down* into a triplet. *Sleep and Poetry* doesn't resolve the tonal question of such over-the-top, down-driving energy: brave risks, campy extravagance, or just Icarus-foolishness?

From these serial positions and poses, postures and posturings, *Sleep and Poetry* comes to rest in the scene of its composition, a couch in Hunt's library, with its disparate sculptures and paintings, in effect, indexing the inventory: "bards who sung / In other ages – cold and sacred busts"; "fauns and satyrs taking aim / At swelling apples with a frisky leap"; "a train / Of nymphs"; "Sappho's meek head... half smiling down / At nothing," "Great Alfred's too, with anxious, pitying eyes," and hero-patriot "Kosciusko's worn / By horrid sufferance – mightily forlorn"; poet Petrarch, who "Starts at the sight of Laura; nor can wean / His eyes from her sweet face"; and last, "The face of Poesy," which "overlook'd things that I scarce could tell" – among them, the paradoxically "sleepless" poet of *Sleep and Poetry* (381–400). The poem, and volume, end with patrilineage curved back to produce filial Keats as the father of his present lines:

> And up I rose refresh'd, and glad, and gay,
> Resolving to begin that very day
> These lines; and howsoever they be done,
> I leave them as a father does his son.
>
> (401–04)

Keats wittily plays the conventional *envoi*, "go little book," into autogenesis: go little son-lines. *I leave* signs both a bequest and a relinquishment to indeterminate worldly fortune – delight and liberty perhaps, but also uncertainty. The month after *Poems* was out, Keats manned up for his most resolved project ever – a poem of soaring and sinking, *Endymion: A Poetic Romance.*

CHAPTER 3

Falling in and out of love with Endymion: A Poetic Romance
Rereading King Lear

Contest, test, trial

"I stood tip-toe" closes in a relay of mirrorings: a moon-enchanted poet conceives a moon-raptured shepherd conceiving a mythic shepherd (Endymion) beloved by a Moon-goddess. All are inspired poets, with Keats in the production-line. The worldly genesis of *Endymion: A Poetic Romance* (the longest poem he'd ever write, ever publish) was a compact made in spring 1817 with Hunt and Shelley to see who could finish a 4,000-line poem by the end of the year. With *Poems* just out, Keats was eager for a major project. He wrote through 1817, had proofs by the next winter, and a publication at the end of April 1818 – the only one of the three to succeed.

He was doubly energized: *A Poetic Romance* was not only a venture into a promising genre but also keyed to Keats's romance of being "a Poet." "As to what you say about my being a Poet," he wrote to George, and Bailey,

> I have no right to talk until Endymion is finished – it will be a test a trial of my Powers of Imagination and chiefly of my invention which is a rare thing indeed – by which I must make 4000 Lines of one bare circumstance and fill them with Poetry . . . why endeavor after a long Poem? To which I should answer . . . a long Poem is a test of Invention which I take to be the Polar Star of Poetry . . . Did our great Poets ever write short Pieces? . . . I put on no Laurels till I shall have finished Endymion.[1]

In vocation as well as theme – visionary imagination with an erotic vibe – *Endymion* would be a test of length and strength, a work of invention that would prove Keats's poetry to the world. In the "old tale" (4.786), a young man's dreams of a Moon-goddess end in his being "Ensky'd" (778) with her – its "felicity" (782) an embodiment of Keats's "favorite Speculation" to Bailey: "we shall enjoy ourselves here after by having what we call happiness on Earth repeated in a finer tone and so repeated" (*K* 70).

Translated into vocational desire, this thing of beauty would accomplish a few "paces towards the Temple of Fame" (*K* 61).

Yet nearing the end, its poet-narrator is oddly mourning for Endymion, as if things hadn't worked out this way, "Forgetting the old tale" (4.782–87). This may be because Keats's line of conception had become "a trial" in a different sense, a misgiving about visionary desire – its erotic fuel, its psychological and social fallout, its pathology, its self-indulgence, its comedy, and, not least, its poetry. *Endymion* takes several turns around these core concerns, from enchanted to severely critical. We get scenes of dreaming as inspiration, as obsession, as disease, as fatal addiction; of bowers as paradises, as cradles, as prisons, as tombs. We encounter a succession of young men who reflect and qualify each other (Endymion; suicidal genius Chatterton; luxuriously doted-on Adonis; enthralled then deformed Glaucus) and a fraternity of lovers, self-lovers, and beloveds from myth and legend (Pan, Ganymede, Hyacinth, Narcissus).

Z had no trouble parodying Keats into this company: "Mr Keats has thoroughly appropriated the character, if not the name . . . Endymion is not a Greek shepherd, loved by a Grecian goddess; he is merely a young Cockney rhymester dreaming a phantasic dream at the full of the moon" (*Blackwood's Edinburgh Magazine* 3 [Aug. 1818] 521–22). This investment notwithstanding, *Endymion* is noticeably uneven, its hero pitied and idealized but also pathologized and parodied. The narrator's tone shifts too, from visionary devotion, to tragic pathos, to exasperation; and the denouement is magical and factitious at once. If this array suggests Keats testing himself, it has also proven a test for readers. Some get testy at the disparities; others try to coordinate a romance allegory. My view (not mine alone) is that the variety is its own allegory: Keats's pro and con about what he's doing, and his discovery, if not yet a theorizing, of this mode of imagination. "In working out the destiny of his hero," writes Stuart Sperry, Keats was "working out his own." I'll take "working out" as exercise and process rather than resolution.[2] The perplexities of *Endymion* involve questions that Keats will be returning to, turning over, and ultimately making brilliant poetic capital out of for the rest of his career. And for all the welter, *Endymion* contains some pretty impressive stretches of poetry.[3]

The melodious plot

Notwithstanding its famous opening line, "A thing of beauty is a joy for ever," *Endymion* is not known to many these days. Reading it all can be both absorbing and tedious – in any event a challenge to merely sequential summary. Here's a recap (with no claim to allegory):

Book I opens with the poet elaborating a dialectical principle of beauty as solace (in the world, and in beautiful poetry) for "despondence," "gloomy days," and "all the unhealthy and o'er-darkened ways / Made for our searching" (8–11). He projects a schedule of writing on a calendar of nature, from spring budding to fall harvest. The fable proper opens in Latmos, a pastoral mountain community governed by Endymion and devoted to the great god Pan, who is being honored in a morning festival (the setting of "Hymn to Pan"). Endymion is oddly out of it, withdrawn in a "fixed trance" among the tribal elders, "Like one who on the earth had never stept. / Aye, even as dead-still as a marble man" (403–05), rapt by their talk of bliss in the hereafter. His sister Peona, worried about this torpor and neglect of civic responsibility, coaxes him to a favorite bower for an affectionate inquest. Endymion recounts a dream of lovemaking in the night sky with the Moon-goddess, not untouched by lunacy: her tresses were "bright enough to make me mad" (613). She vanished in this dream, leaving him to a "human neighbourhood" that felt only envenomed (622); then she returned, and they coursed "along the dangerous sky" (646) – and he fell again "into stupid sleep" (678), to wake into the present dark, pestilent "down-sunken hours" (708). When practical-minded Peona tsks reproof, Endymion replies with a gorgeous lyric on the sensuous infusions of visionary imagination – leading to "richer entanglements, enthralments far / More self-destroying" (799–800), its "unsating food" making even the most ambitious men ready "to let occasion die, / Whilst they did sleep in love's elysium" (817–24). Daytime Endymion promises to resist fatal melancholy.

Book II begins with an ode to the "sovereign power of love!" – at once a "grief" and a "balm" for our restless, "Brain-sick shepherd-prince" (1–43). Keats summons an old epic pattern to send the hero questing to the underworld. Here Endymion stumbles onto the Bower of Adonis, where Venus's gorgeous young lover slumbers and dreams six months each year, wakened each spring to return to earth with her. Witness to their latest reunion, Endymion is stung anew with his own misery, but hears assurance of eventual bliss from Venus herself. Conveyed to a "jasmine bower" (672), he again dreams of his goddess, who again vanishes, leaving him forlorn and deranged. The book closes as he harkens to the echoed torments of separated lovers river-Alpheus and Arethusa, a nymph devoted to chaste goddess Diana.

Keats launches **Book III** with an anti-monarchal tirade – a bantling's "Cockney poetry" lisping sedition, said Z, while *The British Critic* warned of a "jacobinical apostrophe."[4] The poet wonders if love is freedom, or another tyranny. Endymion encounters a superannuated old man, Glaucus, who tells another story of romance in a bower, turned to a degraded farce. In youth, he had fallen for nymph Scylla. One morning (a pattern now familiar) he woke to find her gone. Deep in a forest resonant with groans, he finds enchantress Circe surrounded by groveling beasts, formerly her enraptured suitors. She flaunts the body of Scylla (drowned) at him, gloats, and curses him to a millennium of bitter wisdom in bodily decrepitude. Glaucus recounts a later shipwreck. Amid the corpses of many lovers he found a cryptic scroll promising restoration to all when a certain youth appears to decipher it. "Thou art the man!" he hails Endymion (234). He is. The lovers, including Glaucus and Scylla, are reunited and proceed to the palace of Neptune for a celebration. Endymion falls asleep and hears from the sky the voice of Cynthia (the Moon-goddess) prophesying their "*Immortal bliss*" in "*endless heaven*" (1022–27).

Book IV brings new trails, new trials. Endymion discovers a forlorn Indian Maid and, despairing of his elusive goddess, swoons for her. Soaring the night sky on winged steeds, they suffer "cold moonshine" (the forgotten goddess), and the Maid dissolves – then reappears and returns with Endymion to Latmos. Realizing "I have clung / To nothing, lov'd a nothing, nothing seen / Or felt but a great dream!" (640–42), Endymion decides to love the one he's with – only to hear from her, "I am forbidden" (757). Bummer. Peona arrives to wonder at her brother's melancholy on the eve of a festival to Cynthia. He tells her that he wants to "live in mossy cave" as a hermit (869). The Indian Maid chimes in that she'll give herself to "Chastity" and join "Dian's sisterhood" (892–95). Gloomier than ever, Endymion wishes that he could "have command" over their "sad fate" (984–85). Presto! the Indian Maid, morphing blond and white, becomes "Cynthia bright" (the Moon-goddess) and tells Endymion that he is to be "spiritualiz'd" (1002) and they'll range the forests together evermore. "They vanish'd far away! – Peona went / Home through the gloomy wood in wonderment" (1010–12). "THE END" (p. 207).

Preliminary signs: dedication, motto, Preface

Happy ending yes; and Keats's publishers played it all with antique flourish, setting the subtitle in antique black-letters: 𝔄 𝔓𝔬𝔢𝔱𝔦𝔠 𝔕𝔬𝔪𝔞𝔫𝔠𝔢 (Fig. 3). But this genre-tag contends at the front of the volume with several signposts of imaginations in trouble.

For a title-page epigraph, "THE STRETCHED METRE OF AN ANTIQUE SONG," Keats drew on Shakespeare's Sonnet XVII ("Who will believe my

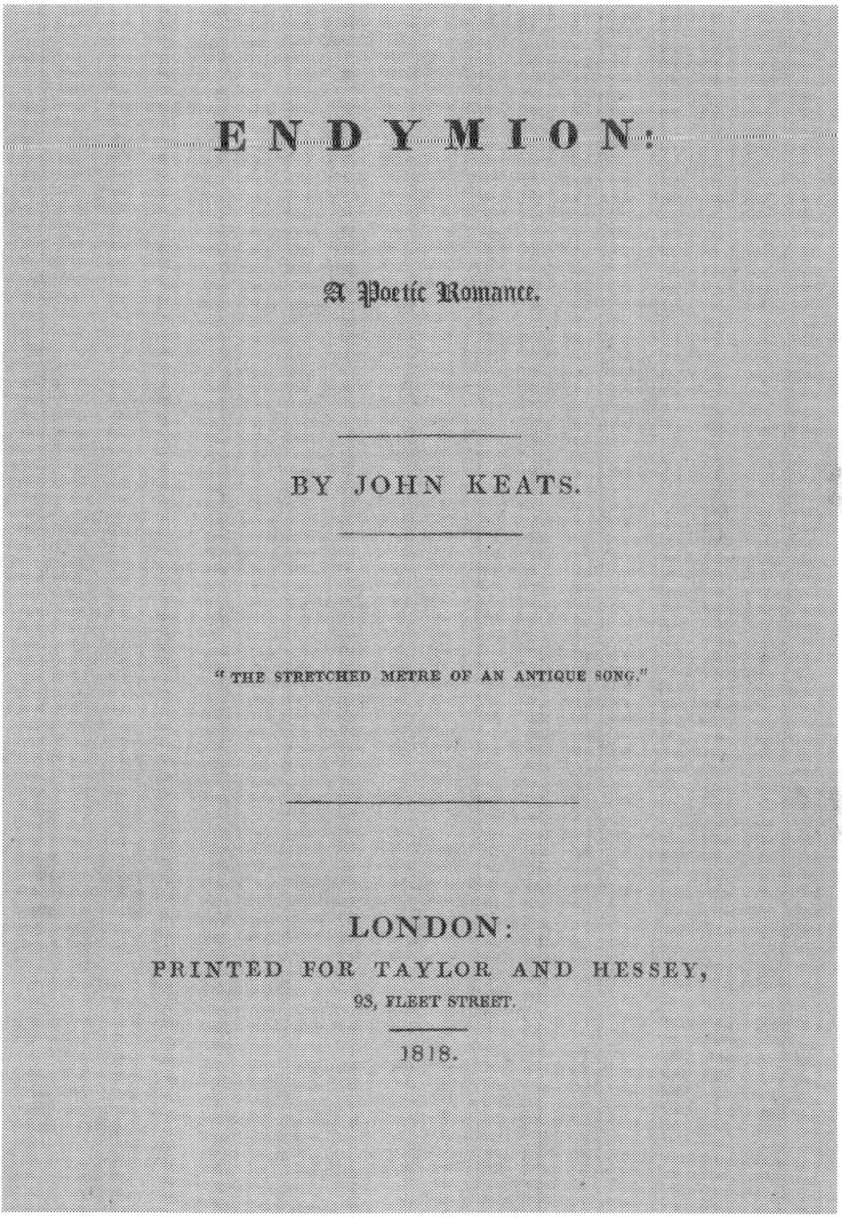

ENDYMION:

A Poetic Romance.

BY JOHN KEATS.

"THE STRETCHED METRE OF AN ANTIQUE SONG."

LONDON:

PRINTED FOR TAYLOR AND HESSEY,
93, FLEET STREET.

1818.

Fig. 3 Title-page, John Keats, *Endymion* (London: Taylor & Hessey, 1818). Department of Rare Books and Special Collections, Princeton University Library. Interested in new talent, the publishers gambled on Keats after the Olliers dumped him. The longest poem Keats would ever write or publish, *Endymion* appeared at the end of April 1818, a larger-page octavo than *Poems*, and priced 9 shillings.

verse in time to come?") – a poet's fear that his heartfelt lines will "be termed a poet's rage / And stretchèd meter of an antique song." This "will be a capital Motto for my Poem," he jokes to Reynolds in November 1817, loving how it "overwhelms a genuine Lover of Poesy with all manner of abuse" (*K* 72–73) – the very class Keats had identified as his likely readers and in which he included himself (*K* 61). Shakespeare's "stretchèd" is a disyllabic jest, enacting what it describes, with a slang joke at the sexual self-stimulation in such a measure.⁵ The Elizabethan pronunciation of *antique* as *antic* is another poke at love-songs (twin to the "antique vows" in a belated *Ode to Psyche*). Two pages on (v) is Keats's dedication, a serious one:

INSCRIBED
TO THE MEMORY
OF
THOMAS CHATTERTON

Keats ranked Chatterton with Shakespeare in "purest" English (*K* 115, 266), a muse of the "native land" for the poet of *Endymion* (4.354). But his suicide at age seventeen casts a shade over Endymion's long melancholy. In an early sonnet to Chatterton (1815), Keats had exclaimed

> How soon that voice, majestic and elate,
> Melted into dying numbers! Oh! how nigh
> Was night to thy fair morning. Thou didst die
> A half-blown flow'ret which cold blasts amate
>
> (6–9; *K* 81)

Sounding *dying* into *nigh* and *nigh* into *night*, Keats makes the night of death nigher yet, pulsed again in *thy* and a closing rhyme in *die*. So relentlessly do these sorrowing numbers work proximate sounds into dramatic consequence, that *morning* cannot but sound *mourning*. A bloom nipped by "the ingrate world" deaf to a "voice, majestic and elate," and now a singer "among the stars," Chatterton is the celebrity of such translation. For Keats, it is a "Memory" with a potential script for Endymion (and salvation for any "Young Poet").

Then there's the Preface (vii–ix). Keats's friend Reynolds urged the publishers to reject this severely self-critical draft.⁶ But even the more moderate one they accepted was a downer – less an introduction than an abject disclaimer:

> KNOWING within myself the manner in which this Poem has been produced, it is not without a feeling of regret that I make it public.
>
> What manner I mean, will be quite clear to the reader, who must soon perceive great inexperience, immaturity, and every error denoting a feverish

attempt, rather than a deed accomplished. The first two books, and indeed the two last, I feel sensible are not of such completion as to warrant their passing the press . . . the foundations are too sandy. (vii–viii)

The "wand'ring spirit" of "I stood tip-toe" falls to its Latin-punned twin, "every error." When Keats rendered his sentence on this feverish attempt – "It is just that this youngster should die away" (viii) – he gave a fatal prescription to the critics. The plan of maturing with *Endymion* had a narrative of immaturity on a parallel track.

Critical mirrors

On these two tracks *Endymion* proceeds: there is the romance-fable and there is the *Romance*-narrator's concern with its theme and its implications for poetic vocation, poetic credit, poetic prospects. The dream-goddess is lover and muse, and Endymion is poet-prone could he but "tell / The enchantment" (1.572–73). Setting out in "full happiness" to "trace the story of Endymion" (1.34–35), Keats's narrative winds up on a devious course. The hero's "wandering in uncertain ways" (2.49) mirrors its poet's "uncertain path" (1.61); "as I proceeded my steps were all uncertain," Keats admits in that rejected Preface (*K* 116) – not yet the aesthetic master of "uncertainties, mysteries, doubts" (*K* 78). In May 1817 Keats could fancy "a good Genius presiding" over him; but he's never free of that "state of Mind" (he confesses to Haydon) "as to read over my Lines and hate them." "I cannot write while my spirit is fevered in a contrary direction," he sighs about an onset of worldly troubles, as if he were the unhappy twin of his "Brain-sick" hero.[7]

Endymion is fraught with its contrary directions, for hero and poet. In Book I the hero is sent "high soaring" in "airy trance" with his goddess, "Spreading imaginary pinions wide" (584–86). And by Book IV the poet is "inspir'd" to try on such pinions: "This is the giddy pair, and I must spread / Wide pinions to keep here" – but the disclaimer that continues the same metrical line exposes the risk: "nor do I dread / Or height, or depth, or width, or any chance / Precipitous" (356–60). Risk is the figure not too many pages on, in the hero's latest perplexity: elusive goddess or a palpably near "panting . . . delicious lady" (442–43)?

> He who died
> For soaring too audacious in the sun,
> Where that same treacherous wax began to run,
> Felt not more tongue-tied than Endymion.
> (443–46)

The triple rhyme diminishes, and the comparison to Icarus travesties. Being "tongue-tied" is the least of this lad's problems. Yet the impending fate blows back to the poet of Book I who petitions his muse, "let not my weak tongue faulter" (1.128), a nice Keats-compounding of *fault* and *falter*. In his first weeks of devoted work, Keats could waver into self-parody. Writing to Hunt about his aspiration "to be in the Mouth of Fame" he reviews himself: "at last the Idea has grown so monstrously beyond my seeming Power of attainment that the other day I nearly consented with myself to drop into a Phæton" (*K* 50–51). The sporty carriage – built for speed, an often reckless drive for young Regency bucks – takes its name from the inept godling-son (twin to Icarus) who crashes and burns Apollo's sun-chariot.

Endymion is the fever and the fervor of Keats's conception. When Peona chastises her brother's enchantment by the "fitful whims of sleep" (1.750), Keats knows the telling train of the adjective. OED lists the first event of this pathological sense (and the only one in Shakespeare's works) in King Duncan's release from "Lifes fitfull Feuer" (*Macbeth* 3.2.23). The Keats-train stopped in *1817* for a sonnet that begins speaking of the "Keen, fitful gusts" of a November night; the poet walking many miles back home in this chill is warmed by a counter-*ful*, an evening "brimful" of social friendliness. Fitful dreamer Endymion is the fever. Even he can recall himself in better health, once an epic hero, kin to the heroic spirits of the natural world:

> I, who still saw the horizontal sun
> Heave his broad shoulder o'er the edge of the world,
> Out-facing Lucifer, and then had hurl'd
> My spear aloft, as signal for the chace –   (1.529–32)

The sun god (in conquest of the morning star) and the shepherd rise shoulder to shoulder. ("What an image that is—'*sea-shouldering whales!*'" Keats exclaimed to Clarke about a phrase in *The Faerie Queene*, as he mimed such physical energy, "*hoisted* himself up, and looked burly and dominant."[8]) Endymion's default has this foil. "*Shame / On this poor weakness!*" Peona itches to scold her sulky brother (1.718–19). She doesn't, but Keats writes the impulse in these italics. At the same time, he exploits what he has her say to this truant prince –

> wherefore sully the entrusted gem
> Of high and noble life with thoughts so sick?
> Why pierce high-fronted honour to the quick
> For nothing but a dream?   (1.758–61)

– as a set-up for Endymion to issue a memorable visionary ode.

Keats put a lot of work into this ode, sending the lines off to Taylor in January 1818 for late insertion (*K* 93–94). It begins:

> Wherein lies happiness? In that which becks
> Our ready minds to fellowship divine,
> A fellowship with essence; till we shine,
> Full alchemiz'd, and free of space. Behold
> The clear religion of heaven! ...
>
> (1.778–82)

And it climaxes with a voluptuous paean to erotic love as the principle of life:

> who, of men, can tell
> That flowers would bloom, or that green fruit would swell
> To melting pulp, that fish would have bright mail,
> The earth its dower of river, wood, and vale,
> The meadows runnels, runnels pebble-stones,
> The seed its harvest, or the lute its tones,
> Tones ravishment, or ravishment its sweet,
> If human souls did never kiss and greet? (1.836–43)

This "Argument" was "a regular stepping of the Imagination towards a Truth," said Keats (with a happy meta-poetics as *stones* double-steps into "its *tones*," and turns again at *s, / Tones*"). "It set before me at once the gradations of Happiness even like a Kind of Pleasure Thermometer."[9]

By Book IV, however, the temperature has sunk. The poet confesses "lowliness of heart" (29) and the hero scarcely has a pulse:

> There never liv'd a mortal man, who bent
> His appetite beyond his natural sphere,
> But starv'd and died. (4.650–52)

Endymion's appetite has been a perpetual caution, now a "breath of life" (2.689), now a lure to "that region / Where falling stars dart their artillery forth," to "frightful eddies" (1.641–42, 648), now a surrender "to death" (1.655) and "the deep abyss" (2.233). He reels helplessly: "lapp'd and lull'd" (1.646), cast "into nothing – into stupid sleep" (678), or enslaved to a "chain of grief" (980). Such toils make it hard to tell "love's elysium" (1.824) from "Love's madness" (2.863).

Every key trope proves as variable. There are lasses alluring, nurturing, and inspiring; protective, calming, and cradling; treacherous, poisoning, and forsaking. There are poet-bowers "Full of sweet dreams, and health, and quiet breathing" (1.4–5), Peona's "bower" of "quiet shade" (1.437), a lush infant-chamber for "embowered" Adonis (2.382–95), and the "jasmine bower, all bestrown / With golden moss" (2.672–73) that couches Endymion's most erotic dream. Keats's sensuous intensity with this last one was ridiculed as childish and censured for prurience. In "soft ravishment," the lovers "trembled into each other" (2.717–18), "kissing . . . Those lips, O slippery blisses" (760) – the words slipping into each other ("thos(e)lips; O slip-"), sounding "swoon'd / Drunken from pleasure's nipple" (870–71). It's telling that *The British Critic*'s livid reprimands nearly slip into advertisement: "the gross slang of voluptuousness . . . immoral images . . . impurity . . . the artifices of vicious refinement . . . imaginations better adapted to the stews" (9:652). Make this lust only, and you've arrived at Circe's "twilight bower," a "specious heaven" that unveils "real hell," a "dark lair of night" (3.420, 479, 563). Book IV has the gravest bower of all, the Cave of Quietude, numbing all sensation.

Latmian patron Pan shifts across various aspects: a Keatsian aesthete who loves "to see the hamadryads dress / Their ruffled locks" (1.236–37);[10] a "melancholy" lover, bereft of "fair Syrinx," who courts "The dreary melody of bedded reeds — In desolate places" (239–43); a "Dread opener of the mysterious doors / Leading to universal knowledge" (288–89), model for Endymion "to follow / Where airy voices lead . . . The silent mysteries of earth" (2.213–15). The lover who "wander'd . . . oft wondering" (2.681) is less a character than a site of reiterated desire:

> Whence that completed form of all completeness?
> Whence came that high perfection of all sweetness?
> (1.606–07)

> My breath of life, where art thou?   (2.689)

> Cynthia! where art thou now?   (3.72)

> Where didst thou melt to?   (4.636)

Supplementing all this *ubi est* (iterating the Latin trope *where is . . . ?)* the goddess of love turns fatal muse: "What, not yet / Escap'd from dull mortality's harsh net?" (3.913–14). With "no self-passion or identity," Endymion worries "Some fearful end must be: where, where is it?" (4.479–80), courting the darkest of love's "enthralments far / More self-destroying" (1.797–800). "I can see / Nought earthly worth my compassing; so stand / Upon a misty, jutting head of land," he moans at midpoint (2.162–64), out-Childe-Harolding Childe Harold (Byron's world-weary, titanically alienated wandering hero), the code tipping to parody.

The two most critical figures on the parody-thermometer are boy-toy Adonis and aged, pining Glaucus. Sleeping away "on a silken couch of rosy pride" staged for "the filled sight / Officiously," Adonis is the centerpiece of a dewy infant's chamber "Full of light, incense, tender minstrelsy," his "faint damask mouth" "tenderly unclos'd" to "slumber pout" like "a dew-lipp'd rose" (2.393–407). A guardian cupid offers accidental tourist Endymion wine, "juicy pears," cream, and "blooming plums / Ready to melt between an infants gums," and exclaims, "Who would not be so prison'd?" (442– 62). But even Endymion winces "in embarrassment" (430), on track to Victorian critic Alexander Smith's term for the spectacle, "babyish effeminacy."[11] Just as embarrassing is Glaucus's tale of his fall to siren Circe.

> With tears, and smiles, and honey-words she wove
> A net whose thraldom was more bliss than all
> The range of flower'd Elysium   (3.428–30)

In *Endymion*, this could've been any lover's case, falling for "Cupid's sake" (432) with a seed of *ache* in the charming syllables:

> Who could resist? Who in this universe?
> She did so breathe ambrosia; so immerse
> My fine existence in a golden clime.
> She took me like a child of suckling time,
> And cradled me in roses.   (3.455–59)

Who could resist the comparison to Adonis, or enchanted Endymion? "This is a Circe who has read Keats" (remarks one critic). It's a Circe Keats wanted to caricature this way.[12] "Ha! ha! Sir Dainty!" she taunts; she's no "nurse / Made of rose leaves and thistledown, express, / To cradle thee, my sweet, and lull thee" (573–75). Sighs Glaucus, "I sought for her smooth arms and lips, to slake / My greedy thirst with nectarous camel-draughts" (481–82). The first instance of *nectarous* cited in OED is the "nectarous draughts" Eve pours for Adam (*PL* 5.306); Keats underlined this[13] and, recalling Endymion's raptures, set it to exhilarating parody:

> I was distracted; madly did I kiss
> The wooing arms which held me, and did give
> My eyes at once to death: but 'twas to live,
> To take in draughts of life from the gold fount
> Of kind and passionate looks; to count, and count
> The moments, by some greedy help that seem'd
> A second self   (1.653–59)

In the course of *Endymion*, this second self gets named "Glaucus," degraded to animal appetite. Cynthia coos "Lispings empyrean" (2.821) and Venus consoles; Circe's "rich speech" of "honey-words" sours to a "pale laugh, and curse" (3.572). Under this "arbitrary queen of sense" (461), lovers turn into a "herd" of "wailing, groveling, serpenting . . . deformities" (503–34). Glaucus's sentence is to "live and wither, cripple and still breathe / Ten hundred years" (600–01) in an un-Adonis blazon: "Gaunt, wither'd, sapless, feeble, cramp'd, and lame" (641).

Hopeful allegorizers see Endymion (at least) in spiritual development, as he forgets his woes for a while to restore the "tempest-tost" lovers, and poor Glaucus too, to their hearts' desires. But in Keats's write-up, this business seems more accidental, dreamlike and magical than ethically volitional. Book IV is a dispirited affair, its poet uttering a global "despondency": "I move to the end in lowliness of heart" (22–29) – as low a moment as any in Keats's poetry and a rare glimpse of the person in the persona. On 28 September 1817, having finished Book III, Keats sifted the project for Haydon:

> My Ideas with respect to it I assure you are very low—and I would write the subject thoroughly again. but I am tired of it and think the time would be better spent in writing a new Romance which I have my eye on for next summer—Rome was not built in a day. (HKI.12.38; *L* 1:168)

Even in low spirits, Keats can't resist punning the realms of Rome and Romance arrayed around I and eye.

And so, bottomed out, Book IV manages to eye the modes of irony, subversion, and satire that will shape the "new Romance" poetry of *Isabella*, *The Eve of St. Agnes*, and *Lamia*. When the Indian Maid appears on the scene, the narrator smirks at what has by now become his hero's predictable predicament. The Maid barely sings a stanza of a "sorrow song" before Endymion is swooning. Keats's narrator here could have auditioned for Byron's *Don Juan*:

> Thou, Carian lord, hadst better have been tost
> Into a whirlpool. Vanish into air,
> Warm mountaineer! for canst thou only bear
> A woman's sigh alone and in distress?
> See not her charms! Is Phœbe passionless?
> Phœbe is fairer far – O gaze no more: –
> Yet if thou wilt behold all beauty's store,
> Behold her panting in the forest grass!   (4.52–59)

(Phœbe is another name of the Moon-goddess). Before the main verb ("behold"), *if thou wilt* weighs in as its own verb, setting the stage for Endymion to mime Glaucus's abject farce:

> Fair Melody! kind Syren! I've no choice;
> I must be thy sad servant evermore:
> I cannot choose but kneel here and adore ...
> I'm giddy at that cheek so fair smooth;
> O let it blush so ever!   (4.302–04, 313–14)

The narrator plays Circe: "Ah, what perplexity! Ah, well a day! /... He could not help but kiss her" (449–51). Keats even sets up Peona's reappearance for Circean fun: "O treachery! / Why does his lady smile, pleasing her eye / With all his sorrowing?" (805–07). "Nothing strikes me with a sense of the rediculous as love," Keats wrote of a smitten friend (in the very months he fell to passion for Fanny Brawne), "A Man in love I do think cuts the sorryest figure in the world – Even when I know a poor fool to be really in pain about it, I could burst out laughing in his face – His pathetic visage becomes irrisistable."[14] Christopher Ricks comments on the punning capital in the spellings, the blush in *rediculous* and the risible *irrisistable*.[15] In September 1819, as he was polishing up *Lamia*, Keats dashed off a twenty-three-line satire of such men in love: "Pensive they sit, and roll their languid eyes" (*L* 2:188), sequel to a brutal squib from 1818, skewering the "silly youth" who would wax "Divine by loving, and so goes on / Yawning and doating a whole summer long" (*1848* 1:283) – both redoing Endymion as farce.

In *Endymion*, Keats sends his hero for therapy to a Cave of Quietude: ultimate insensation, modeled on Spenser's Cave of Despair (*FQ* I.IX.28–47). From rehearsing the hell of love's perpetual pain, its atmosphere turns narcotic, shutting the eyes in a long "dreamless sleep," the soul "lull'd" from all "grievous feud" (4.544–52). If this seems Spenser's Cave of Despair redux, Keats's Cave of Quietude is no site of moral trial. Its motto is "Enter none / Who strive therefore: on the sudden it is won" (534–35). The more visible Spenserian blueprint is the "still / And calmy bay" to which mermaid-sirens beckon "weake traveillers": "the port of rest from troublous toyle, / The worldes sweet in from paine and wearisome turmoyle" (*FQ* II.XII.32).

The rest and resolution of Endymion's turmoil is the lulling that leaves him "So happy" (4.552–55). From such Quietude, Endymion is wafted back to Latmos, not knowing that he is to be delivered from his "mortal state ... by some unlook'd for change" (1000–01). Peona sighs, "Unhappy wight! ... What wouldst thou ere we all are laid on bier?" In a heartbeat Endymion answers, "I would have command, / If it were heaven's will, on our sad fate" (980–85). It's about time! Invoking "Cupid's dove," the Indian Maid morphs into his dream-goddess, announcing that he is to "Be spiritualiz'd" to "range / These forests" with her (988–1002). A "patent *dea ex machina*" is Sperry's term, wish-fulfillment at one with fictive unreality.[16] After a "blissful swoon," Endymion with "Cynthia bright / . . . vanish'd far away! – Peona went / Home through the gloomy wood in wonderment" (1008–12): these are the Romance's last words, with Peona as our proxy in this anti-climax of spiritless spiritualizing (every reader feels it). Never again would Keats end a poem in lovers' blissful meeting, free from danger, free from fear.

The Tory reviewers who savaged *Poems* were ready for *Endymion*, cued by the Preface, disgusted by the sensuality and Book III's anti-monarchal rant. But Keats had already moved on, even saying in that Preface he was "plotting, and fitting myself for verses fit to live" (viii). For all its turmoil, writing these 4,000 lines had given him confidence. "I cannot help looking into new countries with 'O for a Muse of fire to ascend!'" he tells publisher Taylor, tacitly assuming the rest of the sentence in the Prologue to *Henry V* ("The brightest heaven of invention"). "If Endymion serves me as a Pioneer perhaps I ought to be content" (*K* 113). Proof-reading in the winter of 1818, he was restless. Although he appreciated his friends' praises and Taylor's careful attentions, he was unhappy with this trial and alert to Hunt's and Shelley's reserve. "I have lately read your *Endymion* again," Shelley wrote to Keats in 1820, meaning to be complimentary about an ever "new sense of the treasures of poetry," but tipping a critical hand: "though treasures poured forth with indistinct profusion" (*K* 425).

As a reader (and poet) who looks "upon fine Phrases like a Lover" (*L* 2:139), Keats curated such treasures, and with genius. Who could not love his conceit of "lowing heifers sleeker than / Night-swollen mushrooms" (1.214–15)? Or the way sounds not only echo but issue the sense of "there*in* / A *mel*ancholy spirit *well might win* / Oblivi*on*, and *melt* out his essence *fine* / *In*to the *win*ds" (1.97–100)? Or the lovely meta-metrical artistry of "when the airy stress / Of music's kiss impregnates the free winds, / And with sympathetic touch unbinds / Eolian magic from their lucid wombs" (1.784–87)? Or this set-piece on Cybele, the divine mother, Keats taking pains (*P* 152) to get its silent dark splendor just right:

> alone—alone—
> In sombre chariot; dark folding thrown
> About her majesty, and front death-pale,
> With turrets crown'd. Four maned lions hale
> The sluggish wheels; solemn their toothed maws,

Their surly eyes brow-hidden, heavy paws
Uplifted drowsily, and nervy tails
Cowering their tawny brushes. Silent sails
This shadowy queen athwart, and faints away

(2.641–49)

Shelley had sent Keats his recent tragedy, *The Cenci* (an Italian Renaissance horror of rape, savagery, parricide, and state power – legible for modern times). Keats replied that he wouldn't judge the moral "purpose," only "the Poetry, and dramatic effect." For this, "an artist must serve Mammon," Keats advised, using the epithet for worldly (as opposed to divine) riches; "you might curb your magnanimity and be more of an artist, and 'load every rift' of your subject with ore" (*K* 426). Keats's quotation alludes to a famous Spenserian site of trial, the Cave of Mammon, its loads of "rich metall" boding "heavy ruine" to the macrostructure.[17]

In Keats's treasuring of sensuous luxuries, Yeats (who was trying to train his own aestheticism to the demands of modern/Modernist purpose) saw something revolutionary enough. In 1917, he said he was reminded of the way the pleasure islands in *The Faerie Queene*, an epic of patent moral purpose, elude the domain of moral probity: "In those islands certain qualities of beauty, certain forms of sensuous loveliness were separated from all the general purposes of life, as they had not been hitherto in European literature – and would not be again . . . till Keats wrote his *Endymion*."[18] Keats's thinking about his "endeavour after a long Poem" charts such a map: "Do not the Lovers of Poetry like to have a little Region to wander in where they may pick and choose, and in which the images are so numerous that many are forgotten and found new in a second Reading?"[19] This is an alternative to narrative plot: the long poem as an anthology for readers to "wander in" with no moral errancy. *Do not* . . . solicits for this strong suit. It's what Keats enjoyed rereading Shakespeare, the sensation of ever-new findings. But it was Shakespeare who also pulled him into wider regions of fierce dispute.

New Romance, Old Romance

Keats gave his romance with "Romance" its own second reading in January 1818, as he was revising *Endymion*. He wrote to his brothers of wanting to ripen his "intellectual powers" for some great(er) production, and toward this end,

I sat down yesterday to read "King Lear" once again: the thing appeared to demand the prologue of a sonnet. I wrote it and began to read ...
On Sitting Down to Read *King Lear* Once Again

> O golden-tongued Romance, with serene Lute!
>   Fair plumed Syren! Queen! of far-away!
>   Leave melodizing on this wintry day
> Shut up thine olden Pages, and be mute.
> Adieu! for once again, the fierce dispute,
>   Betwixt Damnation and impassion'd clay
>   Must I burn through; once more humbly assay
> The bitter-sweet of this Shakspearian fruit.
> Chief Poet! and ye Clouds of Albion,
>   Begetters of ~~this~~ our deep eternal theme!
> When through the old oak forest I am gone,
>   Let me not wander in a barren dream:
> But when I am consumed with the fire,
> Give me new Phœnix-wings to fly at my desire.

So you see I am getting at it with a sort of determination and strength, though, verily, I do not feel it at this moment.[20]

The event of "reading" is crucial. In the theaters, Shakespeare's *Lear* had been usurped by Nahum Tate's "Romance" revision (1681), of which even Dr. Johnson approved ("so shocked by Cordelia's death" that he could not endure "to read again the last scenes of the play, till I undertook to revise them as an editor").[21] Tate keeps Lear alive to regain the throne, then happily abdicate to newly married Edgar and Cordelia (she survives, too). Keats's determination to "reread" is more than a return of Shakespeare's severity. It's a rereading, a "once again": a disciplined detox after his own long binge on Romance.

For all its specious allure and known danger (she's a Syren), Romance is ever-seductive. "Helen's golden tongue" (Helen of Troy, cause of a long war) is a phrase Keats underlined in *Troilus and Cressida*.[22] The very terms that indict Romance – *golden, serene, fair plumed, far-away* – are also its attractions. Breaking up is hard to do, though Keats does his best in turning the sonnet from a Petrarchan octave (*abba, abba*) to a Shakespearean sestet (*bcbcdd*), as if to signal a move away from doting to dispute. Yet even at its most imperative, the octave is only a prospect: *Shut up ... and be mute; Must I ... When ... Let me not ... But when ... Give me.* And *Adieu!* is a rather fond form of farewell.

No wonder Keats sets the volta as soon as line 4 (not the usual "turn" at line 9), with a point-by-point refusal of Romance for tragedy. He wants fierce dispute instead of melodizing; "this" rereading instead of a dreamy "far-away," "burning through" instead of serene mooning. Yet even as the prospect, "When through the old oak forest I am gone," points beyond romance (*old* echoes Romance's "*gold*en-tongued" "*old*en Pages"), the closing couplet reprises the lover's quarrel. It's partly the phoenix's fault. Rising from the ashes of an old phoenix, a new phoenix is a birth and a cyclical repetition. Then there's the stretched meter of the last line, a hexameter born out of pentameters, analogous to the last line of the Spenserian stanzas that build *The Faerie Queene*. Keats talks tragedy, but lingers in a form from Romance.

Romance returns, again and again, in Keats's imagination, but with an edge. It's a subject for tantalizing, cautionary negotiation, tagged by the phrases "new Romance" (dark, stark *Isabella*) or "old Romance" (the whims of Madeline in *The Eve of St. Agnes*, a Spenserian-stanza romance that alternately indulges and ironizes the genre) or honey words with a bite in the catastrophe of *Lamia*. Flirting with and subverting Romance arguably becomes Keats's modern mode. In a playful-serious verse letter to his friend Reynolds, March 1818, he virtually reviews *Endymion* in a campy lament:

> O that our dreamings all of sleep or wake
> Would all their colours from the sunset take:
> From something of material sublime,
> Rather than shadow our own Soul's daytime
> In the dark void of Night.   (67–71; *K* 120)

If the sigh is for dreams materialized, Keats's impulse is a question. Is it enlightenment to say "Things cannot to the will / Be settled, but they tease us out of thought" (a tease replayed at the end of *Ode on a Grecian Urn*)? Or is it the failure of "Imagination brought / Beyond its proper bound, yet still confined," to discern "any standard law / Of either earth or heaven?" (76–82).

Keats proposes to take refuge "from detested Moods in new Romance" (111; *K* 121). This is *Isabella; or, The Pot of Basil*. And it's no refuge.

CHAPTER 4

Venturing "new Romance"
Isabella; or, The Pot of Basil. A STORY FROM BOCCACCIO

On its way to Keats's generation, the genre of "romance" devolved from Spenser's national epic of moral trial to escapist fantasia – at best, picking up some credit as passionate resistance to the regime of things as they are. Keats called on this spirit in subtitling *Endymion* "a Romance," insisting to his publishers in March 1818 that "a ramance is a fine thing notwithstanding the circulating Libraries" (*L* 1:253). The wry spelling parodies the popular fiction loved by female library patrons and some men slumming on the sly. The "new Romance" that Keats projected to Reynolds would ruffle the market on two fronts, and with gendered force: exposing the delusions of "old Romance" and casting modern meta-Romance, its devices demystified, its spells spelled out, and with such ultimate severity against fair-lady readers as to give *Isabella; or, The Pot of Basil* the cast of an "anti-Romance."[1]

Keats took an outline from a tale in Boccaccio's *Decameron*.[2] Isabella and her brothers' clerk Lorenzo are passionately in love. The brothers regard Isabella as a capital asset, on ice for one of their ruthless "trade designs," namely, marriage to "some high noble and his olive-trees" (XXI). Luring Lorenzo off on a hunt, they murder him, telling Isabella that he had to leave suddenly on business. His ghoulish ghost appears to her in a dream to report his woe and where he's buried. Isabella digs up his body, severs its head, brings it home, pretties it up, and hides it in a pot of basil, the plant flourishing from her incessant tears and then some. Detecting her doting on the basil-pot, her brothers filch it and uncover its ghastly secret. In panic of exposure, they flee and Isabella goes mad in mourning her lost basil, dies in misery, survived by a song of grief.

"Ah! wherefore all this wormy circumstance?"

Doomed love, murder, horrid dreaming, exhumation, corpse-decapitation, pathological fetish, and fatal melancholy: quite a shift from the sky-enchanted poet of *Endymion*! Keats is retailing wares worthy of a circulating

library (gothic shelf). His campy narrator is not shy about provoking readers' imaginative complicity, gothic-dieted, in the rampant graveyard romp:

> Who hath not loiter'd in a green church-yard,
>   And let his spirit, like a demon-mole,
> Work through the clayey soil and gravel hard,
>   To see scull, coffin'd bones, and funeral stole;
> Pitying each form that hungry Death hath marr'd,
>   And filling it once more with human soul?
> Ah! this is holiday to what was felt
> When Isabella by Lorenzo knelt.   (XLV)

What is holiday for a dear reader is horror for Isabella pitying Lorenzo's
corpse. Fascinated by some prints from Boccaccio's era, "Full of Romance
and the most tender feeling . . . But Grotesque to a curious pitch" (*L* 2:19),
Keats pitches his Boccaccio on this arc.

Giovanni Boccaccio survived the Black Death that ravaged Florence in
1348–49, killing his father, stepmother, and many friends. He wrote the
Decameron in its wake, drawing it into his frame-narrative: some young
Florentine aristocrats seek refuge in a country estate, with servants, and
pass the time with music, feasting, dancing, and storytelling. Keats subverts
the escape, not only by planting disease and death at the center of the tale
but doing so with gothic extravagance and brutal political disturbance.
His setting cancels Messina for Florence, major European financial hub
and seat of the powerful, unscrupulous Medici family. Having banished
"golden-tongued Romance" from melodizing on a "wintry day" (the *Lear*
sonnet), Keats cued *Isabella* for telling "among the Snows of next Winter."[3]
Tendering a ritual apology to "eloquent and famed" Boccaccio for "ventur-
ing syllables that ill beseem / The quiet glooms of such a piteous theme,"
his narrator brands a modern "verse in English tongue, / An echo of thee in
the north-wind sung" (XIX–XX). The turn is not so much against Boccaccio as against those readers ready to murmur "ill beseem." After loitering
for five stanzas in a graveyard plot, Keats ventriloquizes the "Fair reader"
distressed by this indulgence, stylizing the lament for parody:

> Ah! wherefore all this wormy circumstance?
>   Why linger at the yawning tomb so long?
> O for the gentleness of old Romance,
>   The simple plaining of a minstrel's song!
> Fair reader, at the old tale take a glance,
>   For here, in truth, it doth not well belong
> To speak: – O turn thee to the very tale,
> And taste the music of that vision pale.
>   (XLIX)

Setting the stresses on *where-, wormy, cir*cum-, a "Fair reader" – implicitly a polite female reader – is dismissed to the sorority of the "FAIR Isabel, poor simple Isabel," doomed from line one.

Trading in gold

For such a reader (and for more sophisticated tastes, too), Keats sets out wonderful treats in the early stanzas. In a compound of poetry-making and lovemaking, he coined the verb *poesied*: kissing Isabella, Lorenzo's lips "poesied with hers in dewy rhyme" (IX). "We speak of the poetry of life," said E. S. Dallas in 1852, but only Keats could image "the rapture of a kiss" in "lips *poesied* with each other" – refuting *The British Critic*'s snort that the conceit was "exquisite nonsense."[4] Christopher Ricks nicely elaborates Dallas's appreciation: "The kiss is a rhyme because it rhymes (pairs) their lips."[5] And who could not love this intricate conceit in stanza X?

> Parting they seem'd to tread upon the air,
>   Twin roses by the zephyr blown apart
> Only to meet again more close, and share
>   The inward fragrance of each other's heart.

Yet any fair reader expecting passage to "the gentleness of old Romance" is in for a rough ride.

Keats's most striking ungentleness is his foregrounding, for critical recognition, the economic base of the old Romance. In Boccaccio, the brothers are mostly motivated by class pride, resenting the insult of lowly Lorenzo's attention to their sister. Keats makes them "ledger-men" and "money-bags," their wealth not even symbolic power (a means) but self-identity in a world where every thing and every person is a commodity. Yet the lexicon of gold and riches is not restricted to them; it also gilds Isabella's romance-world and extends, in relentless thrust, to readers of "old Romance." The case of the brothers is the most obvious, inspiring five stanzas of bitter explication (XIV–XVIII). Here's the first:

> With her two brothers this fair lady dwelt,
>   Enriched from ancestral merchandize,
> And for them many a weary hand did swelt
>   In torched mines and noisy factories,
> And many once proud-quiver'd loins did melt
>   In blood from stinging whip;——with hollow eyes
> Many all day in dazzling river stood,
> To take the rich-ored driftings of the flood.

OED cites Keats here for condensing the hard labor of *swelter* into a terse *swelt*, intensified by the reduction of human beings to the instruments of "many a weary hand." The adjective "proud-quiver'd" is no less pungent, a one-word history: the capture of aboriginal hunters into slave labor. The brothers' empire is global, everywhere pounded with that repeated *for them*:

> For them the Ceylon diver held his breath,
>   And went all naked to the hungry shark;
> For them his ears gush'd blood; for them in death
>   The seal on the cold ice with piteous bark
> Lay full of darts; for them alone did seethe
>   A thousand men in troubles wide and dark:
> Half-ignorant, they turn'd an easy wheel,
> That set sharp racks at work, to pinch and peel.
>
> (XV)

Conceived in the orbit of Hunt's *Examiner* and in the teeth of "old Romance," these stanzas were hailed by G. B. Shaw for their political penetration: "if Karl Marx can be imagined as writing a poem instead of a treatise on Capital, he would have written *Isabella*" – a virtual chapter, he said, in those "Factory Commission Reports" that issued the "immense indictment of the profiteers and exploiters with which Marx has shaken capitalistic civilization to its foundations." He loved that transformation of the brothers into their chief care, "ledger-men" ("Marx is more euphuistic in calling the profiteers bourgeoisie").[6]

Yet the brothers' gold-love is not singular; it's a repetition in a crasser tone of what sustains Isabella's "golden hour" (XXXI) in a station in life in which the only dart (not the weapon for piteous seal-slaying) is love's "honey'd dart" (X), echoing the medium, "honey'*d art*"; the only misery is "some stir of heart, some malady" (I) and desire's "sick longing" (III). Keats's worry about "too much inexperience of live, and simplicity of knowledge" in *Isabella* holds at least for the heroine.[7] In economic logic, the reiterated naming of the beneficiaries of horrific labor, "for them," has to underwrite her, too, unawares. In a poem written the same winter and published in *1820*, Keats quipped that in the modern commercial world, "honey / Can't be got without hard money!" (*Robin Hood* 47–48). In *Isabella* he draws the golden vein from her brothers to Isabella's world in a winter-western sky bereft of "gold tinge" (XXXII) and her grooming Lorenzo's head "with a golden comb" (LI). Keats makes Isabella's grief an awakening from innocence: "I knew not this hard life, / I thought the worst was simple misery," she sighs to Lorenzo's ghost; "thou hast school'd my infancy" (XLII). Her "dismal labouring" and "travail sore" in the graveyard (XLVIII) is a correction with Marxian force.

The lexicon for Isabella's sequestered simplicity is set for repetition in her brothers' worldly business, wrapping their lives around one another. Lest a reader feel free of this rap, Keats catches our collusion in the rich entanglements. In XIII, we're urged, "for the general award of love," to "kill" the "bitterness" of lovers' sorrows by remembering "The little sweet" of these tales' happiest moments. The generic bargain invokes a natural emblem: "Even bees, the little almsmen of spring-bowers, / Know there is richest juice in poison-flowers." Rich poisoned becomes poisoned riches in the very next stanza. The baleful brothers are "Enriched from ancestral merchandize," as slaves, "with hollow eyes / Many all day in dazzling river stood, / To take the rich-ored driftings of the flood." Dazzling river-light, which bids fair as a picturesque treat, is no such thing here. It's the incessant glare of pain on the miners' hollow eyes. What is the economy of romance-reading? Keats (the banisher of golden-tongued Romance) asks:

> Were they unhappy then?——It cannot be——
> Too many tears for lovers have been shed,
> Too many sighs give we to them in fee,
> Too much of pity after they are dead,
> Too many doleful stories do we see,
> Whose matter in bright gold were best be read.
>
>   (XII)

Now it's the reader who gets gold from misery, refusing the fee of pained sympathy. About the necessary secrecy of Isabella and Lorenzo's illicit romance, "Unknown of any, free from whispering tale," the narrator has just sighed in a summary couplet, "Ah! better had it been for ever so, / Than idle ears should pleasure in their woe" (XI). Idling pleasure in the woe of others is the very project of old Romance, for tellers and listeners alike. The graveyard all around the golden world relays the critical, and political, force of *Isabella*. By LVI, we know Isabella's doom: "She withers, like a palm / Cut by an Indian for its juicy balm" – or like doleful tale relished by readers for the "richest juice" within. "Each richer by his being a murderer," Keats writes of the ledger-men (XXVIII), and literary riches rotate on the same axis. Even Keats is in the whirl, having listened attentively to Hazlitt's suggestion that "a modern translation" of Isabella "could not fail to succeed in the present day."[8]

Melody, Melancholy, Melpomene

The presiding spirit of this Romance is no Moon-goddess, but "Melancholy," hailed in a set of stanzas that in effect are Keats's first *Ode on Melancholy*, including a theatricality that verges on camp: "O Melancholy, linger here awhile!" This is the artistry of "cypress glooms, / Tinting with silver wan your marble tombs" (LV), a syntax that lets *wan* play as an adjective for silver, and as a Keats-coined substantive (with *silver* the adjective) for the inspiration. Keats expertly sounds the "syllables of woe" in Melpomene, the tragic muse, into the sounds of *Melancholy, mournfully* and even *Isabel* (LVI).

At the center of this artistry is the artifact that brands Keats's "new Romance": the pot of basil holding Lorenzo's head. Before this urn burial, Isabella dotes on her lover's head, pointing his eyelashes and combing his locks, turning to a most wormy circumstance Venus's embowered Adonis. This is romance only by perversion. Like the leaf-fringed legends of romance, the pot of "Basil green" flourishes "as by magic touch" (LVIII), but beneath its "thick, and green, and beautiful" foliage (LIV) is death "vile with green and livid spot" (LX), the balmy fragrance drawing nurture "From the fast mouldering head there shut from view" (LIV). Woodhouse, sensitive to the smirks at Keats's "prosodial notions of our English heroic metre," wanted to regulate the meter by deleting *fast*, but Keats wanted the alliteration and the stress.[9]

Keats modernizes Boccaccio not only in these local poetics but also in the drama of his stanza-form. Just before he began *Isabella*, Byron's *Beppo* was published, showing the satiric potential of *ottava rima*, with its six-line swell and couplet-snap of epigrammatic wit. The form was familiar in Italian comic romances, and I think Keats was paying attention.[10] Stanza II surely has this fun in its closing line:

> With every morn their love grew tenderer,
>   With every eve deeper and tenderer still;
> He might not in house, field, or garden stir,
>   But her full shape would all his seeing fill;
> And his continual voice was pleasanter
>   To her, than noise of trees or hidden rill;
> Her lute-string gave an echo of his name,
> She spoilt her half-done broidery with the same.

Several stanzas, including XIII and XLV (quoted above), play the closing couplet for sudden and unsettling concentrations of information.

The poem Keats described as having "an amusing sober-sadness about it" (*K* 267) earns this aura by poisoning the "ditty fair" of Isabella's love-song (X) and utterly ruining its opening keynote of a merely lovesick "FAIR Isabel, poor simple Isabel!":

> And a sad ditty of this story born
>   From mouth to mouth through all the country pass'd:
> Still is the burthen sung—"O cruelty,
> To steal my basil-pot away from me!"   (LXIII)

This is how Boccaccio's tale ends, too, in the genesis of the popular folk-song; but in his frame the economy of literary pleasure is equivocal, even indeterminate. When the story "came to be publikely knowne, an excellent ditty was composed thereof beginning thus": the song's first two lines. The prologue to the next day's tale reports that the entertainment "was highly pleasing" to the "Ladies; because they had oftentimes heard the Song, without knowing who made it, or upon what occasion it was composed" (*K* 337). Is the pleasure darkened by the back-story, or is the back-story another pleasure? Boccaccio doesn't settle this question, although his "Introduction" registers it. Worry not, he says to the "Gracious Ladies" among his readers, that the "fearefull beginning" of the plague-frame will "cost you sighes and teares" on every page. Think of it

> but as an high and steepy hil appeares to them, that attempt to travell farre on foote, and ascending the same with some difficulty, come afterward to walk upon a goodly even plaine, which causeth the more contentment in them, because the attayning thereto was hard and painfull. For even as pleasures are cut off by griefe and anguish; so sorrowes cease by joyes most sweete and happie arriving. (Florio's translation)

Keats takes his tale back to Florence, whence these pleasure-travellers escape, and writes disease into its very heart. Against the tendering of pleasures earned through sorrowful passage, Keats's syllables give no quarter. The pleasures of "old Romance" die soon and hard.

Reynolds, who thought to join Keats in the Boccaccio venture, read the draft of *Isabella* in October 1818, and urged Keats to publish it right away to "answer" the attacks in *Blackwood's Edinburgh Magazine* and *The Quarterly*.[11] But Keats couldn't shake the worry that even edgy *Isabella* was too "smokeable" – liable to "be laugh'd at."[12] "I intend to use more finesse with the Public," he alerts Woodhouse (*L* 2:174). In the spring of 1818, he had been rereading Wordsworth, Shakespeare (always, soon and late), *Paradise Lost*, and enjoying Dante's *Divine Comedy* in H. F. Cary's recent translation – prepping for a new venture: no romance, except in futile nostalgia. If the theme-song of *Isabella* is "melancholy," the score of *Hyperion* would counterpoint with Apollo, god of light, music, and "the Father of all verse" (3.13). To a prescient Apollo, Keats attached the determinations of a prescient poet, in control of his materials, primed for vindication after "the slipshod *Endymion*" (he tells Taylor's publishing partner in October 1818) and set, he underscores, to "write . . . with judgment hereafter" (*K* 207).

What was waiting, however, was a new trial by melancholy, and more.

CHAPTER 5

Falling with Hyperion

A political impulse and proof on the pulses

With *Endymion* out, Keats relaxed into a sociable spring and hoped for better reviews than the forecast of *Blackwood's Edinburgh Magazine* May issue. Bailey got his praises into an Oxford paper, and more favor (probably via Reynolds) came in *The Champion*. But *The British Critic* was savage and by summer's end *The Quarterly* and *Blackwood's* piled on. Keats's sights were already set on new work. He headed north for a walking tour with Brown and kept writing – sonnets (on Robert Burns, on the summit of Ben Nevis, on beholding Ailsa Rock), a meditative ramble, and doggerel (an amusement for his sister, "There was a naughty boy"). His new project had been in prospect since January, when he reread *King Lear*. Explaining his ambition to Haydon (go-to interlocutor on matters heroic) Keats pledged that the "sentimental cast" of *Endymion* would yield to "a more naked and grecian Manner," with forward thrust: "the march of passion and endeavour will be undeviating." Unlike "mortal" Endymion, "led on, like Buonaparte, by circumstance," his new hero, Apollo, "being a fore-seeing God will shape his actions like one" (23 January 1818; *K* 88).

The reference to Napoleon was loaded. Defeated at Waterloo (June 1815), the emperor-general left the liberal hopes of a generation in disarray. The seeming savior of the Revolution's principles and rattler of monarchal cages all over Europe had turned imperialist and tyrant. Coleridge, ardent Liberal in the 1790s, likened him to Satan in pride, vanity and sheer evil.[1] "Notwithstand [*sic*] the part which the Liberals take in the Cause of Napoleon," said Keats, "he has done more harm to the life of Liberty than any one . . . not that the divine right Gentlemen have done or intend to do any good" but "he has taught them how to organize their monstrous armies."[2] Keats could still give a liberal cheer to Milton analogizing "the excess / Of glory obscured" in fallen Satan to the way "from behind the moon / In dim eclipse disastrous twilight sheds / On half the nations, and

with fear of change / Perplexes monarchs" (*PL* 1.594–99).³ "How noble
and collected an indignation against Kings," he writes in his margins; "His
very wishing should have had power to pull that feeble animal Charles
from his bloody throne... he hit the new System of things a mighty
mental blow; the exertion must have had or is yet to have some sequences"
(*K* 229–30). Keats wanted to add his sequences. *Endymion* had that rant on
their "baaing vanities" and "gilded masks" (3.1–22). "It will easily be seen
what I think of the present Ministers," he said to Woodhouse.⁴ In 1818 the
political prestige of *Paradise Lost* had Keats exercising a Miltonic blow to
the restored post-Waterloo monarchies.

The prevalent post-Waterloo climate, however, was a "melancholy desolation of... cherished hopes" in the face of deplorable events – so Shelley
put it. In a long, analytical Preface to *The Revolt of Islam* (1818), he named
an "age of despair," gripped by a "disappointment that unconsciously finds
relief only in the wilful exaggeration of its own despair... Our works
of fiction and poetry have been overshadowed by the same infectious
gloom."⁵ Some works sought a "vision of the past," in implicit rebuke to
the Regency regime.⁶ But this is oblique politics at best, and in Keats's
version of this move, *Endymion*, the hero was too led on by circumstance.
Keats wanted to test what a regime-change would look like in the glow
of a capably fore-seeing, "enlighten'd" hero. Convinced as he was that
as civilized countries "become gradually more enlighten'd... there should
be a continual change for the better," Keats understood the dialectics.
England's revolutions had seeded the principles of the French Revolution, which ironically had given "a handle" to the British government to
"undermine our freedom" and oppose "all inovation and improvement."
Britain's blatant tyranny, however, had so re-energized the progressive
movements that the Crown was reluctant to prosecute dissident publishers,
for fear of a "defence" that "would be published in all the papers all over
the Empire... the Trials would light a flame they could not extinguish"
(*L* 2:193–94), and enlightenment would blaze. It was this potential that
Leigh Hunt discerned in the "transcendental cosmopolitics" of *Hyperion*.⁷

Yet the poem Keats was meditating was never going to be named *Apollo*.
It was always keyed to Hyperion, a god foreseeing his own doom in his
fallen brothers. The intensity was more than speculative exercise. When
Keats returned to London in August 1818, it was to his own brother dying,
painfully. Sitting down to write *Hyperion*, he found himself on no march
of passion and endeavor but halted in a horrible contradiction. The plan
was to hail Apollo "the Father of all verse" (3.13), but life had made him
"father of" that "tremendous" knowledge "that the World is full of Misery

and Heartbreak, Pain, Sickness and oppression" (as he had spelled it out the spring before to Reynolds). A few paragraphs earlier, Keats insisted that "axioms in philosophy are not axioms until they are proved upon our pulses," comparing "Miltons apparently less anxiety for Humanity" to Wordsworth's poetry of "the human heart" (*K* 129–30). Philosophy is no settled creed for Keats; it is always the work of philosophy. "I wish I could say Tom was any better," he sighs to a friend (Dilke) in September; "His identity presses upon me so all day that I am obliged . . . to write, and plunge into abstract images to ease myself of his countenance his voice and feebleness" (*K* 200).

"I am gone / Away from my own bosom: I have left / My strong identity, my real self," is the voice he writes for dethroned Saturn (1.112–14). In late October Keats would theorize a "camelion" poetics for conceptual power (including what it's like to be this Saturn). Proximate to Tom's suffering, however, the dynamic presses the inner life of this "other Body" on his consciousness with such pain that he turns to poetry-writing for ease, only to feel sympathetic disease.[8] "I live now in a continual fever," he tells Dilke, caught between a sense of "crime" in wanting to "ease" himself of Tom's suffering by thinking "of fame of poetry," or having to "suffer" if he does not. "Imagine 'the hateful siege of contraries,'" he sighs, summoning a phrase he underlined from Satan's survey of an Eden he can only ruin.[9] "I am sorry to give you pain," he apologizes of his contagion, "but I really have not self possession and magninimity [*sic*] enough to manage the thing otherwise" – no junior Apollo, he. While he can tell Reynolds the next morning that "Poetry has conquered . . . I have relapsed into those abstractions which are my only life," *relapse* names a fall of another kind. Poetry is only "feverous relief" next to "Poor Tom" (*K* 201) – an epithet Keats underlined in his copy of *King Lear*, dating it 4 October.

With the epic action all over or to come, Keats can make an epic of reaction, a genre, on the analogy of Wordsworth's experiment in states of mind in feeling in *Lyrical Ballads*, that could be called "lyrical epic."[10] Mere plot summary seems painfully irrelevant. Here's a bare overview. **Book I** opens into a panorama of the fallen Titans, stunned, confused, and aching, then shifts to Hyperion, still with "His sov'reignty, and rule, and majesty," though sensing a darkening. He tests his powers by trying to launch the dawn before the natural hour and is defeated. His father Cœlus urges him instead "to the earth" to rouse his comrades, and he plunges into the night. **Book II** stages the Titans' debate about what to do, interrupted by the arrival of Hyperion, who is "dejected" at the misery he beholds.

Book III turns away, to Apollo's awakening to divine power, and breaks off mid-sentence after 135 lines.

That was it in April 1819. Yet Keats's publishers were so impressed by the poetry that they put *Hyperion, A Fragment* at the end of the 1820 volume, allotting it more than a quarter of the volume's pages (143–99). Shelley preferred it above all: "an astonishing piece of writing . . . the very highest style of poetry," destining Keats as one of "the first writers of the age."[11] It was "second to nothing that was ever produced by a writer of the same years," he said in his Preface to *Adonais* (1821/1829). Even Byron came round. But Keats, thinking a "Fragment" would signify incapability, was livid at the Advertisement at the front of the volume, which reported the publication as "contrary to the wish of the author" and, worse, that he had been "discouraged . . . from proceeding" by the "reception" of *Endymion*. (Woodhouse drafted it, Taylor tweaked it, and Keats didn't see it until publication.) "This is none of my doing – I was ill at the time – This is a lie," Keats scrawled on one copy (Fig. 4). It wasn't those reviews. It was the contraries in the new project – ones Keats had figured with considerable intensity, but had not figured out.

Fallen Titans

In any fall, *Paradise Lost* looms. Keats meant to write "with judgment" (*K* 207) but not with any Miltonic argument to "justify" the mysteries of "Eternal Providence." His turn to classical myth was calculated against Milton's Biblical code and Milton's argument of culpable disobedience. Keats wanted an epic venture into those Wordsworthian "dark Passages" where "we see not the ballance of good and evil" (*K* 130). What is it like to fall into this experience? The Titans are this language. Thea, in tender sympathy for Saturn, presses her hand "upon that aching spot / Where beats the human heart, as if just there, / Though an immortal, she felt cruel pain" (1.42–44). Cœlus beholds in his children "fear, hope, and wrath; / Actions of rage and passion; even as / I see them, on the mortal world beneath, / In men who die" (1.332–35) – the *as* at the line's turn compacting analogy and simultaneity. Even Apollo's deification, in a language of physical convulsion, pain, struggle, anguish, is intimate in a knowledge of dying bodies. Tom's last days, said Keats, were of "a most distressing nature." Still reeling from grief and exhaustion, he returned in late December to a project he was now thinking of as "the fall of Hyperion."[12]

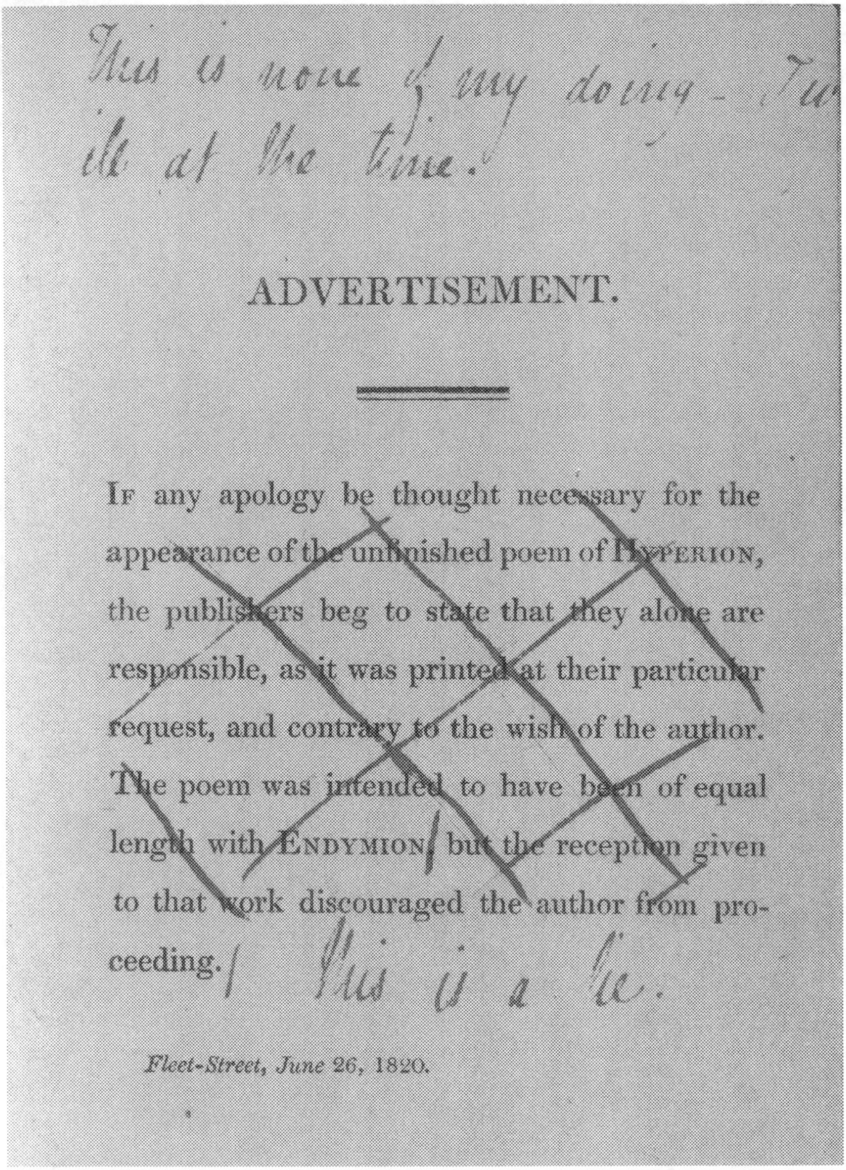

This is none of my doing — I w[as]
ill at the time.

ADVERTISEMENT.

IF any apology be thought necessary for the
appearance of the unfinished poem of HYPERION,
the publishers beg to state that they alone are
responsible, as it was printed at their particular
request, and contrary to the wish of the author.
The poem was intended to have been of equal
length with ENDYMION, but the reception given
to that work discouraged the author from proceeding. *This is a lie.*

Fleet-Street, June 26, 1820.

Fig. 4 Keats's protest on the Advertisement page of the *Lamia* volume. Houghton Library,
Harvard University. Not seeing the Advertisement until its publication, Keats was
dismayed by the inclusion of "A Fragment" and outraged by the well-meaning explanation
(with Woodhouse's advice) of his discouragement.

Reading *Paradise Lost*, Keats marked out the way "the immediate topic of the Poem opens with a grand Perspective" (*K* 233), the action beginning with Satan: "the first step must be heroic and full of power; and nothing can be more impressive and shaded than the commencement of the action here – 'round he throws his baleful eyes'" (1.56). Keats underlines this, along with what these eyes behold in aching recognition (*K* 226):

> At once, as far as Angels' ken he views
> The dismal situation waste and wild:
> (59–60)
>
>   sights of woe,
> Regions of sorrow, doleful shades, where peace
> And rest can never dwell, hope never comes
> That comes to all   (64–67)

Keats takes even Satan off the "ballance of good and evil" and weighs instead the "epic passion" (*K* 129–30). *Hyperion* opens with no ritual invocation to a muse, setting out instead a fallen scene in a one-sentence stanza of relentless intensifications, layer by layer, line by line, word by word. Its fourteen lines shape a sonnet that now truly rereads *King Lear*:

> DEEP in the shady sadness of a vale
> Far sunken from the healthy breath of morn,
> Far from the fiery noon, and eve's one star,
> Sat gray-hair'd Saturn, quiet as a stone,
> Still as the silence round about his lair;
> Forest on forest hung about his head
> Like cloud on cloud. No stir of air was there,
> Not so much life as on a summer's day
> Robs not one light seed from the feather'd grass,
> But where the dead leaf fell, there did it rest.
> A stream went voiceless by, still deadened more
> By reason of his fallen divinity
> Spreading a shade: the Naiad 'mid her reeds
> Press'd her cold finger closer to her lips.   (1.1–14)

This sonnet imprints epic impotence, an anti-inspiration of no breath. From the first spondee, *Deep in* (sounding *deepen*, echoed by *sunken*), the clauses sink down, as far from heaven as fallen divinity can be, into epochal obituary. No initial iamb lilts until "Like *cloud* on *cloud*" (7). Keats loads the blank verse with relentless repetitions, stresses and internal chords of arrest: *Far sunken . . . far from*, then *far* rhymed to *star*; the phonic zoning of *dead, still as the silence, still deadened more; gray-hair'd, his lair, no stir of air, where, there; sadness, voiceless, Press'd; Shady sadness . . . spreading a shade*. A dirge pounds out all that's lost: the healthy breath of morn, leaves that live, a summer day, a breeze, a stream singing. For this effect, Keats devised the negations he needed: Saturn's *realmless* eyes (1.19), to register the lost survey, versus (to come) Apollo's *gloomless* eyes casting across the *liegeless* air he's born to rule (3.80–92).

In the phrasing "Robs not one light seed," the Titan light-robber Prometheus seems an impossible actor. Saturn can murmur only astonishment: "Who had power / To make me desolate?" (1.102–3). There is no sin to arraign, no moral fault, just "epic passion" (*K* 129). Keats's epic narrator, audience to "that large utterance of the early Gods," concedes a "woe, / Too huge for mortal tongue or pen of scribe" (1.151, 159–60). From downbeat trochees to stressed echoes that pulse with a medical student's witness, Keats's poetry churns the agony. Keats underlines Milton's phrasing of the black bituminous <u>gurge</u> that boils from hell's mouth into the fallen world, and injected it into these suffering bodies:[13] "Heaving in pain, and horribly convuls'd / With sanguine feverous boiling gurge of pulse" (2.27–28), the very pulse of *pulse* in con*vuls*'d. Feeling "the full weight of utterless thought," Saturn can riddle no "reason" in his fall – especially to forces that seemed so "untremendous" (2.129–55). Keats had to coin that last word, perhaps *utterless*, too.[14]

The congress in Book II rallies these gods into "alternate uproar and sad peace" (the recap at the top of Book III). *Paradise Lost* Book II is the template (with no Satan working a hidden agenda), and Keats underlined several verses, but none of Milton's moral glosses.[15] Against Cœlus's urging Hyperion to seize "the van / Of circumstance" (1.343–44), Oceanus would "envisage circumstance, all calm" (2.204), reading the signposts on the "avenue" to "eternal truth": "A power more strong in beauty, born of us / And fated to excel us" (186–87; 213–14). There's a critical tradition of hearing this as Keats's proxy, and not without Keats's help.[16] Yet not for nothing was Keats a student of Shakespeare. Like Ulysses in Agamemnon's camp (*Troilus and Cressida*, Act I), Oceanus is one voice among many, and a character study. Shakespeare represents a master-strategist, and Keats nicely camelions a complacent sophist, exempla and clichés ready at hand:

> Say, doth the dull soil
> Quarrel with the proud forests it hath fed,
> And feedeth still, more comely than itself?

> Can it deny the chiefdom of green groves?
> Or shall the tree be envious of the dove
> Because it cooeth, and hath snowy wings
> To wander wherewithal and find its joys?
>
> (217–23)

"Receive the truth, and let it be your balm" (243) is the bottom line for this "Sophist and sage" (168). Clymene, "the simplest voice" (252), gives the pure lament: "joy is gone, / And this thing woe crept in among our hearts" (253–54). Enceladus embodies wrath and contempt for anything else, shouting down Clymene and rebuking Oceanus: "Dost thou forget, sham Monarch of the Waves, / Thy scalding in the seas?" (319–20). Yet it is he who is the voice of epochal elegy as much as Clymene: "Much pain have I for more than loss of realms: / The days of peace and slumberous calm are fled; / Those days, all innocent of scathing war" (334–36).

Keats read *Paradise Lost* for these affective aesthetics. "In Demons, fallen Angels, and Monsters, the delicacies of passion living in and from their immortality, is of the most softening and dissolving nature" – softening and dissolving of their immortality, that is, and so recognizable to mortal readers. If there is a divine force in Milton's epic, it is Milton in this temper, "godlike in the sublime pathetic" (*K* 231), and Keats brings this epic temper into the Titan conclave. Having focused their hope on Hyperion's "radiance" still "undisgraced" (2.344–45), they behold a "dejected King of Day" (380), already fallen in his soul. Impressed by the "Magnitude of Contrast" in Milton's scene of fallen angels gaining heart for another battle, Keats fiercely underlined it all, writing in the margin of "The light and shade—the sort of black brightness—the ebon diamonding . . . the sorrow, the pain, the sad-sweet Melody—the Palanges of Spirits so depressed as to be 'uplifted beyond hope'—the short mitigation of Misery the thousand Melancholies and Magnificences of this Page."[17] He also underlined Satan's rally, how the mighty Cherubims' "Millions of flaming swords" in a "sudden blaze / Far round illumin'd Hell" (1.664–66).

And so he shaped Hyperion's "terrible" revelation as "he stay'd to view / The misery his brilliance had betray'd / To the most hateful seeing of itself" (2.368–70). Catching a rhyme with *he stay'd*, *betray'd* plays brilliantly double: *revealed to* and *subverted*. "Regal his shape majestic, a vast shade / In midst of his own brightness" (372–73) is the outward figure and the inner brooding. The genealogy is Satan's ruining into an "excess / Of glory obscured; as when the sun new risen / Looks through the horizontal misty air / Shorn of his beams" (1.593–96). Keats underscored this, too; it weighs on Hyperion as an allusion.[18]

Keats's Epic Voice and the "Apollonian" poet

Reading (and raiding) *Paradise Lost* for such artistry, Keats took notes on how Milton opened and ended scenes, how he moved from voice to voice, from scene to psychology. The term Keats uses for the entire "management" of Milton's first three books is "Apollonian" (*K* 233), as if discerning in Milton a ghost of the kind of genius he wanted for his "fore-seeing" hero.

But the plan swerves away from the outline in the old mythologies. In this archive, Hyperion was a primitive force ("the Sun's God"), while Apollo advanced sun-lighting into cerebral brilliance: prophecy, philosophy, poetry, music, even medicine. What's not to love for a Keatsian poet? Young Apollo is ignorant in a Miltonic way ("dark, dark, / And painful vile oblivion seals my eyes"; 3:86–87) and set for an upgrade. He has dreamed of a goddess and awoke, like Milton's Adam, to find it truth, with divine musical power:

> "Yes," said the supreme shape,
> "Thou hast dream'd of me; and awaking up
> Didst find a lyre all golden by thy side,
> Whose strings touch'd by thy fingers, all the vast
> Unwearied ear of the whole universe
> Listen'd in pain and pleasure at the birth
> Of such new tuneful wonder."   (3.61–67)

Keats's pauses the meter at the stress of "strings touch'd" as if to play the chord anew in the poetry itself. No sooner does Apollo moan of "aching ignorance" than he knows the goddess as Mnemosyne, repository of memory and the mother of muses. "I can read / A wondrous lesson in thy silent face: / Knowledge enormous makes a God of me" (111–13). Thus "enkindled" and "Trembling with light,"

> Soon wild commotions shook him, and made flush
> All the immortal fairness of his limbs;
> Most like the struggle at the gate of death;
> Or liker still to one who should take leave
> Of pale immortal death, and with a pang
> As hot as death's is chill, with fierce convulse
> Die into life: so young Apollo anguish'd:
> His very hair, his golden tresses famed
> Kept undulation round his eager neck.   (3.121–32)

Yet his initial figuring – numb, melancholy, alienated, restless, longing for "other regions" (3.86–96) – has more than a few readers sensing Endymion

Redux or 2.0. Bower-born, accessorized with a mother and a sister, Apollo is in a heat for a "beauteous star": "I will flit into it with my lyre, / And make its silvery splendour pant with bliss" (100–2). Even Hunt (poet laureate of luxurious foliage) thought the scenario a bit "too effeminate and human"; Apollo "weeps and wonders somewhat too fondly," and "undergoing his transformation into a Divus Major, suffers a little too exquisitely among the lilies."[19] It's not just that no god should flush thus; no man should. It was more Divus-Diva yet in Keats's earlier draft, where commotions

> made flush
> All the immortal fairness of his limbs,
> Into a hue more roseate than sweet pain
> Gives to a ravish'd nymph when her warm tears
> Gush luscious with no sob – (HK3.2.199; *P* 356)

The Bower of Adonis seems muse of the front-rhyme, *Flush* and *Gush*, oozing into *luscious*. Though he rewrote, Keats kept the flush of erotic excitement, and so Apollo is Endymionized.

As with that mortal led on by circumstance, "on the sudden it is won." It's a spectacle "without any momentous depth of speculation" (as Keats grumbled of Benjamin West's *King Lear* [*K* 77]). Betraying no internal agency or volition, his rehearsal of "Names, deeds, gray legends, dire events, rebellions, / Majesties, sovran voices, agonies, / Creations and destroyings" (3.114–16) had Keats sketching an undeviating march of empty nouns. What's left to say? "Apollo shriek'd; —and lo! from all his limbs / Celestial glory dawn'd. he was a god!" The fragment in *1820* breaks off at "Celestial," trailed by fourteen un-symbolic asterisks to fill out this line and another.[20] Typography instead of typology.

"shady visions come to domineer"

If Apollo's apotheosis figures Keats's desire, in April 1818, for "continual drinking of Knowledge" (*L* 1:271), the Titans pulse with his sense (he said to Reynolds a few weeks on) that no draught of knowledge can console us for "the death of a friend or the 'ill that human flesh is heir to'" (*K* 128) – his voice at one with Hamlet's. Apollo is a theoretical ideal; Hyperion is experiential imagination.

Midway in Book I Keats pans over to this uneasy god, with a double-packed word, *still*, to mark time and station: "Blazing Hyperion on his orbed fire / Still sat" (166–67). It's also a devastating repetition: "Sat gray-hair'd Saturn . . . / Still as the silence" (1.4–5) is the textual past, relayed into Hyperion's temporal future. Epic similes and analogies thicken the intimations of mortality:

> For as among us mortals omens drear
> Fright and perplex, so also shuddered he—
>   (169–70)

>   sometimes eagle's wings,
> Unseen before by Gods or wondering men,
> Darken'd the place; and neighing steeds were heard,
> Not heard before by Gods or wondering men.
>   (182–85)

"We see the ebb and flow of the feeling, its pauses and feverish starts, its impatience of opposition, its accumulating force when it has time to recollect itself, the manner in which it avails itself of every passing word or gesture, its haste to repel insinuation, the alternate contraction and dilation of the soul": this is Hazlitt's measure of the power of *King Lear*, deeming it one of the "great master-pieces in the logic of passion." Keats marked and underlined a good deal of this sentence in *Characters of Shakespear's Plays* (seq. 185) taking its logic for Hyperion. Nightmares invade his "palace bright," making it ache with his fever. It "Glar'd a blood-red through all its thousand courts, / Arches, and domes, and fiery galleries" (1.179–80). The very "clouds / Flush'd angerly" (181–12), hailing Hyperion, "full of wrath" (213):

> His flaming robes stream'd out beyond his heels,
> And gave a roar, as if of earthly fire   (1.214–15)

The *as if* is more than analogy; it is history, projecting Hyperion into earthly fire, already effective. It "Jarr'd his own golden region" (224), altering sensation: "Instead of sweets, his ample palate took / Savour of poisonous brass and metal sick" (1.188–89). Keats would recall this for his own mortal savor: "The last two years taste like brass upon my Palate," he tells Fanny Brawne in August 1820, preparing to leave England and her, forever he feared, and feeling Hyperion on his pulses (*K* 423).

He gives Hyperion a horrible parody of Adam's Dream, his "dreams of day and night" issuing paradise-poisoning "monstrous forms," "spectres," "Phantoms" (1.227–30, 255). The "shady visions come to domineer" (244) not as external forces but as presences already in the mind, turning language to questions, echoing "why," and trailing clouds of glory lost that Keats summons from literary memory:

Why do I know ye? why have I seen ye? why
Is my eternal essence thus distraught
To see and to behold these horrors new?
Saturn is fallen, am I too to fall?
Am I to leave this haven of my rest,
This cradle of my glory, this soft clime,
This calm luxuriance of blissful light,
These crystalline pavilions, and pure fanes,
Of all my lucent empire?   (1.231–39)

In the poetry of these anguished questions, Keats's anaphora of elegiac cadences echoes (and enlists by allusion) John of Gaunt's dying hymn to an England lost and gone in an internecine usurpation ("this sceptred isle, / . . . This other Eden, demi-paradise, / . . . This blessed plot, this earth, this realm, this England") and Satan's survey of hell: "this the region, this the soil, . . . this the seat / That we must change for Heav'n, this mournful gloom / For that celestial light."[21] Wordsworth magnificently wrote it out in the mortal shades of immortality: "Blank misgivings of a Creature / Moving about in worlds not realized" (*Ode, Intimations* 146–47). Keats relays this misgiving to Hyperion in a register of epic negation, a haven

Deserted, void, nor any haunt of mine.
The blaze, the splendor, and the symmetry,
I cannot see – but darkness, death and darkness.
                              (1.240–42)

Hyperion's darkening Chamber of Maiden-Thought is the antagonist. The symmetry of existence can rhyme, on the fly, only with "I cannot see," evoked only in this radical negation.

For this assault from within, Keats reworks Satan's insinuation into Eden "wrapt in a mist / Of midnight vapour . . . Like a black mist low creeping, he held on / His midnight search" for a place to hide, and finds that sleeping coil of a serpent, entering in at his mouth. Underlining all of this,[22] Keats fits it to Hyperion's agony (1.175):

A mist arose, as from a scummy marsh.
At this, through all his bulk an agony
Crept gradual, from the feet unto the crown,
Like a lithe serpent vast and muscular
Making slow way, with head and neck convuls'd
From over-strained might.   (1.258–63)

We are "in a Mist," said Keats of Wordsworth's dark passages (*K* 130). What a devastating touch is Keats's use of *crown* – from empire to imperiled body.

In a brilliant firing of divinity into human history, Keats writes Hyperion's deteriorating wrath into that futile, premature assault on the gates of dawn, and sends the action into "hieroglyphics old." In the resistance of nature's law, the sun is counter-scribe. It

> wrought upon the muffling dark
> Sweet-shaped lightnings from the nadir deep
> Up to the zenith, – hieroglyphics old,
> Which sages and keen-eyed astrologers
> Then living on the earth, with labouring thought
> Won from the gaze of many centuries:
> Now lost, save what we find on remnants huge
> Of stone, or marble swart; their import gone,
> Their wisdom long since fled.   (1.275–83)

How poignant, in a magnitude of contrasts, that sunlight should become "Sweet-shaped lightnings" – no lightening, but the lost import of divine agony, *wrought* finding its symmetry with the labors of human *thought*. The relay rhyme of remnant *stone* and import *gone* is the harmonized pathos of a ditty of no tone.

Keats knows he has to close Book I with Hyperion's thwarted reading, and his course downward to darkness, himself an uncommunicating text: "Forward he stoop'd over the airy shore, / And plung'd all noiseless into the deep night" (356–57) – *noiseless*: without words, still (quiet) in the extreme. This is the "sublime pathetic" at its keenest: grand, dark, silent. "His fragment of 'Hyperion' seems actually inspired by the Titans, and is as sublime as Æschylus," none other than Byron would say.[23] What was left for Keats to do after this stunning sublimity? Just the fated business that Woodhouse noted: "dethronement of Hyperion . . . by Apollo," and "the war of the Giants for Saturn's reestablishment." With only "very dark hints in the mythological poets," Woodhouse adds, these "incidents would have been pure creations of the Poet's brain."[24] All brain, maybe, with no heart in it. "You must be wondering where I am and what I am about," Keats writes to Haydon, then saves him the trouble. "I am about nothing; being in a sort of qui bono temper, not exactly on the road to an epic poem" (*L* 2:42). *Qui bono/cui bono: for whose benefit?* The rise of celestial Apollo over sublimely dark Hyperion had not been an undeviating march after all, but a design derailed into doubt.

Yet the derailment was hardly a halt. The year begun with *Hyperion* (September 1818–September 1819) "may be soberly described as the most productive in the life of any poet of the past three centuries," says Keats's celebrated biographer, W. J. Bate.[25] The next venture would leave epic on the side, to drive a romance with a foreseeing hero, and a witty, sober-sided, though no trivial pro and con about what the burning lad is up to and what we're to make of it all.

CHAPTER 6

Still Romancing
The Eve of St. Agnes; *a dream-sonnet;* La belle dame

But let me laugh awhile, I've mickle time to grieve:
The Eve of St. Agnes

– so sighs old beldame Angela, accessory to a young knight's romantic adventure on a winter night (XIV). As if in recoil from the exhaustion of *Hyperion*, Keats found himself writing *The Eve of St. Agnes* in late January 1819, on a vacation from London, during which he may have had a light romantic affair. Its Spenserian stanzas are at once homage to *The Faerie Queene* (*The Eve* has a medieval décor) and a display of intricate poetic skill. Its nine lines rhyme *ababbcbcc* are iambic pentameter (a ten-syllable line), except for the final line, which is a hexameter (six iambs). The rhymes are artfully interwoven, with two opportunities for making the most of couplet rhymes (for close relations of sound and sense) and with the final line offering an opportunity for medial caesura (a pause in the syntax half way through). Keats is also mindful of a spectacular modern-retro site of this stanza, Byron's *Childe Harold's Pilgrimage, A Romaunt* (1812), which turned the stanza into an energetic serial extravaganza. *Childe Harold* Canto III appeared in 1816 and Canto IV, the last, in 1818, each installment an astonishing success. "I was surprised to hear from Taylor the amount of Murray the Booksellers last sale – what think you of £25,000? He sold 4000 coppies of Lord Byron," Keats writes to George and Georgiana in February 1819, about Canto IV.[1] Having this news from his own publisher must have been hard, especially in tandem with the report, "I have not gone on with Hyperion" (*L* 2:62). What Keats could go on with was "new romance" – not only from aptitude but also on the pulse of the market.

The Eve of St. Agnes summons a rather severe history: this patron saint of young virgins was a thirteen-year-old Christian martyr (fourth century), saved by a miracle of storm and lightning from a brutal sentence of gang rape in the brothels on the eve of her execution. Save the stormy weather, Keats suppresses all of this and focuses his romance on a reception history of sorts: a legend, or superstition, curated by "old dames," that if on this Eve (20 January), young virgins observe ritual fasting and prayer, they "might have visions of delight, / And soft adorings from their loves receive / Upon the honey'd middle of the night" (V–VI). Madeline is "Full of this whim" (VII), on both a visionary and erotic pulse. Her love is "young Porphyro, with heart on fire" (IX). A "purple riot," throbbing with rapture, braving perils, he is also a foreseeing hero: in a "full-blown rose" of inspiration, he plans to inhabit Madeline's dream (XVI) and warm her silvery, chilly, saintly virginity into passionate lovemaking.

In *The Eve of St. Agnes*, artifice is never invisible. It is everywhere, not only in the high art of its Spenserian stanzas (some, such gorgeous set-pieces as to inspire several painters),[2] but also in its confection of legends, rituals, schemes, and literary riffs galore. Keats's romance is a complex production: camelion-immersed in sensuous intensity, coyly (sometimes puzzlingly) allusive, ironic, meta-fictive, light and dark, sophisticated and enchanted, sentimental and skeptical, comic and thrilling. In contrasts that Keats works for both dramatic effect and critical point, the lovers tryst amid a freezing winter night fraught with Romeo-and-Juliet-like family feuds, a rising storm of sharp sleet, iced gusts and roaring wind, and a seduction by manifold delights that is part of an artful stratagem on (or against) a hoodwinked dreamer.

In an epiphenomenon of these various turns, mid-twentieth-century Keats studies became a field of debate, not only about what we are reading but how we are to read. Earl Wasserman, out to advance Keats as a serious as well as a sensuous poet, cast *The Eve* as a spiritual allegory: a lover-knight on a quest to the shrine of his beloved, rescuing her from chilly innocence into a vitality of sense and spirit that transcends the material antagonisms of clan-hostility and winter weather. Yet so carefully culled was his "mystic oxymoron" that Jack Stillinger issued an "admittedly exaggerated" rejoinder, quite controversial at the time, titled "The Hoodwinking of Madeline." Arguing that *The Eve* is a spiritual pilgrimage only in "satire," he tagged Porphyro as a schemer from the fraternity of Tereus (rapist of Philomena, one of the allusions for Madeline), Peeping Tom, Shakespeare's treacherous Iachimo, Milton's Satan, Richardson's rapacious Lovelace; and he read Madeline as a perilously blind dreamer, of the cohort everywhere rebuked in Keats's mature work.[3] Her very name evokes "Maiden" innocence (dreaming in a "Chamber of Maiden-Thought") and synonymizes "Magdalene," patroness of fallen women.

Keats serves all parties. "God's help! my lady fair the conjurer plays," sighs Angela (XIV) after the narrator has described her "hoodwink'd with faery fancy; all amort": dead to (or "regardless" of) the waking world, yet panting in passion, "Anxious her lips, her breathing quick and short" (VIII). Keats first wrote "Her anxious ~~lips~~ mouth full pulp'd with rosy thoughts."[4] In this flush Madeline could be a sleeping beauty ripe for wakening (Keats's first unravish'd bride of quietness); or she could be on track to Magdalenizing. Porphyro, straight from romance-central, is a plumed knight streaking "across the moors" (IX), braving a dangerous castle gothic-printed with "a lowly arched way," a "moonlight room" (XIII), "many a dusky gallery" (XXI), guarded (sort of) by a drunken porter and a sleeping bloodhound, and packed with a "blood-thirsty race" of "barbarian hordes, / Hyena foemen, and hot-blooded lords, / Whose very dogs would execrations howl / Against his lineage" (X). Keats liked his "fine mother Radcliff names" (*L* 2:62) for this race: "dwarfish Hildebrand" and "old Lord Maurice" (XII).[5] By "happy chance," Porphyro finds "mercy" in a "beldame" – no *belle dame sans merci* but an *Angela ex machina*, replete "with ivory-headed wand" (X–XI) to bring him to Madeline's chamber.

There are fictionists abounding. Madeline reads herself into a legend. Porphyro tells Angela and himself a story of his honorable quest, plays the "ancient ditty" of "La belle dame sans mercy" to Madeline, and spins the weather into an elfin storm from faery land that will cover their escape to the southern moors. The narrator, with a store of literary echoes and allusions, is also a literary performer. He begins with a stagey conjuration, "St. Agnes' Eve – Ah, bitter chill it was!," sprinkles melodramatic punctuations ("Ah!" "lo!" "aye!" "woe betide!"), gives on-site commentary – "He ventures in: let no buzz'd whisper tell, / All eyes be muffled, or a hundred swords / Will storm his heart" (X) – or stage-manager cues: "Now prepare, / Young Porphyro for gazing . . . " (XXII). The first conjurer in the tale is the castle's "ancient Beadsman" (IV), a hired prayer for his employers' souls. Keats enlists him as a camelion poet, in for and feeling how the "sculptur'd" effigies in the cold winter chapel "seem to freeze" and "ache in icy hoods and mails" (II). Then there's the party's "revelry," glimpsed and dismissed as a "rich array, / Numerous as shadows haunting fairily / The brain, new stuff'd, in youth, with triumphs gay / Of old romance" (V). We are solicited to wish this world away for the sake of turning to Madeline, in a panting whimsy fueled by the tales of those old dames.

Tale-telling, fiction-making, tale-reading: all this is in play. Madeline is the intersection of imagination, dreaming, excited love, and sensuous rapture, Keats's poetic anatomy from his own reading and first writings. She's inspired, she's blinded, she's vulnerable, she's ready to be thawed, she's deluded, she's doomed, she's enchanted. She's "Blissfully haven'd both from joy and pain" and "Blinded alike from sunshine and from rain" (no reader ready for *King Lear*). If the analogy for her is "As though a rose should shut, and be a bud again," she's also marked by weakening repression: "she panted . . . her heart was voluble, / Paining with eloquence her balmy side." Legible are those anti-Catholic discourses of virgin hysteria (in, say, Burton's *Anatomy of Melancholy*, which Keats had), which manifests in dreams, visions, and suppressed speech, "As though a tongueless nightingale should swell / Her throat in vain, and die, heart-stifled, in her dell" (XXIII).

If dreamer-Endymion had cut an unmanly figure, Keats reworks the gender-issue into a female dreamer as a focus for rapture, witty demystification, and critical consequence (the tongueless nightingale is rape-victim Philomel). Porphyro is a new kind of Keatsian hero. He's an artful adventurer affecting the vassal, hoping to "gaze and worship" unseen − or if things go well, "Perchance speak, kneel, touch, kiss" (IX), all chastely. He has a bit of comic macho brio in "Brushing the cobwebs with his lofty plume" as he follows Angela to the safe haven of a closet (private room) next to Madeline's chamber (XIII). And he's the resourceful manager of a "stratagem" (XVI), ready to avail himself of the "cates and dainties" (XX) as well as a lute stored in a nearby room. His agenda just to worship heats up with the narrator slyly goading: "Now prepare, / Young Porphyro, for gazing on that bed; / She comes, she comes again, like ring-dove fray'd and fled" (XXII) − like a bird in the eye of a predator, or a voyeurism we're all to share in (Keats will stage Lamia stalking Lycius with a similar appetite [*Lamia* 1.237−41]).

Is this why Keats wanted *1820* "to commence with St Agnes' Eve" (*L* 2:276)? *Isabella* applies a brutal corrective to "old Romance" delusions; *The Eve of St. Agnes* capitalizes on its conspicuous illusions. Instead of fragrant basil nurtured by the hidden head of a murdered man, the meta-emblem here is a gorgeous work of art:

XXIV

> A casement high and triple-arch'd there was,
> All garlanded with carven imag'ries
> Of fruits, and flowers, and bunches of knot-grass,
> And diamonded with panes of quaint device,
> Innumerable of stains and splendid dyes,
> As are the tiger-moth's deep-damask'd wings;
> And in the midst, 'mong thousand heraldries,
> And twilight saints, and dim emblazonings,
> A shielded scutcheon blush'd with blood of queens and kings.

If the term of lineage, *blood*, accidentally evokes the "blood-thirsty race," its aesthetic is a blush, as if the entire race could be beautified, even a bit

aroused in excitement, by such artwork. Madeline, too, seems recreated by
its stains and splendid dyes:

> Full on this casement shone the wintry moon,
> And threw warm gules on Madeline's fair breast,
> As down she knelt for heaven's grace and boon;
> Rose-bloom fell on her hands, together prest,
> And on her silver cross soft amethyst,
> And on her hair a glory, like a saint:
> She seem'd a splendid angel, newly drest . . .
>
> (XXV)

Keats worked hard to get the blend of spirit and sense just right, arriving
at *warm* gules after trying out *red* then *rich*. He wanted a vital body in the
saint-like figure. Yet illusion it is, optical magic through "panes of quaint
device" on the other side of which is the winter world. Keats underscored
"quaint Device" in his copy of *The Tempest* – part of a stage-direction for
how sprite Ariel makes a sumptuous banquet suddenly vanish.[6]

It's a question "whether most to admire the magical delicacy of the
hazardous picture, or its consummate irresistible attraction," said reviewer
John Scott, italicizing the last two lines of my quotation of XXV (above,
ending *newly drest*). He's referring to the stanzas that follow, too, which
involve *un*dressing.[7] In one of the bravura moves of this romance, Keats
turns his artistry to the seductive choreography. "Porphyro grew faint"
at the saint-like splendor of Madeline praying (XXV) – but not for
long:

> Anon his heart revives: her vespers done,
> Of all its wreathed pearls her hair she frees;
> Unclasps her warmed jewels one by one;
> Loosens her fragrant bodice; by degrees
> Her rich attire creeps rustling to her knees:
> Half-hidden, like a mermaid in sea-weed
>
> (XXVI)

Scott loved the last three lines, italicizing them, too. Keats paces words,
phrases, lines, one by one, "in for and feeling" *camelion-wise* every degree
of unrobing, soliciting our imagination of the body heat of warmed jewels,
a mermaid half-not-hidden, an "empty dress" that reports an undressed
body (XXVIII). He expended considerable labor on the poetry of this
rising Pleasure Thermometer (Fig. 5):

> ~~Unclasps her bosom jewels~~
> ~~Unclasps her warmed jewels one by one~~

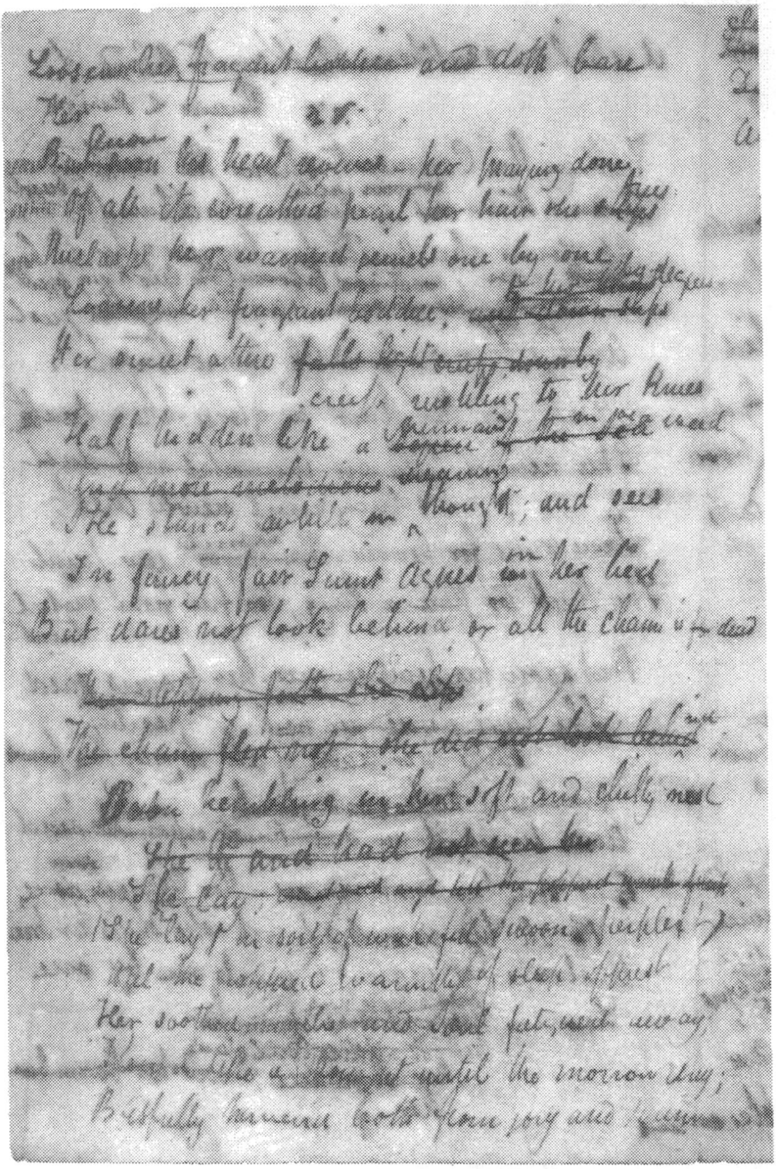

Fig. 5 Keats, manuscript page of *The Eve of St. Agnes*. Houghton Library, Harvard University, MS Keats 2.21.15. Keats's assiduous work on the stanzas of Madeline's unrobing, unaware of Porphyro's voyeurism; Keats implicates the reader, line by line.

> ~~her bursting~~
> ~~Loosens the bodice from her~~
>
>   ~~her bodice lace string~~
>   ~~her Boddice; and her bosom bar~~
> Loosens ~~her fragrant bodice and doth bare~~
> ~~Her~~
>
>   frees
>   Of all her wreathed pearl her hair she ~~strips~~
>
>   ~~to her knees~~
>   Loosens her fragrant bodice; ~~and down slips~~
>
> Her sweet attire ~~falls light creeps down by~~
>   creeps rusteling to her knees
>   Mermaid   in sea weed
>   Half hidden like a ~~Syren of the Sea~~
>   (MS pp. 14–15)

Keats means to make his readers partners in Porphyro's purple riot, a striptease out of thought.

Shifting tone just a jot, Keats flirts with suspenseful farce:

> Stol'n to this paradise, and so entranced,
> Porphyro gazed upon her empty dress,
> And listen'd to her breathing, if it chanced
> To wake into a slumberous tenderness;
> Which when he heard, that minute did he bless,
> And breath'd himself: then from the closet crept,
> Noiseless as fear in a wide wilderness,
> And over the hush'd carpet, silent, stept,
> And 'tween the curtains peep'd, where, lo! —how fast she slept.
>   (XXVIII)

On the cue of "paradise," here is avatar-Satan, stolen into Eden and gazing on Eve. While the main sense of *entranced* is the iambic one, the word, in the company of *Stol'n*, has a hint of a Keats-nonce-verb: having "gained entrance." Keats blends calculating seduction, nervous voyeurism (just a peep) and a bit of awkwardly tense comedy.

The chamber-banquet Porphyro produces from the closet's stores yields another set piece of Keatsian art, sequel to window-blazon, in a gusto of display for eye and appetite:

> Of candied apple, quince, and plum, and gourd;
> With jellies soother than the creamy curd,
> And lucent syrops, tinct with cinnamon;
> Manna and dates, in argosy transferr'd

From Fez; and spiced dainties, every one,
From silken Samarcand to cedar'd Lebanon.

> These delicates he heap'd with glowing hand
> On golden dishes and in baskets bright
> Of wreathed silver: sumptuous they stand
> In the retired quiet of the night,
> Filling the chilly room with perfume light. —
>   (XXX–XXXI)

How delicate of Keats to make it seem that perfume is another glow in the room (though we know *light* means airy), and how sensuous to have a hiss of delight in these words, a seduction for any reader to vocalize. Keats turns the truth-sensed adjective *sooth* into this new blend of *soothing* and *smooth*.[8]

In an amusing irony, Porphyro can hardly avail himself of all his success. His arm is "unnerved" as he slips into Madeline's bed, and when she opens her eyes, he buckles in self-ravishment: "Upon his knees he sank, pale as smooth-sculptured stone" (XXXII–XXXIII), about to join the company of the chapel-effigies. Then in a moment of coincidental magic, dreaming Madeline calls out in distress to him, changed from a sweet-voiced wooer to one "pallid, chill, and drear" (XXXV). From this near-death arrest, Keats recovers Porphyro to throbbing life:

> Beyond a mortal man impassion'd far
> At these voluptuous accents, he arose,
> Ethereal, flush'd, and like a throbbing star
> Seen mid the sapphire heaven's deep repose;
> Into her dream he melted, as the rose
> Blendeth its odour with the violet—
>   (XXXVI)

Flush'd and throbbing: this isn't about stars. (They twinkle).[9] To rhyme *arose* and *rose* is an outrageous erotic pun, a "Pun mote" as Keats might write it up (*L* 2:214). Porphyro's stratagem had come to him like a "full-blown rose" (XVI). More explicitly sexy was the draft Keats purveyed to a nervous Woodhouse in September:

> So while she speaks his arms encroaching slow
> Have zon'd her, heart to heart—loud, loud the dark winds blow:
> . . .
> More sooth for that his close rejoinder flows
> Into her burning ear: . . .
> With her wild dream he mingled, as a rose
> Marrieth its odour to a violet . . .[10]

In both this draft and the publication, Madeline is in a trance (a spell, an undisturbed sleep) during all this, awakening to find Porphyro in her bed and herself "a deceived thing" (XXXVII). Keats resolves the lad's rosy opportunism (had Madeline been complicit, it might have been a detriment to her character) with protestations of spiritual honor and honorable intentions.

Even with these safeties, Woodhouse felt he had to alert Taylor to the likely shock that "we innocent ones (ladies & myself)" might feel at "all the acts of a bonâ fide husband." Woodhouse hoped (a bit disingenuously) that "all is left to inference" and noted how "the Interest on the reader's imagination is greatly heightened" – even if this might "render the poem unfit for ladies." He had hinted to Keats about this last limit, and was taken aback by Keats's vehement response, à la Byron, which he conveyed to Taylor:

> He says he does not want ladies to read his poetry: that he writes for men— & that if . . . there was an opening for doubt what took place, it was his fault for not writing clearly & comprehensively—that he sh^d despise a man who would be such an eunuch in sentiment as to leave a ~~Girl~~ maid, with that Character about her, in such a situation . . . &c &c &c—and all this sort of Keats-like rhodomontade. (19 September 1819; *L* 2:163)

This was the same conversation in which Keats judged *Isabella* too "mawkish" to publish (162). His sensitivity to the reviews of *Endymion* as puerile fantasy was not helped by Woodhouse's news that it had been a big hit with a female cousin and the author Miss Porter ("of romance celebrity"). "I must needs feel flattered by making an impression on a set of Ladies," Keats too-politely replied, with gender-inoculation: "I should be content to do so in meretricious romance verse if they alone and not Men were to judge."[11] In *The Eve* he sexed the sentiment, even demystified it as a polite front for sexual appetite (men who protest this are eunuchs).

Taylor, his eye on "Decency & Discretion" and "the Suffrages of Women," and impatient with Keats's "Vaporing . . . as far from sound Fortitude, as the Conduct itself in the Instances before us," said that if Keats refused to emend, he'd have to be content to read the poem under "some other Imprint" and spare his own "Imprimatur."[12] After he cooled down, Keats agreed to some Tayloring, turning the poetry back to the initial codes of flowers and stars – and perhaps gaining more of an effect in the arousal of a reader's decoding. And he doubled down on the unappeasable winter world, returning to it in the very line of lovemaking consummation:

Solution sweet: meantime the frost-wind blows
Like Love's alarum pattering the sharp sleet
Against the window-panes; St. Agnes' moon hath set.
(XXXVI)

It's not a rose that blows (blooms) now, but the antagonist world. Keats weakens the stanza's closing couplet-rhyme for the sake of pulling *sweet* against *sleet*. The stanza widens in a heartbeat to this weather-world and stays there, carrying *sleet* into the *a*-rhymes of the next stanza: "'Tis dark: quick pattereth the flaw-blown sleet . . . / 'Tis dark: the iced gusts still rave and beat" (XXXVII) – beat on the very meters. Feeling this beat, Keats underscored Milton's Hellscape: "a frozen continent / Lies dark and wild, beat with perpetual storms / Of whirlwind and dire hail," and the winter visited on fallen earth, "ice, / And snow, and hail, and stormy gust and flaw."[13]

Keats's last stanzas stay in storm-world but (in another surprising shift) with a shimmer of romance. The lovers move along "a darkling way," evading the "sleeping dragons all around, / At glaring watch" (XL), dragoon-guards enchanted into fairytale dragons, with no glare of watch. It seems, even, that all feudal violence can be left to a tapestry, passed by the lovers in escape:

The arras, rich with horseman, hawk, and hound,
Flutter'd in the besieging wind's uproar;
And the long carpets rose along the gusty floor. (XL)

What waits beyond, however, is another siege. XL's alexandrine feels longer for two syllables of *long*, and *rose* is now no flower but an index of the storm outside. There is thrilling immediacy in the present participles (*besieging* but also *sleeping, glaring, flickering*; even *darkling* feels like a participle). Then suddenly, in the next stanza, the lovers enter a present tense that seems produced from another fictive order: "They glide, like phantoms, into the wide hall; / Like phantoms, to the iron porch, they glide" (XLI). The chiasmus, *glide, like phantoms/ Like phantoms . . . glide*, encloses them as wisps for another order of being. The next and final stanza conveys them into a history far gone from the sensuous immediacy of everything before: "And they are gone: ay, ages long ago / These lovers fled away into the storm" (XLII).[14]

What's left in the rest of the stanza (the poem's last lines) is ice-cold comfort, a romance brutally dispelled into wormy circumstance, as if outtakes from *Isabella*. The Baron "dreamt of many a woe," his guests are left "be-nightmar'd" (another Keats-coinage) by "shade and form / Of witch, and demon, and large coffin-worm," and the two castle-servants wind up in grotesque parodies of angel and worshipper:

> Angela the old
> Died palsy-twitch'd, with meagre face deform;
> The Beadsman, after thousand aves told,
> For aye unsought for slept among his ashes cold. (XLII)

Keats wanted to "leave off with this Change of Sentiment," and was glad to see from Woodhouse's response (so he sighed to Taylor) "that he had succeeded." Angela dies horribly, and nothing could be more abject than a beadsman not even missed by his patrons. Keats, added Woodhouse, seems to have "had a fancy for trying his hand at an attempt to play with his reader, & fling him off at last... the 'Don Juan' style of mingling up sentiment & sneering."[15]

A dreamy sequel?

If Keats leaves the fate of *St. Agnes*'s lovers a mystery, the lovers in a sonnet from the spring, *A Dream, After Reading Dante's Episode of Paulo and Francesca*, are damned to eternal storm. But where Dante sentenced them to *Inferno* for adultery, Leigh Hunt pitied them without judgment in *Story of Rimini*, and took a lot of heat for this liberty. Giving his sonnet to Hunt to publish in *The Indicator*, Keats converted hell to melancholy, in a camelion feeling for Paulo, and signed himself "Caviare" (Hamlet's trope for delicacy wasted on vulgar palates).[16] Even as Porphyro and Madeline evade the dragon-guards, the poet-dreamer, twinning himself to artful dragon-slayer Hermes, wields an "idle spright" (3) to defeat the "dragon world" of a "hundred eyes" (5). His course is to become Paulo in "that second circle of sad hell" (9), with verbal tracks across Adam and Eve's eviction from Eden into the storms of history. This is managed by hyper-panoptical Cherubim who derail the analogy to Hermes's magic. They are "Spangl'd with eyes more numerous than those / Of Argus, and more wakeful than to drowse, / Charm'd with Arcadian Pipe, the Pastoral Reed / Of Hermes" – lines in *Paradise Lost* Keats underscored.[17] If the dreamer read no more that day, it is only to become what he reads:

> Where in the gust, the whirlwind and the flaw
> Of Rain and hailstones lovers need not tell
> Their sorrows—Pale were the sweet lips I saw,
> Pale were the lips I kiss'd and fair the form
> I floated with about that melancholy storm—
> (10–14)

In *The Indicator*, the atmosphere is "world-wind": maybe an error; maybe a punning revision to *whirl'd* and an imprint of the dragon-*world*. In the currents of the whirl are *hell, hail, tell, Pale, Pale.* The lull of "fair the form / I floated with" is no lullaby, but a sonic stream to *storm* at the end of the final, metrically extended line.

This is a hell not of morals but of melancholy, the way lovers are battered by forces they can't control. The prologue in Keats's letter is his macrotext in this key. It begins, "I had passed many days in rather a low state of mind and in the midst of them I dreamt of being in that region of Hell." A dream may change to delight, low moods to warm uplift:

> The dream was one of the most delightful enjoyments I ever had in my life—I floated about the whirling atmosphere as it is described with a beautiful figure to whose lips mine were joined at it seem'd for an age—and in the midst of all this cold and darkness I was warm—even flowery tree tops sprung up and we rested on them sometimes with the lightness of a cloud till the wind blew us away again . . . o that I could dream it every night—— (HK1.53.247)

Cold and darkness are not dispelled, just suspended, by a dream. And not every night.

A cold hillside: *La belle dame sans merci*

Keats wrote out *A Dream* on 16 April 1819, then on the 21st, *La belle dame sans merci.*[18] In *Hyperion* the critical event is past, and the epic is a lyric anthology. In the lyrical ballad that is *La belle dame*, the events are not only past but may be only a dream conjured in sequel, as sense-making logic for present arrest.

For three stanzas, an unidentified voice questions a curious spectacle, a Knight at arms loitering where life has withered or fled, his own at seeming peril:

> O what can ail thee Knight at arms,
>   Alone and palely loitering?

The caution reverberating in *ail thee / palely* gets amplified as the stanza rounds to a loaded seasonal report, culminating in the alarm of three stressed syllables:

> The sedge has withered from the Lake
>   and no birds sing!

Still monologic, the question repeats, now with adjectives pressing interpretation:

> O what can ail thee, Knight at arms,
>   So haggard and so woe begone?

Something has *gone* to produce *woe*, and *haggard* hints a cause: commerce with a hag, "a wild or intractable person" (usually female) with a "'wild' expression of the eyes" (OED). And so the questions shift to proto-narrative diagnosis:

> I see a lilly on thy brow
>   With anguish moist and fever dew,
> And on thy cheeks a fading rose
> Fast withereth too.

Reading becomes sign-reading by-the-book for a fatally failed romance. (Keats canceled a too redundant "death's lilly" and "death's fading rose".)

In symmetry with "I see a lilly on thy brow" an answer (with no punctuation of a new voice) emerges, to tell a story: "I met a Lady in the Meads." What unfolds is a point-by-point contrast to the aftermath: a lady "full beautiful," song, magical food ("roots of relish sweet, / And honey wild, and manna dew") and lovemaking with a "sweet moan." A sensuous playland absorbs all: "And nothing else saw all day long," the Knight recalls, kin here to "hoodwink'd" Madeline (*Eve of St. Agnes*) and "blinded" Lycius (*Lamia*). We catch terms of potential delusion in "She look'd at me as she'd did love . . . And sure in language strange she said / I love thee true – ." If the syntax of *as she'd did love* lets the temporal conjunction *as* host *as if*, the assertion of *sure* can't really be sure. Keats stages a "language strange" strained into interpretation by desire.

It matters that the Knight is not just a lover but a truant Knight at arms. There's a long literary lore of such truancy, usually from she-enchantment, with severe consequences. Spenser's Bower of Blisse is the north star of the Keatsian map. The gendering of the temptation is critical, because it credits the slander and the logic of the ballad's title (language not so strange in import). This identification is announced in a post-coital dream:

> And there she lulled me asleep,
>   And there I dreamd Ah woe betide!
> The latest dream I ever dreamt
>   On the cold hill side.

> I saw pale Kings and Princes too
>   Pale warriors death pale were they all
> They cried• La belle dame sans merci
>   Thee hath in thrall•

Recalling the symptoms "woe-begone" and "pale," the dream seems to spell it all out: an identity unveiled, love's power to enthrall parsed into the literalism of thrall, "beautiful" distilled as "La belle" sans merci, a merciless traitor to a mistaken tacit contract. The dream comes in the voice of the patriarchal order: Kings, Princes, warriors, *all* literally in thr*all*.

As the Knight tells it, the answer to "what can ail thee?" is "La belle dame sans merci." But as Keats's ballad arrays it, such a story, especially in its gender-scheme, can also seem a fabulated "cause": a Lady gets conjured from legend to take the rap for a scandalously truant Knight at arms.[19] The word *man* is nowhere in the ballad, except as a syllable in the poisonous *man*na. The enchanted Knight seems kin to the female melancholics in Burton's *Anatomy*, who "cannot tell what ails them; you . . . cannot well tell what to make of their sayings . . . they think themselves bewitched; they are in despair."[20] Keats leaves indeterminate the ballad's involute of cause and effect: a "cause" retrojected from, and so a consequence of, this endpoint. No less determinate is the shape of the ballad itself, ending it where it began:

> And I awoke and found me here
>   On the cold hill's side
>
> And this is why I ~~wither~~ sojourn here
>   Alone and palely loitering;
> Though the sedge is withered from the lake
>   And no birds sing ——

"And I awoke and found me here," disjoins *I* and *me* in a "here" suspended between a location and a state of mind. Who is questioning? who else would be out in this withering world? Not for nothing does the verb *met* in medieval literature denote both encounter and dream, what Keats's Victorian biographer nicely calls "the union of infinite tenderness with a weird intensity."[21] *And this is why* answers in echo of the question, with a variant *Though* to concede a paralysis. With such repetition, absent of punctuation to distinguish questioner and Knight (even in *The Indicator* text), the ballad shimmers as a dialogue of the mind with itself, a voice addressing an identity now alien. If this feels like a stretch, you're still left with an "answer" involved with questions – about its gender array, its cultural lore, its explanatory validity, its deepest motivations.

Keats leaves everything darkly, brilliantly, double-bound: fairy's child and merciless enchanter; sweet food and fatal poison; love and enthrall-ment; awakening and still loitering; alienation from a life at arms and truancy from knightly manhood – and, not least, a twinning of question and answer, of questioner and answerer. In this lyricized ballad (its action not just over, but unknowable), Keats is on the verge of conceiving a deliberate poetry from self-questioning.

Is there a lyric genre for such a drama in the mind? This is the genius of some of the "Other Poems" in *Lamia &c*, ones now synonymous with Keats's fame: the "Great Odes."

CHAPTER 7

Reforming the sonnet and forming the Odes *of spring 1819*
Psyche; Nightingale; Grecian Urn; Melancholy; Indolence

Another sonnet

The Spenserian stanza of *The Eve of St. Agnes*, rhyming *ababbcbcc*, offered two couplets to exploit, and the Shakepearean sonnet, typically arraying its rhymes *ababcdcdefefgg*, had a dramatically pregnant last couplet. Keats is always thinking of sonnets, in sonnets. The journal-letter of 1819 that has *La belle dame* and the Dante dream-sonnet holds several sonnets, among them (on 3 May) one headlined "Incipit altera Sonneta" – Latin for "Here begins another sonnet" ("Here endeth the other Sonnet" is the postscript). The word *altera* means not just *other* but also *alternative*. Keats had no love for the "pouncing rhymes" of the Italian octave (*abbaabba*, three couplets in eight lines of only two rhymes) and was no warmer to Shakespeare's closing couplet, nor even its quatrains of alternating rhymes. "I have been endeavouring to discover a better sonnet stanza than we have," he writes. *Incipit* enacts this discovery, animated by another round with "Romance": the Sonnet as chained maiden liberated by a Keatsian poet-hero.[1]

With no aim of publication, Keats works out an argument, moving from a condition, *If*, to a proposal, *Let us* (us: the English poets among whom Keats would be), to a happy prospect, *so that* – indeed, an achievement on this very page (Fig. 6):

> If by dull rhymes our english must be chaind
> And, like Andromeda, the Sonnet sweet,
> Fetterd in spite of pained Loveliness;
> Let us find out, if we must be constrain'd,
> Sandals more interwoven and complete
>   To fit the naked foot of Poesy.
> Let us inspect the Lyre, and weigh the stress
>   Of every chord and see what may be gain'd
>   By ear industrious and attention meet.
>   Misers of sound and syllable no less
>   Than Midas of his coinage, let us be

87

Fig. 6 "If by dull rhymes"; journal letter, 1 May 1819 entry, to George and Georgiana Keats. Houghton Library, Harvard University, MS Keats 1.53.270–71. Keats's heading, "Incipit altera Sonneta," is a plausible title. Also known by its first words, "If by dull rhymes," this meta-sonnet was first published in a newspaper in 1836, then in *1848* (2:303).

Jealous of dead leaves in the bay wreath crown
So if we may not let the Muse be free,
She will be bound with garlands of her own.

Keats splurges the sonnet-budget of fourteen lines on three sentences of wreathed rhymes, with just a few strong pauses: *abc*[;] *abd*[.] *cab*[.] *cdede*[.], punctuated with trochees, spondees, and elided stresses. There is no couplet-rhyme. Only three lines (8, 13–14) play out in iambic pentameter, while the most meta-poetic one, "To fit the naked foot of Poesy" (8) conspicuously trips up: just four iambs, and the weakest end-rhyme (or no rhyme at all) on the front-stressed *Poesy*.[2]

On more than this keyword *Poesy*, this sonnet enacts its aims, turning its puns to make its points. Take the first rhyme, *chaind-constrain'd* – figuratively fit (with a link of *pained*) for a Petrarchan quatrain (four lines rhymed *abba*). But Keats drives his syntax against this promise, with a re-launch of the *If*-clause at line 4, and with fuel from the stressed syllables at the front of lines 3 and 4, *Fettered / Let us*, and with a charge from *to fit* (as if sprung from *Fettered*). *Let us*, the front of two lines and echoed inside 7 and 11, forges its own rhyme-chain, with help from *stress, no less, jealous*. Keats's chords are no cords. A sonnet about rhyming with ear industrious might have taken a scheme from *bound* (rhyme's principle) and *sound* (rhyme itself), but Keats softens this to a subtler internal chime. And if the concentrated syntax of his final lines mimes a Shakespearean couplet, no rhyme pounces. The final rhyme, *crown/own*, is not just atonal but a visual pun on this effect: "her *own*" takes four letters from *crown* but refuses its reign of sound.

The gendering of this meta-formal wit winks at all those Keatsian men in thrall to female spells. Keats's master-trope for the constrained resources of "our english" is Andromeda, the cue of her name ("men's ruler") subverted by her fettering as prey for a sea-serpent. In Ovid's fable (Keats knows) her liberator is the icon of masculine poetic force, Perseus on his winged steed Pegasus – already famed as decapitator of Medusa, she whose gaze turns men to stone. Taking her head as a trophy, Perseus assumes its power, and Pegasus is born from her corpse. Writing himself as a twin liberator, Keats shapes the sonnet in a romance of garlanding more supple, various, and lovely, and "natural" to "english."

This sonnet-thinking is legible in the odes he starts writing this spring. *Ode to Psyche* pivots from antiquity to modernity with a sonnet-stanza (36–49): an octave (Shakespearean *abab*, Petrarchan *cddc*) with a volta (formal and rhetorical "turn") at 9, "So let me be thy choir..." And a

Shakespearean quatrain and Petrarchan sestet form the ten-line stanzas of *Ode to a Nightingale, Ode on a Grecian Urn, Ode on Melancholy,* and *Ode on Indolence.*[3]

Ode poetics: reading actions

These odes are more than sonnet-reforms, of course. Just before relinquishing *Endymion* to his publisher, Keats argued to his theology-friend Bailey that "nothing in this world is proveable" – not to justify any nihilism but to consider how "every mental pursuit takes its reality and worth from the ardour of the pursuer – being in itself a nothing." "Nothings" (including "Poetry itself") are potentials in this way, "made Great and dignified by an ardent pursuit."[4] Keats writes these odes to stage this ardency in a poet's energetic pursuit and, correspondingly, a "perpetual activity of attention required on the part of the reader" (to cite Coleridge on Shakespeare's poetry).[5] The odes are about Keats's way of reading. With a concentration and subtlety of wording and a technical brilliance of form, he casts arcs of speculation and critical reflection, from first lines to last, with ventures of desire evolving complications and qualifications, ironies and reversals. Their language is a force-field, no less gorgeously wrought than fraught with fault-lines: words (even syllables) play repetitions with a difference, double into puns and paradoxes, command re-auditions. As a reader acutely tuned to etymologies, Keats exploits the "powerful effect" he notices in Milton's precision with a word, "its original and modern meaning combined and woven together, with all its shades of signification."[6]

These lines vibrate with echoes and allusions, as resonant as casual, ranging through the Bible, poetry, and the intertext of Keats's images and figures. Their contextual climate is personal, cultural, and historical: the ache for love and ease, the pharmacology of opium, the press of social misery, Tom's dying and Keats's acute sense of his own mortal lease, the mystery of ancient art, and, always, what modern art can and cannot do. Working its lines of inquiry from ode to ode, and in relay with its other poetry, Keats's volume is in effect a macrotext.[7]

The grammar that sustains negative capability amid positive pursuit is interrogative. "A Question is the best beacon towards a little Speculation," Keats once proposed to Bailey (*L* 1:175). "But who was thou, O happy, happy dove?" heralds one encounter. "Was it a vision, or a waking dream? . . . Do I wake or sleep?" is the morning-after musing on a nightingale's song; "What leaf-fring'd legend haunts about thy shape?" is the interview of a Grecian

Urn; "How is it, Shadows! that I knew ye not?" spells another morning's reflection. "Where are the songs of Spring? Ay, where are they?" plays the old *ubi sunt* trope for critical review. Answers, if they come, linger in pro and con: a poet's mind as a "fane" of "feign"; "easeful Death" latent in the lure of "full-throated ease"; "Spring . . . For ever" set in "Cold Pastoral"; a "Melancholy" of mutability as the contract of all "Delight"; a tribute to "Indolence" contradicted by busy thought and more ode-writing. Keats writes the odes less as designs for certain interpretation than as calls for readerly participation.

Ode to Psyche: soul-thoughted poetry

Just above that headline "Incipit altera Sonneta" Keats renders a faux-arty postscript to the piece just prior: "Here endethe yᵉ Ode to Psyche." The sonnet and ode are close company not just on this page but also in the genre of autogenesis (a poem about itself); and both star a she possessed by a modern-minded poet. "Psyche was not embodied as a goddess before the time of Apulieus the Platonist who lived afterr the Agustan age, and consequently . . . never worshipped or sacrificed to with any of the ancient fervour—and perhaps never thought of in the old religion," Keats writes as headnote to the history his *Ode* means to reclaim; "I am more orthodox than to let a hethen Goddess be so neglected."[8] The surmise "never thought of" cutely cues Psyche, the old world's word for *soul* and *mind*.[9]

A few pages back in this long letter, as Keats is speculating on mortal life as a "System of Soul-making," he suggests that the vitality of "hethan mythology" is not a metaphysics but a proto-poetic system of "abstractions . . . personified" (*L* 2:103). Recall his enthusiasm for the passage in *Excursion* IV on this score. *Ode to Psyche* renders a poet's discovery of mind personified as the muse of modernity. It is about its production – in effect, an "Ode to *Ode to Psyche*" – and so the logic of its redundant prelude:

> O GODDESS! hear these tuneless numbers, wrung
>   By sweet enforcement and remembrance dear,
> And pardon that thy secrets should be sung
>   Even into thine own soft-conched ear: (1–4)

This is the sole instance in Keats's poetry of *tuneless*, a negative tuned to be wrung and rung (the first of many purposeful puns) into visible as well as audible signs: an *ear* in h*ear* and d*ear* (this lettering, even, in conch*ed ear*). The eye awakened to secrets is the greeting of the poet's spirit:

> Surely I dreamt to-day, or did I see
> The winged Psyche with awaken'd eyes?
> (5–6)

The poetry is a romance of itself, this *or* nicely surrendered to a syntax that lets "with awaken'd eyes" be prepositional to both "I see" and to consonant "Psyche" (especially in the unit of line 6).

The poet starts his story "I wander'd in a forest thoughtlessly" (7), another negative set to be reversed – this, in a surprise by thought, on a scene of secretly quivering, erotic suspense:

> Saw two fair creatures, couched side by side
> In deepest grass, beneath the whisp'ring roof
> Of leaves and trembled blossoms, where there ran
> A brooklet, scarce espied:
> 'Mid hush'd, cool-rooted flowers, fragrant-eyed,
> Blue, silver-white, and budded Tyrian,
> They lay calm-breathing on the bedded grass;
> Their arms embraced, and their pinions too;
> Their lips touch'd not, but had not bade adieu
> As if disjoined by soft-handed slumber,
> And ready still past kisses to outnumber
> At tender eye-dawn of aurorean love: (9–20)

Keats's seeing "I" flirts with the sceptics of *Paradise Lost*: Satan espying Eden's pair "Under a tuft of shade that on a green / Stood whispering soft," then the epic poet sighing of the amorous "two fair Creatures" in an "inmost bower," then "asleep secure of harme."[10] Keats's swerve is not to align his "I" with either spy and the plot of loss afoot, but to key his tuneless numbers to an infinitive readiness "to outnumber." The timing "At tender eye-dawn" is just right, winking at the poet's "eyes" and "I" on the verge of inspiration – all done in arch knowingness:

> The winged boy I knew;
> But who wast thou, O happy, happy dove?
> His Psyche true!   (21–23)

The letter-text has a second question-mark after *true*, but Keats decided that he might as well exclaim what his title has already told.[11]

Such an ode, "too late for antique vows, / Too, too late for the fond believing lyre" (36–37), signals its close company with par-ody, the *antic* of "antique" (how it used to be said), and the shade of naïve-thoughtlessness in *fond*. Keats's inspiration invests in a poetics of double-played words on an historical arc of modernist difference:

Yet even in these days so far retir'd
   From happy pieties, thy lucent fans,
   Fluttering among the faint Olympians,
I see, and sing, by my own eyes inspired.
               (40–43)

41–42 are calculated for smart double-play. In the sequence of words, the preposition *retir'd / From* seems readied to govern all of line 41: these days, retired from the happy pieties of "lucent fans / Fluttering" – with a dying fall on O*ly*mpians, fainting into the sole feminine rhyme in this stanza, a grace note on the ironized antiquity. But 43 corrects this into the syntax of modern inspiration: *lucent fans* turns out to be the object of "I see and sing, by my own eyes inspired." Capitalizing on the "I"-promise of "eye-dawn" (20), this is aurorean wit in poetic grammar, recalling Psyche from retirement into shimmering presence.

    This wit is amplified in the Ode's larger auditorium of knowing puns. The lucent *fans* among the *faint* gods involves the poet "*fainting* with surprise" and keynotes the *fane* planned for his poetry of mind and the *feign* that will name "all" its *Fancy* can produce. The poet who declares at the top of his climactic, prospective stanza, "Yes, I will be thy priest, and build a fane / In some untrodden region of my mind" knows his fictions (Keats tested *frame* as the verb of artifice; HK1.53.270) and knows the impossible reproduction of Spenser's *Amoretti*: "Her temple fayre is built within my mind, / In which her glorious ymage placèd is, / On which my thoughts doo day and night attend / Like sacred priests" (22:5–8). Too, too late for this antiquity, Keats's retro interior décor tenders no claim for a visionary establishment. It is provisional:

And there shall be for thee all soft delight
   That shadowy thought can win,
A bright torch, and a casement ope at night,
   To let the warm Love in!   (64–67)

Here endethe ye Ode to Psyche, deftly qualified, in a loving Chamber of Maiden-Thought.

    As in the letter that spun this simile for awakening thought (*K*130), such residence has a temporal lease. *Ode to Psyche* keeps this development at bay but registers in its wording. Keats knows the severer modernity forecast in Wordsworth's Prospectus to *The Excursion* (1814): to make "the Mind" the "haunt, and the main region of my Song" requires a muse able to "tread on shadowy ground" (xi–xii). Keats pauses his *Ode* in a "shadowy thought" of delight. Its bower is a truce: here, "branched thoughts, new grown with pleasant pain, / Instead of pines shall murmur in the wind" (52–53). If there is a minor *groan* in *grown* by sweet enforcement of pleasant *pain*, the only poetic hazard, for now, is a risk, with a murmuring play on *pines*, of the Cockney tones for which Keats was mocked in the reviews. It's a coterie joke, which Keats was happy to amplify in describing the "moderate pains" he took with this ode (HK1.53.268).

The world beyond is a surreal extrapolation of Psyche from *Fledge*: "Far, far around shall those dark-cluster'd trees / Fledge the wild-ridged mountains steep by steep" (54–55). A ridge of pines that might seem feather-covered figures winged Psyche – or rather, a poet's psyche on the wing. "Psyche" whispers readiness for what later odes will intensify. *Psychology*, says the OED, first names a proto-Enlightenment science of the soul (1654); then an Enlightenment science of cognition, summed up by David Hartley's *Observations on Man* (1749): "Psychology, or the Theory of the human Mind" (1.3.354). Keats's psychology theorizes the mind's workings and wordings, and makes this the far field of poetic figurings, including the dark passages.

Ode to a Nightingale: poetry's darkling sounds

Ode to Psyche is self-reflecting. *Ode to a Nightingale* is self-listening. Phrases, words, and syllables repeat for new auditions, chiming with a difference, and for critical review. Across an eight-stanza drama of a mind yearning for hearts-ease, *Ode to a Nightingale* tolls its words on an arc of wishing, reflecting, rejecting, and lingering, in a thinking poetry that parallels but never coincides with the birdsong it tracks to last fading. The poetry surrounds its speaker as our text.

"My heart aches," it opens, three weighted syllables. While *My* is a personal pronoun, the ache is of all sensate consciousness. Hamlet's sigh at "the heartache and the thousand natural shocks / That flesh is heir to" is Keats's allusion in his comment to Reynolds that life cannot avoid "the ill 'that flesh is heir to'."[12] For such knowledge, a nightingale's song spells the ease of a melodious plot. The poetry has a more devious plot, however, and it courses through another calculated confusion of syntax:

> 'Tis not through envy of thy happy lot,
>   But being too happy in thine happiness,— –
>   That thou, light-winged Dryad of the trees,
>   In some melodious plot
>   Of beechen green, and shadows numberless,
>   Singest of summer in full-throated ease.
>
>   (5–10)

The seeming camelion sympathy of a poet "infor – and filling" the happiness he hears is subverted by line 7 into a radical difference. The nightingale knows nothing of envy; its lot is one where shadows numberless are just nature's variety, no dark passages of heart-ache.

Not opiate or hemlock but a draught "Tasting of Flora and the country green" is the desired dose for a Dryad's full-throated ease:

> That I might drink, and leave the world unseen,
>   And with thee fade away into the forest dim:
>
> (19–20)

So ends stanza 2 – or not quite. The colon at the end cues a continuation – more, we expect, about this forest-retreat. But when stanza 3 reprises the cue, "Fade far away, dissolve, and quite forget" (21), what follows is no fading, but an expansion of *forget* into conceptual impossibility:

> What thou among the leaves hast never known,
> The weariness, the fever, and the fret
>   Here, where men sit and hear each other groan;
> Where palsy shakes a few, sad, last gray hairs,
>   Where youth grows pale, and spectre-thin, and dies;
>   Where but to think is to be full of sorrow
>   And leaden-eyed despairs,
>   Where Beauty cannot keep her lustrous eyes,
>   Or new Love pine at them beyond to-morrow.
>
> (22–30)

Line by line, an epic catalogue in the genre of ode unfolds what a nightingale can never know and what a poet cannot but know, cannot forget. Sounding *Here* into memory's *hear*, Keats adds a relentless anaphora of *Where*, which picks up the *here* inside its lettering. This repeated syntactic anchor (i.e. anaphora) is the stanza's strong rhyme chord. The infinitive *to think* writes the infinite condition of human consciousness. It's sequel to Hamlet's darkest passages and *Tintern Abbey*'s "burden of the mystery" (39), when "the fretful stir / Unprofitable, and the fever of the world, / Have hung upon the beatings of my heart" (53–55), says Wordsworth, with a present perfect re-experiencing this beat in the sensate pulse of composition. It's not just that the world is mortal, but that its youth fades and dies in our eyes; it's not just that we think, but that thinking knows this, is full of sorrow. No deader line than "And leaden-eyed despairs."

Stanza 4 is a thinking poet's turn against such thinking: "Away! away! for I will fly to thee, / Not charioted by Bacchus" (that draught of vintage) "but on the viewless wings of Poesy" (31–33), the poet's trope fledging him for nightingale-company. Yet in the very pitch of this Poesy, Keats releases another subversive grammar athwart the romance:

> Already with thee! tender is the night,
>   And haply the Queen-Moon is on her throne,
>   Cluster'd around by all her starry Fays;
>   But here there is no light   (35–38)

The exclamation seems continuous with "Away! away!": the poet who would "with thee fade away" repeats "with thee" in pursuit of the nightingale's lot (*haply* is happy surmise). Yet the vision is artificial, antique: quaint, fantastic rather than redemptive (thus Fitzgerald's purchase for the title of his last, tragic novel, *Tender is the Night*). And so the recall at line 38: "thee!" (35) seeming to lay a claim to union, is a differential punctuation. The night is tender with the nightingale only, not the poet whose light "here" sifts "Through verdurous glooms" (40). Keats exfoliates the next stanza (5) on this dark pastoral of sensations "in embalmed darkness," of "Fast fading violets" mingling with "The coming musk-rose."

In this *fading* Keats re-hears, to revoke, the wish to *fade away* from this world. So, too, the critical force of another re-hearing, this on *ease*, in the turn to the next stanza (6):

> Darkling I listen; and, for many a time
>   I have been half in love with easeful Death,
> Call'd him soft names in many a mused rhyme
>   (51–53)

The desire for nightingale's "full-throated ease" repeats *ful/ease* as Death's *easeful*, and its elaboration, "To cease upon the midnight with no pain" (56), muse-rhymes *cease* as the contract of such *ease*. The call to "Death . . . To take into the air my quiet breath" (54) courts un-inspiration, a breath taken away, and with it, the voice of human song, human poetry, the poet left a "sod" of earth (60). Keats might have ended the ode here, on this brutal recognition.

But he wanted a reflection, and so stanza 7 turns the line of sympathy (fellow-feeling) from impossible birdsong to the human community joined by the durable enchantment:

> Thou was not born for death, immortal Bird!
>   No hungry generations tread thee down;
> The voice I hear this passing night was heard
>   In ancient days by emperor and clown:
> Perhaps the self-same song that found a path
>   Through the sad heart of Ruth, when, sick for home,

> She stood in tears amid the alien corn;
>   The same that oft-times hath
> Charm'd magic casements, opening on the foam
>   Of perilous seas, in faery lands forlorn.
>   (61–70)

This stanza re-audits the voice as charm for everyone, oft-times, across time, across class (a clown is a peasant), especially in sorrow. In the icon of Ruth (from the Old Testament), Keats arrays his pronouns on the path of sorrow: *through* her sad heart (more piercing than the idiom *in* and a sonic anagram of *Ruth*), sick *for* home, and *in tears*, this idiom getting sudden force from the immediately following *amid* alien corn – a sociology of migrant labor in three words. Home-sickness, the nostalgia of pained dislocation, was a fairly recent terminology, and Keats, medical student and poet at once, gives it such an evocative figuring here that it seems like staged etymology.[13] This is why *Bird* gets a capital and "immortal" status (pairing this way with *Death*, the sponsor): *Bird* is reread as a symbol of the desire to fade away, quite forget. Yet Keats's refusal to reduce desire to such reasoning sustains a lull at the stanza's end that enchants, even in naming, the fatality: *ease* reverberates in faery lands' "perilous *seas*."

On this complex recognition of lingering enchantment amid rational disenchantment, Keats might have ended his ode brilliantly here, too. Yet his "pro and con" has one more stanza, which opens on one of the most stark self-listenings in this, or in all of Keats's poetry, a word isolated and activated into reflection:

> Forlorn! the very word is like a bell
>   To toll me back from thee to my sole self!
> Adieu! the fancy cannot cheat so well
>   As she is fam'd to do, deceiving elf.
>   (71–74)

Forlorn! voices recognition and a cry of the heart; so, too, *Adieu!* (73). Everything is double-played this way at the end. Now, no more *Away! away!* (31): charmed magic is stripped to a she-fancy's cheat, a "deceiving elf" trumped by a better-knowing "sole self." Yet, Keats knows, such breakups are not for ever. If it is ultimately the song and not the self that fades away, in the next line, *Adieu* gets sighed twice again as the poetry tracks its fading trace:

> Adieu! adieu! thy plaintive anthem fades
>   Past the near meadows, over the still stream,
>   Up the hill-side; and now 'tis buried deep
>   (75–77)

Past, *near*, *over*, *Up*: the prepositions verge on a recovery-plot for another passing night. The vanishing point, "buried deep / In the next valley-glades" (77–78), is near at hand, ready for revival.

The power of Wordsworth's poetry, Hazlitt comments, is his infusing natural phenomena with "the shadowy brightness of a waking dream," the actual object "lost . . . as sound in the multiplication of echoes."[14] Keats's last lines echo this phrasing for waking thought:

> Was it a vision, or a waking dream?
> Fled is that music. – Do I wake or sleep?
>
> (79–80)

The questions are for a reader, too. When the poet of *Ode to Psyche* asks, "Surely I dreamt to-day, or did I see?" it's prologue to a pursuit in which the difference is so blended that it scarcely matters. The questions that close *Ode to a Nightingale* oscillate in the valences of *vision*, *waking*, and *dream*. Even the referent of *it* is elusive: enchantment? disenchantment? a romance in relay of both? The sequel "Do I wake or sleep?" begs its question: does *wake* signify smartening up, or holding a wake over a forlorn fantasy? Is *sleep* this life waiting for the wakening through easeful death? or does it denote a mind still enchanted? The poet's questions to his sole self are ours to weigh and work out. The sole certainty is "Fled is that music," and even this conclusion is contradicted by the composition of the Ode.

Ode on a Grecian Urn: poetry's rogueglyphics

Keats loved how actor Edmund Kean could voice a "melodious passage in poetry . . . full of pleasures both sensual and spiritual," the spiritual "felt when the very letters and points of charactered language show like the hieroglyphics of beauty."[15] *Ode to a Nightingale* and *Ode on a Grecian Urn* find occasions in art (a song ever heard human history, an art-world for ever) that might inspire poetry to such hieroglyphics of beauty. Yet a variant hieroglyphing that Hazlitt described in Shakespeare's language – "It translates thoughts into visible images" – proves a muse with a difference. Translating thoughts, Keats makes words themselves visible images at key moments in *Ode on a Grecian Urn*.

Every reader comes to feel that *Ode on a Grecian Urn* is a reader's urn in this way – and, with Keats in charge, an ode prone to, or primed for, that Keatsian double-play of parody. This double-play is active from the get-go as the poet tests the urn's rival powers:

Thou still unravish'd bride of quietness,
  Thou foster-child of silence and slow time,
Sylvan historian, who canst thus express
  A flowery tale more sweetly than our rhyme:
                    (1–4)

Not just bride but also foster-child and historian are expressive potentials. Yet this rhyme flexes too: what but our rhyme can evoke slow time in the halted pace of *and slow time?* There is rivalry at hand in the epithet "historian," which derives from the ancient Greek word for "inquiry, knowledge obtained by inquiry" (OED). By this method, the odist, armed with a quiver of questions, turns historian in rhyme:

What leaf-fring'd legend haunts about thy shape
  Of deities or mortals, or of both,
      In Tempe or the dales of Arcady?
  What men or gods are these? What maidens loth?
What mad pursuit? What struggle to escape?
    What pipes and timbrels? What wild ecstasy?
                    (5–10)

Keats's verbal wit is a mimetic mimicry. With the boost of "about," *leaf-fring'd* rounds into "leaf-ring'd": the ring of questions that would ravish, in mad pursuit, this bride of quietness.

"What creates the intense pleasure of not knowing? A sense of independence, of power form the fancy's creating a world of its own by the sense of probabilities," wrote Keats of Milton's imagination of Pandemonium.[16] On a different scale, stanza 2 takes this pleasurable turn to consider what rhyme has to say about intractably silent hieroglyphics:

Heard melodies are sweet, but those unheard
  Are sweeter; therefore, ye soft pipes, play on;
Not to the sensual ear, but, more endear'd,
  Pipe to the spirit ditties of no tone: (11–14)

This is no sooner said than the call to "no tone" is un-urned, turning the rhymes from the sensual ear (baffled by atonality) to the reading eye: *ear* is inside end*ear*'d, as if to figure, visually, and to echo faintly, an inner ear, more endeared to silence. The *ear* is quiet in the first line's lettered frame, "H*ear*d . . . unh*ear*d," the words spelling but not sounding *ear*. In ditties of no tone, the reading eye is liberated to surmise, and surmise to oscillating promises:

> Fair youth, beneath the trees, thou canst not leave
> Thy song, nor ever can those trees be bare;
> Bold Lover, never, never canst thou kiss,
> Though winning near the goal—yet, do not grieve;
> She cannot fade, though thou hast not thy bliss,
> For ever wilt thou love, and she be fair!
>   (15–20)

More than one tone, however, occupies this zigzag syntax. The negatives spell immutability and infinite protraction at once, a heaven that could be hell. Winning near the goal for ever is simulcast as arrest by enforcements for ever most unsweet.

Along the stress of this tension, stanza 3 verges on affective collapse. As one *nor ever* releases *for ever* into five iterations, the ode arrives at its parody of the signatures and extremes of ecstasy. At this limit, *still* transmutes from a tease of silence ("*still* unravish'd") into an illusion of infinite potential, a "happy happy love! / For ever warm and still to be enjoy'd" (25–26). And at this climax Keats pivots into a subversive syntax:

> For ever panting, and for ever young;
> All breathing human passion far above,
> That leaves a heart high-sorrowful and cloy'd,
> A burning forehead, and a parching tongue.
>   (27–30)

As a line-unit, "All breathing human passion far above" seems to sum the surmise of happiness: human passion for ever in a realm far above. The semicolon at "for ever young" (27) looks like a medial pause in this surmise (two manuscripts even show a comma here), appositive to "nor ever bid the Spring adieu;" (22) and "for ever piping songs for ever new;" (24). In this eternal present, *breathing* joins *piping* and *panting*. All the figures, in one way or another, might be breathing "human" passion on a plane far above mortal humanity. But the next line (29) explodes the illusion, syntactically rules it out. What nouns or verbs are these? The phrase "far above" turns out, in a second syntax, to be differential, in distinction to mere "breathing human passion," this human-below breathing aligned with *burning* and *parching*. At the same time, *breathing*, however far below, exposes what marble can't do, and so isn't: human.

To turn musing to the historical bargain entailed in art's "for ever," stanza 4 recruits another scene, a civic group off for a ritual sacrifice. Questions for a Sylvan historian – "Who are these?" "What little town" is theirs? "To what green altar" do they proceed? – evoke no unheard melodies but index the desolation of aesthetic arrest. The Urn's "for ever" is the leaf-fringed legend of history lost for ever:

> And, little town, thy streets for evermore
>   Will silent be; and not a soul to tell
>   Why thou art desolate, can e'er return.
>
>   (38–40)

Tell is Keatsian meta-poetry: a poetic telling against the silence. Keats's rhyme pairs *return* atonally with its schemed partner, the urn-time of *pious morn* (37). Keats mutes this rhyme, I think, to feature an eye-rhyme, lettered inside as *-urn*, to the medium of the title-word, *Urn*.

The last stanza theorizes this return, now reading urn-figurings not as signifiers of any elusive legend but as static art: "O Attic shape! Fair attitude!" (41). In the "brede / Of marble men and maidens overwrought," Keats puns on what a *brede* (design) will never ever do, *breed*, the impossible contract of a *bride* of quietness. The "silent form" to the eye survives in a poetry full of heard melodies, cues, quips, and parodies, what "our rhyme" can express. Keats turns a pun on *overwrought*: a style elaborated into excess, and exhausted or agonized by arrest. At the outset of *Childe Harold III*, Byron describes his "brain . . . / In its own eddy boiling and o'erwrought" (7), and in such an eddy Keats describes his frustrations with *Endymion*: "I found my Brain so overwrought that I had neither Rhyme nor reason in it – so was obliged to give up for a few days."[17] Writing *Ode on a Grecian Urn,* Keats not only does not give up, but reasons *overwrought* (against the Byron line) into a sober corrective rhyme with *thought*:

> Thou, silent form, dost tease us out of thought
>   As doth eternity: Cold Pastoral!   (44–45)

Thought is not only this corrective but it also stages, with the lettering of *Thou*, the expulsion of the thought that the urn's imagery spells anything other than "Cold Pastoral!"

This medium is the muse of the ode's conclusion:

> When old age shall this generation waste,
>   Thou shalt remain, in midst of other woe
> Than ours, a friend to man, to whom thou say'st,
>   "Beauty is truth, truth beauty," —that is all
>   Ye know on earth, and all ye need to know.
>
>   (46–50)

Back in 1817, Keats insisted that "What the imagination seizes as Beauty must be truth" (*K* 69) and in this seeing sharpened to seizing, argued

that "the excellence of every Art is its intensity, capable of making all disagreeables evaporate, from their being in close relationship with Beauty &
Truth" (*K 77*). Because this *Ode* holds onto its disagreeables, the keywords
get sized without capital letters. The syntax "Beauty is truth, truth beauty"
is a perversity of chiasmus and tautology, a signifying so opaque as to
deliver "ditties of no tone" in a verbal figure that parodies the melody one
strains to hear ring'd out from its lettering in "leaf-fring'd legend." It refuses
export to the scenes of the ode, let alone chiseled library walls. The only
knowing is that old age wastes all human generations. For this history, *woe*
and *know* is the key-rhyme, with *all* completing in rhyme and sense what
has to be left to "Cold Pastoral." Ruth "amid the alien corn," generations
ever "midst other woe": Keats's prepositions are the "for ever" of human
desire for an ease that is always a tease.

Nothing could be more tonally, rhetorically elusive than *that is all*. Set at
the end of the line, the words declare sufficiency, plenitude, but the phrase
sounds dismissive. Completion feels indistinguishable from depletion, the
whole business reading like a riddle from a sphinxy bride of silence. How
apt that the voice of this oracle entails some textual uncertainty. The hand
(not Keats's) that guided *1820* into print put "Beauty is truth, truth beauty"
in quotation and in lower-cases shy of Platonic full-dress. In the text
published in Haydon's aesthetic journal, *Annals of the Fine Arts* (working
from a draft likely Keats's), the words are the same, but the style is variant,
amped with capitals and released from quotation-marks:

> Beauty is Truth, Truth Beauty. —That is all
> Ye know on Earth, and all ye need to know.[18]

The textual crux that is produced is a perfect meta-text for Keatsian irony:
we know only the ardent pursuit to know. In pursuit of a "hieroglyphics
of beauty," *Ode on a Grecian Urn* brilliantly distills the parodic aesthetics
of Keatsian "rogueglyphics."[19]

Melancholy's strophe, Melancholy's trophy

If *Ode on a Grecian Urn* tests a romance of timelessness, *Ode on Melancholy*
is relentlessly temporal: it's not just that nothing lasts; it's that this is the
condition of all beauty. The melody of *melody* in the syllables of *Melancholy*
tempers *mel-*, the Greek syllable of sweet song with *melano*, Greek for the
black bile of melancholia. Keats's *Ode* sets every sweetness, every fullness
for dissolution. In three stanzas arrayed on the classical ode-pattern of thesis
(strophe), antithesis (antistrophe), and condensation (stand), the *Ode* issues

a mock-didactic treatise on how to rebrand transience, the Melancholist's lament, as a poetic resource, intensity.

Keats begins *in medias res*, on four stressed syllables, three rhymed:

> No, no, go not to Lethe, neither twist
>   Wolf's-bane, tight-rooted, for its poisonous wine;
> Nor suffer thy pale forehead to be kiss'd
>   By nightshade, ruby grape of Proserpine;
> Make not your rosary of yew-berries,
>   Nor let the beetle, nor the death-moth be
>   Your mournful Psyche, nor the downy owl
> A partner in your sorrow's mysteries;
>   For shade to shade will come too drowsily,
>   And drown the wakeful anguish of the soul.
>
>   (1–10)

This stanza writes a Keatsian palinode (an ode retracting a previous one); "No, no" even re-verses the odal "on." *Ode on a Grecian Urn* ends in parody of *antiquae sententiae*. *Ode on Melancholy* works a rhetoric of serial *sententiae* with a rogue's twist on the litany. For all the large cautions against Lethe above, the tone is tricky. In the "contrariety of pathological splendours" William Empson hears a "parody" that voices "by contradiction . . . the wise advice of uncles,"[20] while Helen Vendler audits a poet "subversively attracted by what he reproves" (172). Keats serves both with his menu of lush antithetical compounds, admonitions rehearsed in melodies of seductive allure. Even that downy owl, rejected mascot for "sorrow's miseries," is more than half in love with the sound of *drowsily* (Keats hit this adverb after trying out *heavily* then *sleepily*[21]) for the sake of a flow from *owl* into *drown*.

This allure is dosed with a new pharmacy in stanza 2, in disdain of the pathology of "melancholy fits" indexed in Burton's *Anatomy of Melancholy* (1621), this phrase appearing therein dozens of times. Keats summons mournful Psyche into a wakeful soul, alive to the intensity of complex compounds, fleeting beauty. A "melancholy fit" is poetic capital, refreshing *fit* (*fytte*) as an archaism of poetry and music:

> But when the melancholy fit shall fall
>   Sudden from heaven like a weeping cloud,
> That fosters the droop-headed flowers all,
>   And hides the green hill in an April shroud;
> Then glut thy sorrow on a morning rose,
>   Or on the rainbow of the salt sand-wave,
>   Or on the wealth of globed peonies;

> Or if thy mistress some rich anger shows,
>   Emprison her soft hand, and let her rave,
>   And feed deep, deep upon her peerless eyes.
>
>   (11–20)

In this one-sentence stanza of luxurious cascades, Keats even hangs *fall* at a line-end, to give it pause before the scenery drops from weeping, to heaven-sent nurture, to funeral shroud. The advice is arrested around its images. The *morning* rose cannot forbid its undertone of *mourning*, nor keep *rose* from ghosting the *fall* of melancholy that might re-call for use the *rosary* refused in stanza 1. The rainbow of a salt-sand wave is a sheen no sooner seen than gone. The adjective *globed* is Keatsian: this for a world in a peony, the flower famed, in old, for medicinal powers, but here a wealth in transience. The diet for these dyings is not mourning, however, but the exhortation to "glut" and "feed."

The odist takes to erotic extravagance (in his dreams!), feeding on a spectacle of female anger, in love with the phonics of *feed deep, deep . . . peerless* (the *peerless* eyes are aesthetic nonpareil, no window to her soul). On this Stuart Sperry paused his critical analysis for a parenthesis: "(Viewed in purely human terms, the situation is the perfect one for a poet having his face slapped.)"[22] The hazard is more than a slap in Keats's plan. The severest reversal impends in stanza 3, and it's related to the gender-spectacle that had Sperry wincing. The opening phrase, "She dwells with Beauty," puns the mistress of stanza 2 into transience too, and then, in a crucial pivot, turns this *She* to an alliance with sovran Melancholy:[23]

> She dwells with Beauty—Beauty that must die;
>   And Joy, whose hand is ever at his lips
> Bidding adieu; and aching Pleasure nigh,
>   Turning to poison while the bee-mouth sips:
> Ay, in the very temple of Delight
>   Veil'd Melancholy has her sovran shrine,
>   Though seen of none save him whose strenuous tongue
> Can burst Joy's grape against his palate fine;
>   His soul shall taste the sadness of her might,
>   And be among her cloudy trophies hung.   (21–30)

The Melancholy-connoisseur of she-anger is set up for a death of luxury. I think that Keats left *eyes/peonies* such a weak rhyme at the end of stanza 2 in order to save *eyes* for this strong chime with *die* at the start of 3. Beauty must die, the present participles spelling not the *for ever* on the Grecian Urn but the rapid transience of life in time: Joy *bidding* adieu; Pleasure *aching* nigh, *turning* to poison in the pitch of sweetness. In an argument pointed by rhyme-echoes, the ruby grape of *Proserpine* returns as Joy's grape bursting against a palate *fine*, the boon of Melancholy's sovran *shrine*. Oscar Wilde would upgrade this intensity to an aggressive crush: "What an exquisite life you have had!" Lord Henry sighs to Dorian Gray; "You have drunk deeply of everything. You have crushed the grapes against your palate" (*The Picture of Dorian Gray*, chapter xix). Keats is more ironic yet than the irony-ready Lord Henry. Wilde celebrates the indulgence; Keats wrings the existential economy. The mighty sadness of ephemeral intensity is inevitable surrender to trophy-status, and no special trophy either – just one "among" many "hung" out in the accounting. Yet to hear the Ode's last words undertoning "trophies sung" is to catch, in verbal embodiment, the soulful inspiration of this wasting muse.[24]

This is ecstasy, transubstantiation, and spiritual apocalypse all at once: the contractual temporality of sensation that is self-surrendering, self-annihilating on principle. Absent from this *Ode* has been "I." It is trumped by an expressive *Ay*, schemed to rhyme with *die*, as the headline for everything on the run, on the wane, "Bidding adieu," "Turning to poison." The qualifier "none save him" is a rich double supplement. Keats first wrote "none but him" (keyed to the willing *burst*);[25] his revision is better for punning the sense of *except* into grammar of *beyond saving*. *Ode on Melancholy* is ultimately a mortality ode. We may feel ourselves bullied into the philosophy of a Melancholist, but the bully wins only by losing all.

Poetry's diligent indolence

Keats would have his fruit and his writing in one moment of luxury. "Talking of Pleasure, this moment I was writing with one hand, and with the other holding to my Mouth a Nectarine – good god how fine – It went down soft pulpy, slushy, oozy," he writes to a friend, 22 September 1819 (*K* 269). Such pleasure feels like a muse for *Ode on Indolence* but its ground is the Melancholist's plot. Keats wrote to George and Georgiana, 19 March 1819 –

> This morning I am in a sort of temper indolent and supremely careless . . . and to such a happy degree that pleasure has no show of enticement and pain no unbearable frown. Neither Poetry, nor Ambition, nor Love have any alertness of countenance as they pass by me . . . This is the only happiness . . . I have this moment received a note from Haslam in which he expects the death of his Father . . . This is the world – thus we cannot expect to give way many hours to pleasure – Circumstances are like Clouds continually gathering and bursting – While we are laughing the seed of some

> trouble is put into the wide arable land of events – while we are laughing it
> sprouts is grows and suddenly bears a poison fruit which we must pluck —[26]

Indolence, like all Keatsian romances, is no escape, just an interval in what
it and *careless* name by negation: *dolens* (pain) and *care*. It's a morning's
temper that can yield in a heartbeat to bids of mourning. It's not just Joy's
grape that bursts into melancholy; it's the circumstances of the world,
continually gathering and bursting, seeding laughter into poison. Such
*circum*stances write life's ringed legend. How deft of Keats to draw *arable*
from (un)be*arable*. The whole "world" is an Ode to Melancholy. Only *To
Autumn* will register this without pain.

Ode on Indolence means to suspend, for a morning, the pains of poetry,
ambition, love. Keats didn't publish it with the other odes, perhaps because
indolence is too readable as unmanly lapse. In the background is unfinished
Hyperion, and maybe Wordsworth, too, naming "the most dishonorable
accusation which can be brought against an Author, namely, that of an
indolence which prevents him from endeavouring" (Preface to *Lyrical Ballads* [1800] I:x). Brown's diligence "affronts my indolence and Luxury,"
Keats sighed in the summer of 1818 (*L* 1:344), revising that "delicious dili-
gent Indolence" he had theorized to Reynolds a few months before:

> let us not . . . go hurrying about and collecting honey-bee like, buzzing here
> and there impatiently from a knowledge of what is to be arrived at: but
> let us open our leaves like a flower and be passive and receptive – budding
> patiently under the eye of Apollo and taking hints from every noble insect
> that favors us with a visit.[27]

The letter of March 1819 is edgier. The morning's indulgence has a masculine prequel: Keats is nursing a "black eye" from a robust cricket game with
the guys the day before (*K* 241–42). Describing his "languour" as a "state
of effeminacy," Keats camps it up: he might have "teeth of pearl and the
breath of lillies," longing after a stanza or two of Thomson's eighteenth-
century cautionary splendor, *The Castle of Indolence*. It's not a default, just
a holiday.

And compromised, at that. If indolence is that "rare instance of advan-
tage in the body overpowering the Mind," *Ode on Indolence* is still buzzing.
It takes a motto (about the lilies of the field) that seems authorizing:
"They toil not, neither do they spin."[28] But this fronts six stanzas that
toil and spin in a visionary masque. The ode begins as a casual anec-
dote, "One morn before me were three figures seen," but by stanza II the
"blissful cloud of summer-indolence" has been disturbed out of a "sense"
devoted to "nothingness." Even as the feminine-prone falling rhyme-chain

(-*ence, sense, -ness*) mimes the spell, the syntax is restless, questioning, sensing those shades of signification in figured Shadows of thought:

> How is it, Shadows! that I knew ye not?
>   How came ye muffled in so hush a mask?
> Was it a silent deep-disguised plot
>   To steal away, and leave without a task
>   My idle days? Ripe was the drowsy hour
>   . . .
>   O, why did ye not melt, and leave my sense
> Unhaunted quite of all but—nothingness? (II)

Haunted is the ode, even inspired, by the "great difference between an easy and an uneasy indolence" that Keats had arrayed just the day before the cricket match (*K* 241).

Indolence becomes an elegy, its drowsy hour roused into knowing, ardent pursuit:

>   to follow them I burn'd
> And ached for wings, because I knew the three;
>   The first was a fair Maid, and Love her name;
> The second was Ambition, pale of cheek,
>   And ever watchful with fatigued eye;
>   The last, whom I love more, the more of blame
>   Is heap'd upon her, Maiden most unmeek, —
> I knew to be my demon Poesy.   (III)

In the story that Keats gives in his letter of 19 March 1819, "Poetry" has no pull. In the story of the *Ode*, "Poesy" is a hot lure, and Ambition, though pale and pooped, is still on watch. And Love? At the turn to stanza IV, it's a question at best. "What is Love? and where is it?" In this sigh, Poesy falls away, too: "she has not a joy,— / At least for me," and "poor Ambition" is dismissed as disease: "a man's little heart's short fever-fit."

Still, for every turn against, there's a return to. If the poet's plea at the end of stanza IV is "O, for an age so shelter'd from annoy" (Keats made *annoy* this noun), that he "may never . . . hear the voice of busy common-sense" (38–40), the poetry keeps busy for two more stanzas. "O" is a cue for an ode, and eleven lines on, "O Shadows! 'twas a time to bid farewell!" is still oding. Despite the poet's adieu – "Fade softly from my eyes, and be once more / In masque-like figures on a dreamy urn" (55–56) – this is no fade-out: it undertones *dreamy yearn*, even as that ear to the "throstle's lay" (48) managed to find a singer whose name puns into a frame for spinning.[29] The last lines, "Vanish, ye Phantoms!, from my idle spright, /

Into the clouds, and never more return!" (60), ends in a lettering of *-turn* and within this syllable, the figural *urn*, the spin to it all.

Writing on *Ode on Indolence* may reflect Keats's being "affraid more from indolence of mind than any thing else" (15 April 1819; *L* 2:83). He would even embrace "a fevrous life alone with Poetry" if ambition is ready: "I would rather conquer my indolence and strain my nerves at some grand Poem" (31 May 1819; *L* 2:113). When Keats tells a female friend in June, "the thing I have most enjoyed this year has been writing an ode to Indolence," he assesses the quantum of enjoyment: "I have been very idle lately, very averse to writing; both from the overpowering idea of our dead poets and from abatement of my love of fame." Within a sentence he's punning *averse* into a cartoon-self he would shed, "a versifying Pet-lamb" (*K* 257), or that "pet-lamb in a sentimental farce" in the *Ode*'s unforgiving figure of success (VI).

"I hate a Mawkish Popularity" he said to Reynolds, despising the public as "an Enemy . . . I cannot address without feelings of Hostility" (*L* 1:266–67). Keats's last address of "Romance" interweaves a maiden unmeek, demon Poesy, and a perverse ambition, and a degraded market. This is *Lamia*.

CHAPTER 8

Writhing, wreathing, writing Lamia

Critical Judgment

The reason he had the truant Knight at arms give La belle dame "kisses four," Keats jests, was a "wish to restrain the headlong impetuosity of my Muse—she would have fain said 'score' without hurting the rhyme – but we must temper the Imagination as the Critics say with Judgment" (*K* 249). If a venture "without Judgment" was the regret of *Endymion* (October 1818; *K* 207), Keats had "great hopes" for *Lamia*, "because I make use of my Judgment more deliberately than I yet have done" (11 July; *L* 2:128). While *Isabella* and *The Eve of St. Agnes* might be "laugh'd at," he was confident of "no objection of this kind to Lamia" (*L* 2:174).

Lamia is saturated with corrosives to "golden-tongued Romance," that Syren bid a too-lingering farewell in the sonnet of January 1818. Keats sets the main scene in urbane Corinth, famed for its "temples lewd" (1.352, hubs of prostitution), its material luxury, and (this is ancient Greece, after all) its school of Platonic philosophy. The characters are insidious caricatures of Keatsian antecedents. Young Lycius is a self-involved, visionary philosopher, then an impetuous swooner, "blind" to the arts of seduction, then a tyrant over his lover, and finally dead from it all. His mentor Apollonius is no Apollo of "knowledge enormous" but an icy un-lyric problem-solver, kin only in snake-killing. And eponym Lamia is a maze of contradictions: snake and woman, predator and victim, yearning lover and specious enchanter, a "sure art" of "mysterious sleights," a voice of teasing and of blunt truth, a fresh life, and a fatal attraction.

Keats's publishers decided to put *Lamia* first in the 1820 volume, with 46 of its 200 pages (only *Hyperion* got more). Even so, Keats was named on the title-page as "Author of Endymion" – the old Romance on the new brand (and still in stock) (Fig. 7). This double-exposure is apt for a volume in which every major poem entertains, ironizes, and elegizes romance. *Lamia* does not so much dissolve in its corrosives as make insoluble its puzzles.

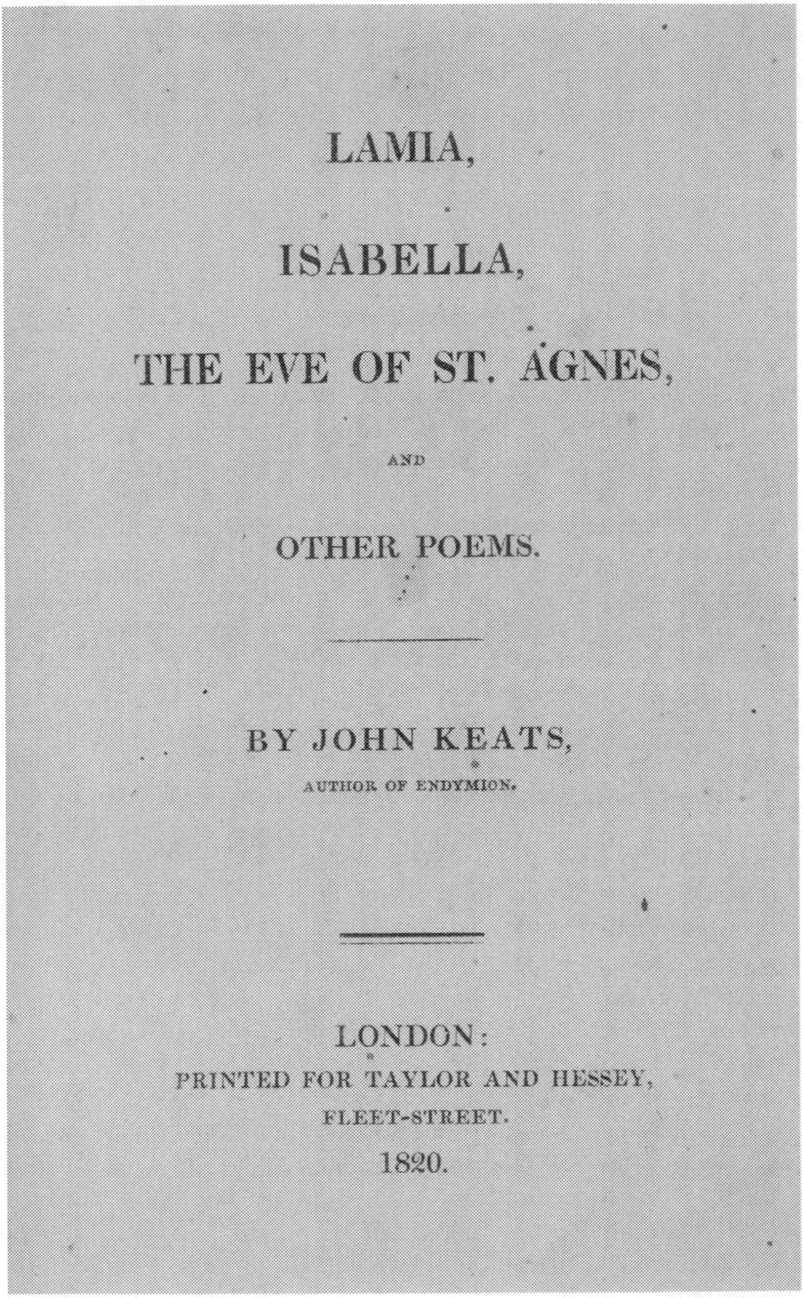

LAMIA,

ISABELLA,

THE EVE OF ST. AGNES,

AND

OTHER POEMS.

———

BY JOHN KEATS,

AUTHOR OF ENDYMION.

———

LONDON:

PRINTED FOR TAYLOR AND HESSEY,

FLEET-STREET.

1820.

Fig. 7 Title-page, John Keats, *Lamia, Isabella, The Eve of St. Agnes, and Other Poems* (London: Taylor & Hessey, 1820). Department of Rare Books and Special Collections, Princeton University Library. Even with print runs of no more than 500 copies, all Keats's lifetime volumes were remaindered, though this last one did well enough, at a lower price of 7 shillings 6 pence, to recover expenses.

"But were there ever any / Writh'd not of passed joy?" Keats wondered in December 1817 (*P* 221). Writhe, write: their involved etymology is deep in Keats's verbal genetics – with a verbal payoff in *Lamia*, a writhe of writing if ever there was one: *interwreathed* (1.52). This was quite a rare word in English poetry. Not for nothing does *Lamia* begin in Crete, site of the famed wreathed Labyrinth. This is such a genius loci that Keats coined it into a transitive verb: Lycius sighs to Lamia of striving to "snare / Your soul in mine, and labyrinth you there" (2.52–53).

Keats's linguistic genius weaves gorgeous phrasings and cutting satires; his allusions issue conflicting signals; Lamia, the site and agent of transformative artistry, is inspired, travestied, and sadly undone; prompts of pathos can be suddenly moving or merely pathetic; reason is brutally administered but not wrong; and the denouement stays knotted. All this threads a narration so disjunctive as to make *Lamia* a mimicry of coherence.

A plot summary is both beside the point and telling. **Part I** opens in a spoof of faery land, where a snake with a woman's voice woos Hermes (god of trade, among his designations) into a business deal. He's in "celestial heat" for a nymph under her protection; she'll give him access if he gives her the woman's body she once had, so she may pursue young Corinthian philosopher Lycius. Hermes gets his nymph, in a blur of predation and seduction. Then follows a dazzling set-piece of Lamia's phosphorescence from snake to woman. The rest of Part I is her seduction of Lycius, and the lovers' retreat, after a troubling brush with Apollonius, to a mysterious house in Corinth. **Part II** opens on a satire of the lovers in their "purple-lined palace of sweet sin" (31). Lycius shifts from sap to show-off, eager for his foes to envy and his friends to cheer his "prize" at a public wedding. Lamia demurs and weeps, he turns tyrant, she succumbs and becomes sad impresario of a feast-hall conjured by her magic and fretted with ruin. Apollonius, daft by the "knotty problem" (160) of this sudden bride, crashes the wedding. The denouement is a brutal pun of un-knotting. Naming Lycius "a serpent's prey," Apollonius fixes Lamia with his (phonically vibrant) "perceant" eye. She vanishes with a scream and Lycius, his "arms . . . empty of delight," dies "that same night" (298–308) – a tale recapped in a rhyme.

Gordian complications

If this arc seems issued by *La belle dame*, it wasn't in that poem's wake that *Lamia* rose. It was on a train of odes, shaped for equivocation and the exercise of negative capability (a poetics of uncertainty, mystery, doubt). In *Lamia*, however, Keats wields a high tonal and stylistic assurance to send negative capability into extremes of positive incapability. The poetics are not the nuanced turns of the odes but feel like calculated perversions.

Lamia opens in romance parody, a faery land mapped onto ante- and post-bellum eras. This gives no historiography of sad fall, however; it's a variation on a power-grid:

> UPON a time, before the faery broods
> Drove Nymph and Satyr from the prosperous woods,
> Before King Oberon's bright diadem,
> Sceptre, and mantle, clasp'd with dewy gem,
> Frighted away the Dryads and the Fauns
> From rushes green, and brakes, and cowslip'd lawns,
> The ever-smitten Hermes empty left
> His golden throne, bent warm on amorous theft:
> From high Olympus had he stolen light,
> On this side of Jove's clouds, to escape the sight
> Of his great summoner, and made retreat
> Into a forest on the shores of Crete.   (I.1–12)

This deftly paced sentence of serial appositives is a masterpiece of poetic art, crafted for a decadent faery land. Keats's couplets are works of wit snapped with masculine rhymes and verbal fun. In the line of escape, "From high Olympus had he stolen light" (9), the artful dodger is no benevolent junior Prometheus, just an appetitive hunter. His regent staff is a "serpent rod" (89): a "caduceus" (intertwined snakes) symbolizing the reciprocity of rivals in the commercial world of which he is patron, and so an apt herald of the bargaining to come. This business begins as he hears a voice sighing of its "wreathed tomb" (38) and longing for a "body fit for life, / And love, and pleasure, and the ruddy strife / Of hearts and lips!" (39–41) – partner to his sorrow's miseries.

Its source is "a palpitating snake, / Bright, and cirque-couchant" (45–46), a "beauteous wreath" (84). Keats writes a blazon at once dazzling and confusing, whether by symbolic lore, allusive reference, or even aesthetic assay. "So varied he, and of his tortuous train / Curl'd many a wanton wreath in sight of Eve" are words of Satanic seduction that Keats underlined in *Paradise Lost*.[1] For the spectacle that is Lamia he stripped off the moral tags (the torture to come; the wanton lust). "She was a gordian shape of dazzling hue" (47). *Gordian!* the very word is like a bell in Keats-land. *Endymion* has Cynthia's "locks" (tresses, with a hint of chains) "gordian'd up" (1.614; a verb Keats coined just for her), and Glaucus likens Circe's bewitching fire to "the eye of a gordian snake" (3.497). The word rings a

Satanic descent: "the serpent sly, / Insinuating, wove with Gordian twine / His braided train" (*PL* 4.347–49; also underlined by Keats).[2]

From 1848 on readers could add to the train Keats's confession (to Bailey) of not having "a right feeling toward women."[3] A "gordian complication" is his ready phrase as he maps a chamber of boy-thought into too dark passages. "When I was a schoolboy I thought a fair woman a pure goddess; my mind was a soft nest in which some one of them slept, though she knew it not." This thought imprints *Sleep and Poetry*, its boyish poet in "the shade / Keeping a silence round a sleeping maid" (67–68). More appetitive, Porphyro gazes on Madeline asleep, "trembling in her soft and chilly nest" (235). As a man among real women, Keats is "full of suspicions," a "perversity" (he tells Bailey) deriving from "being disappointed since boyhood." He then knots the tell-tale phrase for "the root of the evil": "an obstinate prejudice can seldom be produced but from a gordian complication of feelings, which must take time to unravel, and care to keep unravelled." No one can unravel Gordias's intricate knot (Alexander the Great just slices it open). Love-raveled by now with Fanny Brawne, Keats had freshly activated prejudices.

No wonder the "palpitating snake" (45) in Hermes's gaze is so multiple in its motions:

> So rainbow-sided, touch'd with miseries,
> She seem'd, at once, some penanced lady elf,
> Some demon's mistress, or the demon's self.
> (I.54–56)

This list of surmises is a mockery of "consequitive reasoning" (cf. *K* 69 and 94) towards anything decisively, merely, Satanic. Every phrase shifts: now magical art, now pathos, now misery, maybe the art of misery-seeming, a demon familiar or the demon's self or, in a slither of letterings, a lady elf turned demon's *elf*. Even the "swift-lisping" of "I was a woman, let me have once more / A woman's shape, and charming as before" (1.116–18) is slippery: is "woman" origin or phase, essence or guise? When Lamia wins Lycius's "heart / More pleasantly by playing woman's part" (336–37), we may want the key-code: is "woman's part" a cultural role, an achievement in expert camelion imagination, or a bawdy Keats-joke for the male readers he'd like to court?

Lamia, Keats's one-word title (no subtitled genre) may point to the LAMIÆ, for which see Lemprière: "Certain monsters of Africa, who had the face and breast of a woman, and the rest of the body like that of a serpent. They allured strangers to come to them, that they might devour them, and though they were not endowed with the faculty of speech, yet their hissings were pleasing and agreeable." Yet Keats's Lamia eludes such definitional capture. She's from Crete not Africa; her serpent head has a woman's eyes and mouth; she's no devourer (only metaphorically, but is also devoured), and she doesn't have to rely on pleasing hisses – her faculty of speech is quite polished. Any inclination to let Lemprière's *Classical Dictionary* nail Lamia's sorority is going to be thwarted by Keats's assembly of other sisterhoods. Lamia is "Sprinkled with stars, like Ariadne's tiar" (1.58), Keats sprinkling the sound of *star*, as if to make the snake-stars a badge of sisterhood with this lovelorn maid.[4] Then a turn of a line blazons Renaissance love poetry: her mouth has "all its pearls," and her weeping eyes are "so fair" (60–62). The rhyme for *fair* is "As Proserpine still weeps for her Sicilian air" (63) – this *As* casting a simultaneity as well as a sisterhood in sympathy. We're primed, even, to hear in *Proserpine* a hapless *serpentine*: she was forced to be demon-Hades's mistress, with a release for half each year (negotiated by Hermes, no less). A later simile aligns Lamia with nymph Euridyce (daughter of Apollo, no less), doomed to Hades's domain by a fatal snakebite (248).

Is the snake who coos to Hermes here a Satanic artist or an imprisoned lover?

> Her throat was serpent, but the words she spake
> Came, as through bubbling honey, for Love's sake
> (1.64–65)

It's no easier to assess the stakes in Hermes's first view of the snake, "Bright, and cirque-couchant in a dusky brake" (46). Keats invented the faux-heraldic *cirque-couchant* both for this formal artistry and for a lexical affinity with *Circe*. Yet the naming of this snake's "Circean head" (115) is less helpful than might seem: is the head Circe's own, or the effect of a Circean curse? The "very emblems that characterize" her are "bewilderingly varied and contradictory . . . not clearly separated or distinguishable" but playing with "striking mobility and fluctuation."[5] Keats writes this she-serpent with exuberant aesthetic surfeit, the agent and object of romance confected from a wreath of signs that is too readable, and ultimately unreadable.

Hermes's serpent-rod releases the she-serpent into a whirl of letterings: a *serpent* mouth *besprent* on its way to beauty (1.146–48), a disarray "as the lava ravishes" (155–57). *Lamia* is a love-affair with language in its richest energies and potentials. Not for nothing is Lamia reborn syllabling *Lycius!* (168), the first of her "de*licious*. . . words" (249). She materializes with this name and a woman-form in the herald of love's records, a sonnet-stanza (171–84;

the poem's only such inset). The first line puts *Lamia* in metric-phonic symmetry with *lady*:

> Whither fled Lamia, now a lady bright,
> A full-born beauty new and exquisite?
> She fled into that valley they pass o'er
> Who go to Corinth from Cenchreas' shore;
> And rested at the foot of those wild hills,
> The rugged founts of the Peræan rills,
> And of that other ridge whose barren back
> Stretches, with all its mist and cloudy rack,
> South-westward to Cleone. There she stood
> About a young bird's flutter from a wood,
> Fair, on a sloping green of mossy tread,
> By a clear pool, wherein she passioned
> To see herself escap'd from so sore ills,
> While her robes flaunted with the daffodils.
>
> (1.171–84)

The *ubi sunt* of pain in *Endymion* is transposed onto this map of surest location: "There she stood" puns this very *stanza* (Italian: *standing place*), and it was Keats who coined *flutter* as a measure. The daffodils are more than flowers; they are the literary figures of Lamia's latest formation, and for readers in Keats's day, a transformation of the merely natural, glorious daffodils that surprised Wordsworth's lonely wanderings in England's Lake District.

When Lamia teases Lycius that as a scholar he "must know / That finer spirits cannot breathe below / In human climes, and live" (1.279–81), her game of hard-to-get is also the fame of hard-gotten Keatsian knowledge. Keats works out the score with a critical difference for panting Hermes, even though this godling of lies bites the oldest line in the world, "I had a splendid dream of thee last night" (69) – so Lamia has his number, up to speed on the nymph-quest. For Hermes, the dream comes true, with a moral to the tale:

> It was no dream; or say a dream it was,
> Real are the dreams of Gods, and smoothly pass
> Their pleasures in a long immortal dream.
>
> (1.126–28)

The *of* is richly genitive and objective: the Gods' dreams and what we dream of Gods. Four times in three lines Keats writes *dream*, the anatomy coolly nonchalant or just a bit bitter. With mortal Lycius's mistake pre-marked,

Keats ends the vignette on a couplet that wrests (with an extra internal rhyme) the happy conclusion of *Endymion* into a cautionary motto:

> Into the green-recessed woods they *flew*;
> Nor *grew* they pale, as mortal lovers *do*.
> (1.144–45, my italics)

For the Gods, means and ends are simultaneous: "they flew." But such flight, we're advised at the end of Part I, is naïve fantasy for mortal lovers – and romance-readers, too:

> And but the flitter-winged verse must tell,
> For truth's sake, what woe afterwards befel,
> 'Twould humour many a heart to leave them thus,
> Shut from the busy world of more incredulous.
> (1.394–97)

Tipping the hand to woe, the narrator arrays *Lamia*'s readers against credulous dreamers, those consumers of sentiment. The echo of "Love's sake" (1.65) in this "truth's sake" (395) vocalizes an old *ake* (*ache*) for both domains. Keats worked hard on this passage (*P* 463) to tune it for savvy "Judgment," the muse of all those couplets that make foresight a poetic form. The closer rhyme, *incredulous*, is its only instance in Keats's poetry – and a real beaut.

Yet if "Spells are but made to break" (draft, *P* 466) and "truth's sake" is safety, it is cold comfort for readers to find their foresight (how it must end) compounded with Apollonius's buzz-kill: "'twas just as he foresaw" (2.162). It's a spoiler. While truth-sure reading gets narrative endorsement, any interpretive pride in plucking out the heart of Lamia's mystery is set for trouble. In a slippery game of reading skills, Keats works two threads of imagery, optical and gordian.[6] The poetry is designed to make us capable with the optics, only to trap us in the knots.

The optical course is made for the reading, allegorical even. Blindly dazzled sight, fungible invisibility, strategic invisibility, predatory sighting, sharp-eyed suspicion, perceant demystification: a reader has the score-card. It's written by our narrator: "we shall see" (1.201) in compact with him. Lamia can still commission "viewless servants" for her Corinthian arts (2.136) but her prime arena of optical power is Crete. It is here that she keeps that nymph "invisible," "unseen; unseen ... unseen ... veil'd ... unaffronted, unassail'd / By the love-glances of unlovely eyes, / ... free / To wander as she loves, in liberty" (1.94–109) – then, with a breath on Hermes's eyes, renders her "seen" (124). In her Corinthian venture, Lamia wields the

gaze to stalk Lycius – "beheld him coming, near, more near – "; "unseen /
She stood: he pass'd, shut up in mysteries, / . . . while her eyes / Follow'd
his steps" (237–43) – then commands his gaze. It's a matter of seconds
before "his eyes had drunk her beauty up, / Leaving no drop in the bewil-
dering cup" (251–52). He doubts "Whether my eyes can ever turn" away
(258).

Thus "blinded" (347), he's the antonym to Apollonius's "sharp eyes,"
which catch the pair entering Corinth, Lycius quickly trying to "blind"
himself (364–74).[7] Common eyes are baffled: "the most curious / Were
foil'd, who watch'd to trace them to their house" (392–93). The jig is up
once "the sophist's eye, / Like a sharp spear" goes through Lamia (2.299–
300); Lycius "gaz'd into her eyes," eyes unable to return his "lovelorn
piteous appeal" (256–57). Even when the sightline wreathes, the figurings
stay legible. If Lamia is a "beauteous wreath" (1.84), Lycius is the foil, "His
mind wrapp'd like his mantle" (242), ready to be "tangled in her mesh"
(295). When he "awoke into amaze" (322), the syllables break out a pun
on a labyrinth-effect. The skill of Lamia's "sciential brain" unravels what
we know (what Keats knows) is experientially inwrought: no purveyor of
Melancholy-complexities, Lamia's art is to "unperplex bliss from its neigh-
bour pain . . . estrange / Their points of contact, and swift counterchange"
(191–94). "And every word she spake entic'd him on / To unperplex'd
delight" (326–27).

Yet as Lamia is to Lycius, so Keats's *Lamia* proves to us. Keats constructs
a reading practice never really free from a mesh of uncertainty about how
to read. As the poem arrives at the wedding feast, we feel the grounds
of interpretation shifting with an aggressive shove. There's something a
little too baroque (we sense) in the riot of wreathings, as if to parody
the arch-figuring. An incidental detail of "fifty wreaths of smoke / From
fifty censers" seems a little too ready for reading, even preempted by this
centaine dose:[8] "mimick'd as they rose / Along the mirror'd walls by twin-
clouds" (2.179–82). The last of *Lamia's* wreathings is just plain hard to
read, as grammar, rhyme, and sense. Worried for Lycius in the wake of the
catastrophe,

> his friends came round—
> Supported him—no pulse, or breath they found,
> And, in its marriage robe, the heavy body wound.
> (2.309–11)

Is *wound* what they've done to the body? or what they found, *wound* an
agentless past participle, a final metamorphosis, of robe into shroud, with

a hint of snakeskin? In both cases, *wound* ends it all on a triplet dirge. Yet *wound* cannot advert a non-grammatical noun-pun, the wound of injury. The hypermetrical alexandrine final line ends in an ironic roguery of rhymed completion.

Ironies in the fire

There's trouble for a reader well before this. Though the names are the same, Part II seems a different game. It opens with a sarcasm on Love's varieties of torment for the poor and rich. Embodied Love appears as a perverse antagonist to his very charge:

> Love, jealous grown of so complete a pair,
> Hover'd and buzz'd his wings, with fearful roar,
> Above the lintel of their chamber door (2.12–14)

And the pair shifts into nearly opposite characters. No vamp, Part II's Lamia is a damsel nervous and insecure, while Lycius, "a buzzing in his head" (29), is "cruel" (75), jealous grown. Keats writes him up as simile-twin to Apollo, in a mitigated fury, about to "strike" the python,

> The serpent—Ha, the serpent! certes, she
> Was none. She burnt, she lov'd the tyranny,
> And, all subdued, consented . . .   (2.80–82)

Line 80 doubles down on Lamia up to serpent-certainty – *serpent . . . serpent! certes* – then at the turn revokes the sentence. Keats liked this sudden strike, endorsing it with underscoring for Woodhouse: "Women love to be forced . . . by a fine fellow—such as this" (*L* 2:164).

What is the scorecard? When the narrator interrupts the feast to enlist our sense of things, "What wreath for Lamia? What for Lycius? / What for the sage, old Apollonius?" (2.221–22), we confront a test of trick questions matched to tricky answers:

> Upon her aching forehead be there hung
> The leaves of willow and of adder's tongue;
> And for the youth, quick, let us strip for him
> The thyrsus, that his watching eyes may swim
> Into forgetfulness; and, for the sage,
> Let spear-grass and the spiteful thistle wage
> War on his temples.   (2.223–29)

Such assignments can only be buzzed by context into further puzzles, interpretive kin to "that is all / Ye know on earth, and all ye need to

know" *(Ode on a Grecian Urn)*. If willow and adder's tongue signify grief
or sorrow, adder's tongue surely indexes a cause, with a sleight of sound into
adder-stung. And how can we judge kill-joy Apollonius without judging
our foreknowing? Even the narrator, who has set us wise at the outset,
despises cold philosophy. "Do not all charms fly / At the mere touch of
cold philosophy?" (2.229–30) is not a bid for speculation but a cue for a
rant:

> Philosophy will clip an Angel's wings,
> Conquer all mysteries by rule and line,
> Empty the haunted air, and gnomed mine—
> Unweave a rainbow.   (2.234–37)

"Lamia" now stands for an archive of mysteries in accord with Keats's
lament (in a theater review of 1818) that "the failure of our days" is that
"romance lives but in books. The goblin is driven from the heath, and
the rainbow is robbed of its mystery!" (*K* 76). He knew Hazlitt's praise
of Wordsworth for scorning "the cold, narrow, lifeless spirit of modern
philosophy" and any "progress of knowledge and refinement" that tends
"to circumscribe the limits of the imagination, and to clip the wings of
poetry."9

Yet if "Philosophy will clip an Angel's wings" (2.234), clipping this
epigram onto Apollonius and Lamia is an awkward business. Lamia may
be many things but she's no Angel, while Philosophy Apollonius-style is
"Keen, cruel, perceant, stinging" (301). It's not just that romance lives but
in books, but that it cannot live in Keats's book. Lamia and Apollonius,
the warring names for Lycius's mortal division, won't hold as polarized
contrasts. In Lycius's eyes, Apollonius is what he says of Lamia, a worker of
"Unlawful magic, and enticing lies" (286), and he himself is serpentine: "his
lashless eyelids stretch / Around his demon eyes!" (288–89).10 Meanwhile,
Lamia is not just exposed but fatally blighted, and with no little pathos.
Fully informed by Keats's lived experience, Lycius sees the body of his
beloved drained of life and breath, himself following in a heartbeat. When
Keats has him cry out, "Lamia, what means this?" (254), the question, by
this point, is about *Lamia* itself.

This question becomes an epiphenomenon for readers of *Lamia*. In 1917,
Sidney Colvin (Keats's major nineteenth-century biographer) confessed his
"bewilderment" about "the effect intended to be made on our imaginative
sympathies." Writing in 1973, Stuart Sperry, notable as the first critic to
theorize Keats's mode of "irony," still found himself bewildered by "a
bitterness verging at times on self-mockery . . . a work written by a poet

against his better self." Tracking alongside the bewildered is W. J. Bate trying to get his head around "as rapidly shifting an interplay of ambiguity as can be found in any narrative poem in the language" (over and against a fable whose "original simplicity" tempts a reader "to pin the poem to an exclusive interpretation"). The next step was taken by Gene Bernstein, who anatomized *Lamia* as a deliberately conceived "lamia," a work of "twists and turns . . . circular rather than linear, repetitive rather than progressive." He was building on Garrett Stewart's already brilliant explication (and unabashed praise) of a "new language of metamorphosis" – not only in theme or in the whirl of allusions, but in the lexical phenomenology of compositions and decompositions played through grammar, puns, phrases and syllables. *Lamia's* perplexities generate perplexed readers or readings of perplexities.[11]

   One last twist is the text's metamorphosed ending. If Lycius's "wound" (in multiple senses) is the poem's last word, it is not the last word of Keats's text, which winds up this way, with an asterisk on wound* – cuing an addition, on the same page of *1820*, in smaller font:

> *"Philostratus, in his fourth book *de Vita Apollonii*, hath a memorable instance in this kind, which I may not omit, of one Menippus Lycius, a young man twenty-five years of age, that going betwixt Cenchreas and Corinth, met such a phantasm in the habit of a fair gentlewoman, which taking him by the hand, carried him home to her house, in the suburbs of Corinth, and told him she was a Phœnician by birth, and if he would tarry with her, he should hear her sing and play, and drink such wine as never any drank, and no man should molest him; but she, being fair and lovely, would live and die with him, that was fair and lovely to behold. The young man, a philosopher, otherwise staid and discreet, able to moderate his passions, though not this of love, tarried with her a while to his great content, and at last married her, to whose wedding, amongst other guests, came Apollonius; who, by some probable conjectures, found her out to be a serpent, a lamia; and that all her furniture was, like Tantalus' gold, described by Homer, no substance but mere illusions. When she saw herself descried, she wept, and desired Apollonius to be silent, but he would not be moved, and thereupon she, plate, house, and all that was in it, vanished in an instant: many thousands took notice of this fact, for it was done in the midst of Greece."
>
> Burton's 'Anatomy of Melancholy,' *Part* 3. *Sect*. 2. *Memb*. 1. *Subs*. 1.[12]

Far from producing any leaf-fringed legend, Keats's asterisk sprinkles another star onto the puzzle. While Philostratus-Burton Apollonius still unmasks the fair gentlewoman as a serpent, a lamia, there is also the strange detail of a young man (Keats's age exactly) who seems in need of protection from other men's molesting, as if a phantasm-house might front a fortress against the hostile reviewer-men – or their figuring in romance-hostile Apollonius.

The radiating perplexity is the reader's location. Part II shifts the question of dreams/reality to the truth-claims of secret pleasures against a public gaze. For this, the narrator morphs from masterful fabulist to Greek chorus:

> O senseless Lycius! Madman! wherefore flout
> The silent-blessing fate, warm cloister'd hours,
> And show to common eyes these secret bowers?
> (2.147–49)

Keats's draft was harsher yet: "Dolt! Fool! Madman! Lout! / Why would you murder happiness . . . ?" (*L* 2:158). Common eyes are curious, while the palace of art lives and dies on a frail lease:

> A haunting music, sole perhaps and lone
> Supportress of the faery-roof, made moan
> Throughout, as fearful the whole charm might fade.
> (2.122–24)

This is the pathos of the aesthetic contract, and its public execution by the Corinthians:

> The herd approach'd; each guest, with busy brain,
> Arriving at the portal, gaz'd amain,
> And enter'd marveling . . .
> . . . in they hurried all, maz'd, curious and keen
> (2.150–56)

This "busy brain" issues from the "busy world" at the end of Part I, all agog for romance marvels: not for nothing does Keats have *gaz'd amain* chime again in *all, maz'd*. The banquet-hall "is a good sample of the Story," he purred to publisher Taylor (*L* 2:157–59). Getting the insult to Keats's public, Taylor (again) urged some tailoring. Even with this compromise, Keats was "certain there is that sort of fire in it which must take hold of people in some way – give them either pleasant or unpleasant sensation. What they want is a sensation of some sort" (*K* 272). If to read *King Lear* was to "burn through" a "fierce dispute" of "damnation and impassioned clay," *Lamia's* "sort of fire" seems set with malice aforethought against "public opinion" and "the Reviews" on which it battens: "they are like the spectators at the

Westminster cock-pit – they like the battle and do not care who wins or who looses," Keats says in contempt (*L* 2:65).

Keats could throw his own fine poetry into the pit. Here is a bit of *Lamia* in the letter-draft:

> A glutton drains a cup of Helicon,
> Too fast down, down his throat the brief delight is gone.
> "Where is that Music?" cries the Lady fair.
> "Aye, where is it my dear? Up in the air"?   (*L* 2:159)

Melancholy, transience, *ubi sunt*, fair Lady, feeling repetition: all travestied, played for laughs.

As he's working on *Lamia*, he tells Reynolds, "I feel it in my power to become a popular writer—I feel it in my strength to refuse the poisonous suffrage of a public" (*L* 2:146). He ends with a pledge to "the best sort of Poetry—that is all I care for, all I live for" (147). Within a few weeks, he is confessing himself "now & then, haunted with ambitious thoughts" (21 September 1819; *L* 2:209) – the matter of *Hyperion*, it seems, not quite "given up" (*K* 266) after all.

CHAPTER 9

Falling in Fall 1819
The Fall of Hyperion *and* To Autumn

Poetry versus philosophy / poetry reverses philosophy

When *Another Version of Keats's "Hyperion"* appeared in 1857 in *Miscellanies of the Philobiblion Society* 3, it was taken to be the original housing of *Hyperion*, not least because the first half is a dream-frame prequel. This was actually a post-composed back-story, the work we now know as *The Fall of Hyperion, A Dream.*[1] Recasting direct epic narration into the rehearsal of an inward turning of dream-vision, Keats's new version is intensely self-involved. It opens with an "induction" on the character of the poem at hand; then the dream-frame takes the poet to an interrogation by the severest of muses, Moneta, sole survivor and repository of the Titans' catastrophe, whose brain holds it all. The poet enters her memory, its text supplied by a refreshed, refashioned *Hyperion*.

The belated publication of *Another Version* proved timely in its address to mid-century debates about poetic visions and poetic idealism amid the energies of the modern world. Is the poet a relevant philosopher? a potential benefactor? or just a fever? For Keats, the debate had sharpened in the interval between his first attempt, as Tom lay dying, and his return, when, like Hyperion, he had lost his brothers (George to another world). How to write the fall of Hyperion into a philosophy of intellectual ascent was still the question. An entire career of favorite fancies and tropes, of debates about beauty, poetic force and agency, dreaming and awakening, immortality and mortality, come back into play in *The Fall*. Recall Keats thinking with Bailey late in 1817 about the "consequitive reasoning" of the "Philosopher" versus the momentary starts of a poet's "Imagination," or the maturing of a "philosophic Mind" against his sigh, "O for a Life of Sensations rather than of Thoughts!" (*K* 69). The question soon dovetailed into the creative force of "negative capability" over thinking "incapable of remaining content with half-knowledge" (*K* 78). On this track in the spring of 1818 (we recall) Keats tires of Milton's "Philosophy, human and divine," and decides the genius of Wordsworth is in the "dark Passages" rather than his "powers" as "a Philosopher" (*K* 129–31). "What shocks the virtuous philosopher, delights the camelion Poet," Keats parses it out later that year (*K* 214).

Yet this thinking is more zig-zag than linear. "To philosophize I dare not yet," he said in March 1818, writing of provisional incapability rather than negative capability. *Philosophize* is a verb (this is the only time the word appears in Keats's writing). To reject an easy "lore of good and ill" is not to disdain philosophical striving at those limits when imagination, will, and thinking itself "tease us out of thought" (*K* 120). Differential distinction is a philosophical method, and for Keats it's ongoing. In April he describes himself to his publisher as "hovering for some time between an exquisite sense of the luxurious and love for Philosophy" (*K* 125). By March 1819, he is again at pro and con. Poetry is "energy" of "reasoning," that however "erroneous . . . may be fine"; but "if so it is not so fine a thing as philosophy" (*K* 243). By August the Philosopher is still ascendant: "I am convinced more and more every day that (excepting the human friend Philosopher) a fine writer is the most genuine Being in the World" (*K* 264). Within a month Keats confesses, "I have no trust whatever on Poetry" and marvels "how people read so much of it" (*L* 2:179). But he says this as he reads much of it, and theorizes "how." This is the same season he's writing *Lamia*, playing Lycius's deluded dreaming, Lamia's dazzling artistry, and Apollonius's "cold philosophy" against one another, with no champion.

Sitting down to reread *Hyperion* once again, Keats worked the question of dreaming, poetry, and philosophy into a symbolic autobiography: a poet at the remnants of a garden feast, swooning to sleep and wakening into a vast wasteland. Here he experiences, in agonizing degrees of sensation, his own death. Wrought in the shadow of Dante's liminal *Purgatorio* and the doom of *Paradise Lost*, *The Fall of Hyperion* casts no Apollo-god of poetry – just this human poet, who is told he is no poet, merely a useless, fevered dreamer. This sentence is pronounced by Moneta, who sets a test in the theater of her memory. It's Keats's memory, too: her memory is his *Hyperion*. *Hyperion* used the Titans' fall as an epic syntax for mortal knowledge; in the revision, a mortal poet bears this knowledge.

This is the theme, in conception and wording, of the extended figure Keats sketches out in the spring of 1819 for the life in the world. It is a figure of reading in a school he names a "vale of Soul-making" (what beckons beyond the fane in *Ode to Psyche*):

How then are Souls to be made? . . . How, but by the medium of a world like this? . . . a grander system of salvation than the chrysteain religion . . . I will call the <u>world</u> a School instituted for the purpose of teaching little children to <u>read</u>—I will call the <u>human heart</u> the <u>horn Book</u> used in that School—and I will call the <u>Child able to Read</u>, the Soul made from that <u>school</u> and its <u>hornbook</u>. Do you not see how necessary a World of Pains and troubles is to school an Intelligence and make it a soul? A Place where the heart must feel and suffer in a thousand diverse ways! Not merely is the Heart a Hornbook, It is the Minds Bible, it is the Minds experience, it is the teat from which the Mind or intelligence sucks its identity . . . a system of Salvation which does not affront our reason and humanity . . . (21 April 1819; *K* 251)

Learning to read by "the Heart" is the literal *re-cord* of identity-formation. What Keats couldn't figure out for *Hyperion* – an experiential philosophy for Apollo's victory – is now turned into a premise: a poet challenged to earn his identity from the hornbook, half-punned as the school of Moneta's "horned shrine" (1.137). The "vale of Soul-making" imprints the very word that turns *The Fall* to the text of *Hyperion*: "Deep in the shady sadness of a vale" (1.294). This vale will become the poet's for "A long awful time" (1.384) as he feels, with acute sympathy, the suffering that *Hyperion*'s poet-godling Apollo experienced only in rapid transit.

The conceptual stakes are spelled out in the opening lines of *The Fall*. "Fanatics have their dreams" and so do preliterate savages, but these "shadows of melodious utterance" have not been "Trac'd upon vellum or wild Indian leaf"; "bare of laurel" (the poet's honor), their imaginings have been left to "live, dream, and die" (1–7).

> For Poesy alone can tell her dreams,
> With the fine spell of words alone can save
> Imagination from the sable charm
> And dumb enchantment.   (1.8–11)

Keats plays a promising chime from *vell*um to *mel*odious to laur*el* to *tell* to *spell*, but every one of Poesy's claims will be tested – both in the poet's dream, and for the poem subtitled *A Dream*:

> Whether the dream now purposed to rehearse
> Be poet's or fanatic's will be known
> When this warm scribe my hand is in the grave.
>   (1.16–18)

This is a question not just of genre but of narrative genesis: is the dream-rehearsal the distillation of memory (Mnemosyne embodied) or the writing

uncertainly to come (Moneta its medium)? Is the *now* (lettered inside
k*now*n) a temporal indicator (post-dream) or the present of writing? The
question entails its scribe: "this warm scribe" and the fear of the *Hyperion*
poet that his subject may be "Too huge for mortal tongue or pen of scribe"
(1.160) are the sole instances of the word *scribe* in Keats's poetry.

A spell of words and a warm hand figure into the most traumatic dream
of all, the sensation of dying. This is the dreamer-protagonist's ordeal at
Moneta's temple, a site exceeding the mere "faulture" of worldly ruins
(1.70) – a great Keats-coinage evoking fault-line and failure. At the end of
a "patient travail" of "innumerable degrees" (91–92), the dreamer tells how

> suddenly a palsied chill
> Struck from the paved level up my limbs,
> And was ascending quick to put cold grasp
> Upon those streams that pulse beside the throat:
>
> . . . the cold
> Grew stifling, suffocating, at the heart;
> And when I clasp'd my hands I felt them not
> (1.122–25, 129–31)

This agony is *The Fall*'s muse, a death to qualify this poet as witness to the
Titans' desolation. He has "felt / What 'tis to die" and then "live again"
(141–42), in order to watch others die – so Moneta explains the passport to
a vision indistinguishable from a hellish curse.

Keats wrote and rewrote an extended debate between this poet and
Moneta on his (or any poet's) claim to vocation: is such a poet clear-eyed
about "the miseries of the world" or is he a haven-seeker for "thoughtless
sleep" (1.148–53)? Is he among those who "Labour for mortal good" or one
of those "dreamers weak," impotent "vision'ries" unable to "benefit . . . the
great world" and too restless for any "haven" of relief (151–71)? Keats had
to draft another twenty-seven lines of interrogation (187–210) to reach
this judgment: "The poet and the dreamer are distinct, / Diverse, sheer
opposite, antipodes" (199–200).[2] It's no conclusion. As *A Dream*, the poet's
logic is a conundrum. And its muse overwhelms its medium:

> I had no words to answer; for my tongue,
> Useless, could find about its roofed home
> No syllable of a fit majesty
> To make rejoinder to Moneta's mourn.
> (1.228–31)

Immersed as ever in words, Keats found a syllable, coining *visionless* to
write "eyes visionless entire . . . Of all external things" (1.267–68). Moneta

is the one to make rejoinder, with a contract including an *if*-clause so dire as to count as first test, a test not only of aesthetic logic but of aesthetic ethics:

> My power, which to me is still a curse,
> Shall be to thee a wonder; for the scenes
> Still swooning vivid through my globed brain
> With an electral changing misery
> Thou shalt with those dull mortal eyes behold,
> Free from all pain, if wonder pain thee not.
>
> (1.243–48)

Wonder is one of those words with a Keatsian career, tracking from ravishment to curiosity to speculation, to this *if*, and now its impossibility in beholding "a wan face" (256), a sublimity beyond capable imagination:

> Not pin'd by human sorrows, but bright blanch'd
> By an immortal sickness which kills not;
> It works a constant change, which happy death
> Can put no end to; deathwards progressing
> To no death was that visage; it had pass'd
> The lily and the snow; and beyond these
> I must not think now, though I saw that face.
>
> (1.257–63)

"I must not think" halts at this unending present. To the medical term, "mortal sickness," Keats fits a new syllable, and finds the genre of epic tragedy as Moneta discloses the "high tragedy / In the dark secret chambers of her skull" (1.277–78). Dante, said Hazlitt, is "the father of modern poetry" in such a mode of "terrible obscurity, like that which oppresses us in dreams," rendering "the same thrilling and overwhelming sensation, which is caught by gazing on the face of a person who has seen some object of horror."[3] Gaining the power "To see as a God sees . . . And seeing ne'er forget" (1.303–10), Keats writes a genesis of tragedy, the experience and the literary work at once. "Then came the griev'd voice of Mnemosyne, / And griev'd I hearken'd" (331–32). Editors usually propose a slip here for "Moneta" but Keats, whose dreamer has already hailed a "Shade of Memory!" (282), wanted Mnemosyne (Memory and the Mother of the Muses): her "griev'd voice" infuses the poet's "griev'd I."

On this channel the text of *Hyperion* returns, with grieving revision. Of Saturn and Thea *Hyperion* renders epic narrative:

> One moon, with alteration slow, had shed
> Her silver seasons four upon the night,

> And still these two were postured motionless,
> Like natural sculpture in cathedral cavern;
> The frozen God still couchant on the earth,
> And the sad Goddess weeping at his feet
>
> (1.83–88)

It's stately static statuary, the narrator invisible. In *The Fall*'s re-vision the new figure is the poet-witness of the arrest and duration caught by *still*:

> A long awful time
> I look'd upon them; still they were the same;
> The frozen God still bending to the earth,
> And the sad Goddess weeping at his feet;
> Moneta silent. Without stay or prop
> But my own weak mortality, I bore
> The load of this eternal quietude,
> The unchanging gloom, and the three fixed shapes
> Ponderous upon my senses a whole moon.
>
> (1.384–92)

Keats halts and fixes the stresses at *three fixed shapes*. The *pon* syllables in *Ponderous upon* intensify the compounded sensation: the pondering of dream-reading and the affective weight of sympathy. There "is a gloomy abstraction in his conceptions, which lies like a dead weight upon the mind; a benumbing stupor, a breathless awe, from the intensity of the impression," said Hazlitt of Dante.[4] Keats translates this here, but in no abstraction. Dream-reading and dream-poetry measure a physically severe, anti-Pleasure-Thermometer:

> For by my burning brain I measured sure
> Her silver seasons shedded on the night,
> And every day by day methought I grew
> More gaunt and ghostly.   (1.393–96)

In "the vale / And all its burthens" – burthens on the gods, on their witness, on the measures of poetry – the dreamer-poet feels the "burden of the mystery" (the truth of *Tintern Abbey* returns) so intensely that he would die himself (1.396–99). In indelible memory is the stress of Tom's mortal sickness: "His identity presses upon me" (*K* 200). Such press is camelion poetics *in extremis*, the poison fruit of Keats's jesting to Woodhouse how even in a "Nursery of children," "the identity of every one in the room begins to so press upon me that, I am in very little time anhilated" (*K* 215 [*sic*]). If the contract of the Dantean dream is a passge through purgatory, Keats's *Dream* extends the sentence over and over. The floral arbor of the first scene dissolves into a wasteland and a ruined temple; a blissful altar becomes a bar of interrogation and a stage of near death; a "sooth voice" utters contempt; a wonder turns a curse.

Keats closes his first (and only complete) Canto at a threshold, with a gesture to his reader that almost parts company, on the difference between reading and memory:

> —And she spake on,
> As ye may read who can unwearied pass
> Onward from the Antichamber of this dream,
> Where, even at the open doors awhile
> I must delay, and glean my memory
> Of her high phrase—perhaps no further dare. —
>
> (1.463–68)

Poet and reader may be distinct, diverse. Or not: *ye may* rhymes with *I . . . delay. Where* rhymes with *dare,* the text and its challenge.

Canto II opens the doors, with Moneta offering accommodation for her high phrasing, but with no guarantee of unwearied passage:

> Mortal, that thou may'st understand aright,
> I humanize my sayings to thine ear,
> Making comparisons of earthly things;
> Or thou might'st better listen to the wind,
> Whose language is to thee a barren noise,
> Though it blows legend-laden through the trees.
>
> (2.1–6)

Keats liked *legend-laden* for its "fine sound." How canny, perverse even. A *legend* wants interpreting (What leaf-fring'd legend?). Keats wants phonics.[5] And Moneta's humanizing is not so affable as Raphael's to Adam, "lik'ning spiritual to corporal forms" (*PL* 5.572).

When the dream resumes, "Now in clear light I stood, / Reliev'd from the dusk vale" (2.49–50), Keats knows he's writing a short lease of relief, because this dreamer knows "What 'tis to die" (1.142), a severe likening to corporal form. This memory is now the muse, and Keats summons the gates of Purgatory for this doubled knowledge. Here Dante glances a marble stair so "polish'd, that therein my mirror'd form / Distinct I saw."[6] Keats turns this mirror to Mnemosyne – "the polish'd stone . . . reflected pure / Her priestess-garments" (2.50–52) – so that the dreamer's eyes may mirror the god's motion in *Hyperion* ("On he flared, / From stately nave to nave, from vault to vault"; 1.217ff):

> My quick eyes ran on
> From stately nave to nave, from vault to vault,
> Through bowers of fragrant and enwreathed light,

> And diamond paved lustrous long arcades.
> Anon rush'd by the bright Hyperion;   (2.53–57)

The predicate even seems to push this run to 57, overriding 56's period. While the next line – "His flaming robes stream'd out" (58) – realigns the grammar (Hyperion rushed), 57 figures, in the brief pause of its linear poetics and Latinate syntax, the eyes of "camelion Poet... infor – and filling some other Body" (*K* 214). It is such a poet's identification (not Moneta's mediation) that informs, and authorizes, the "comparison of earthly things" (2.3). Hyperion's flaming robes

> gave a roar, as if of earthly fire,
> That scar'd away the meek ethereal hours
> And made their dove-wings tremble: on he flared——
>   (2.59–61)

The words are the same as *Hyperion*'s, but the revision's mainframe adds new sounds: *flared* recalls Canto I's close, *no further dare*, then hits exact rhyme here, on the ferocity of *scar'd*. Yet even as the last word from the warm scribe of Keats's hand, *flared*, rhymes into the end to come, its phrasing is independent: "on he flared—" halts the onward draft of *Hyperion* with a triple-stress propulsion of fierce dispute, an indeterminate dash, and an unwritten future.

Keats said he gave up because he was unable to distinguish "the false beauty proceeding from art" (Miltonic inverted syntax) from "the true voice of feeling" (21 September 1819; *K* 267). Yet these last lines are true in their tracks. The term Keats coined for the history that he couldn't work further to unfold, *legend-laden*, resides in lines of *The Fall of Hyperion* that survive in his own warm hand, in a letter to Woodhouse, just after he transcribed *To Autumn*.

Another Fall: *To Autumn*'s interval

A fall without crisis, *To Autumn* came in relief from the epic labor of *The Fall*: "Somehow a stubble plain looks warm ... this struck me so much in my sunday's walk that I composed upon it ... I have given up Hyperion" (*K* 266). If Keats cites Milton's epic syntax as a baleful influence, he could sense a kin in lyric Milton. On the half-title-page of *Paradise Lost*, he made a note that while Milton's "Genius," especially in "its span in immensity, calculated him, by a sort of birthright," for epic "argument" ("the ardours" over "the pleasures of Song"), Milton also seems to have "had an exquisite passion for what is properly, in the sense of ease and pleasure, poetical Luxury," and so couldn't help "solacing himself at intervals with cups of old wine" – which to Keats inspire some of "the finest parts of the Poem."[7] Keats knew the medical sense of the "interval": a phase between fits of fever. And he would know the original military sense: between the ramparts (*vallum*: rampart); know even Milton's single use of the word in *Paradise Lost*: "'Twixt Host and Host but narrow space was left, / A dreadful intervall" (6.104–5).

So tuned was Keats to interval as a pause with a horizon in view that he used the word, in the wake of his first harsh reviews, to promise Woodhouse that "maturer years" will see him in a Miltonic mode, "ambitious to do the world some good," and "in the interval I will assay to reach to as high a summit in Poetry as the nerve bestowed upon me will suffer" (*K* 215). That was October 1818. But after the impasse of *The Fall of Hyperion*, in September 1819, he was exhausted with the suffering: "I want to compose without this fever" he tells George (*K* 275). To compose this way is to compose himself – for an interval. This is the day he wrote *To Autumn*.

To Autumn is never unconscious of its timescape. In allusions, in imagery, in verbal vibrations, in deft line cuts and finely tuned syntaxes, it works a brilliant poetics of the moment. Here, too, is no scripted "I," but instead an audit and audition. Hailing the season, Keats unfolds the subject in a syntax that so expands from line to line as to seem not to need any predicate:

> Season of mists and mellow fruitfulness,
>   Close bosom-friend of the maturing sun;
> Conspiring with him how to load and bless
>   With fruit the vines that round the thatch-eves run;
> To bend with apples the moss'd cottage-trees,
>   And fill all fruit with ripeness to the core;
>   To swell the gourd, and plump the hazel shells . . .
>   (1–7)

The present participles and infinitives cast grammar's spell of infinite interval. Even those Milton/Keats mists[8] transform into mellow company, while *conspiring* relaxes into the literal sense of companionable breath. Even so, Keats's poetry doesn't stop the clock. The priming of autumn in literary and iconographic tradition as a dying season is averted, knowingly. While bees among late-budding flowers "think warm days will never cease, / For Summer has o'er-brimm'd their clammy cells" (stanza 1's last lines), readers get the jest about magical thinking; for those with brains other than bees', *never cease* has the force of a double negative.

When stanza 2 gives the extravagantly suspended apostrophe an anchor in grammatical form – "Who hath not seen thee oft amid thy store?"

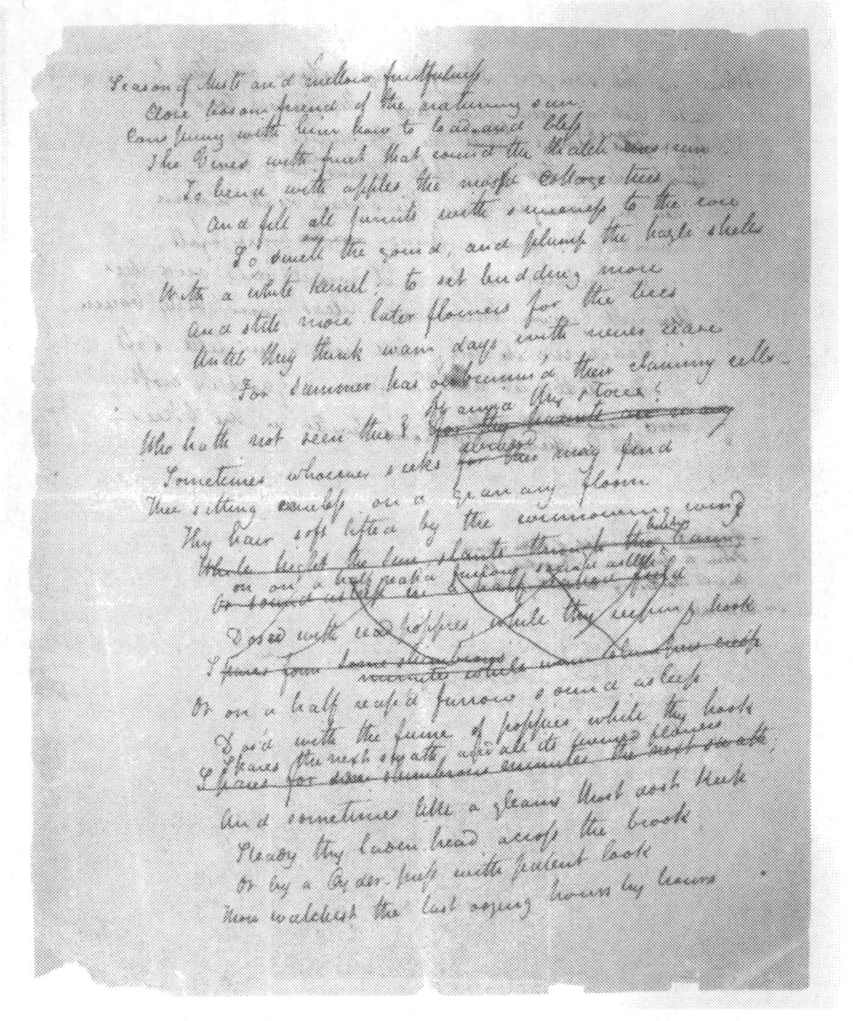

Fig. 8 *To Autumn*, early draft, before 21 September 1819. Houghton Library, Harvard University, MS Keats 2.27.

(12) – it proves a formality to stage another mode of indulged extension, here a poetry of lateral array, of time pictured out in multiple *Sometimes*:

> Sometimes whoever seeks abroad may find
> Thee sitting careless on a granary floor,
>   Thy hair soft-lifted by the winnowing wind;
> Or on a half-reap'd furrow sound asleep,

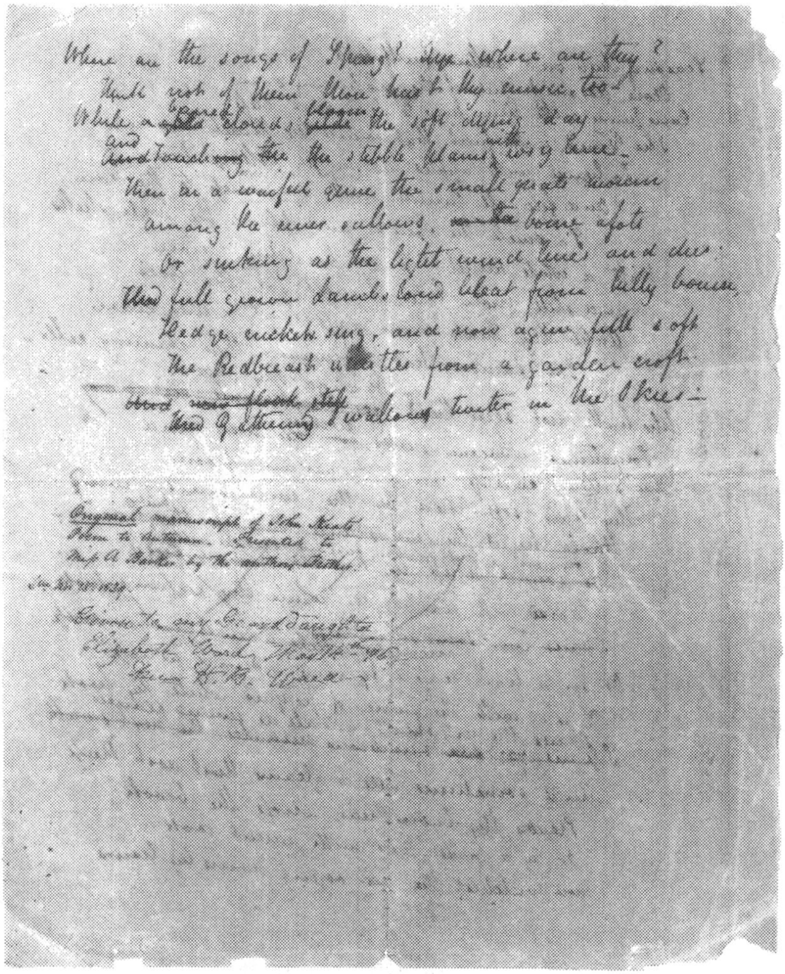

Fig. 8 (*cont.*)

Drows'd with the fume of poppies, while thy hook
 Spares the next swath and all its twined flowers:
And sometimes like a gleaner thou dost keep
 Steady thy laden head across a brook;
 Or by a cyder-press, with patient look,
 Thou watchest the last oozings hours by hours.
(13–22)

Ode on Melancholy turns temporal change in the blink of an eye. In un-melancholy autumn, time-signals seem timed out, factored out from a chronology of seeking and finding and "made prepositional."[9] Those *hours by hours* are more positional than terminally bound (Keats ended the line with a dash: see Figure 8). How notable, comments Stuart Sperry, that the word *adieu* – a theatrical mark in all the other odes of 1819 – makes no show here, though an ode on Autumn is where one might most expect to see it.[10] But qualifiers, if they don't abound, still bind. The wind is busy winnowing (or an evocative elision of wind-mowing to *winmowing* in the letter-draft; MS K.1.64.310), "careless" is the legible binary of care; a "half-reap'd" furrow has more to do; gleaners finish the harvest; "last oozings" will run out.

The temporal consciousness with which Keats headlines the third, and last, stanza is not of these factors, however, but of the season farthest away on the yearly calendar:

> Where are the songs of Spring? Ay, where are they?
> Think not of them, thou hast thy music too.—
>
> (23–24)

Tuning a long *ubi sunt* tradition (Latin *where are?* a sigh for everything gone), Keats takes the formula for mourning into a refusal to mourn. The reply with a mocking repetition that pivots, assertively, into an ode in which the gone *they* is effaced by a present *thy*:

> While barred clouds bloom the soft-dying day,
> And touch the stubble-plains with rosy hue;
>
> Then in a wailful choir the small gnats mourn
> Among the river sallows, borne aloft
> Or sinking as the light wind lives or dies;
> And full-grown lambs loud bleat from hilly bourn;
> Hedge-crickets sing; and now with treble soft
> The red-breast whistles from a garden-croft;
> And gathering swallows twitter in the skies.
>
> (25–33)

Autumn plenitude – hovering in *While, And, Then, now* – seems even to absorb songs of Spring in verbal vibration. The day is "dying" but "clouds bloom" (Keats revised a merely ornamental "a gold cloud gilds"[11]); the plains harvested down to stubble get a "rosy hue"; "gnats mourn" but the verb could recall a *morn* in tune with a *borne* that puns into *born*, and those lambs on the *bourn* might be *born* too. Even the *or* of "borne aloft /

Or sinking" and "lives or dies" feels like pictorial variety rather than fatal sequence (the letter-text has "lives and dies"). Keats first wrote "gather'd Swallows," then revised to "gathering," the present participle playing a chord from from *soft-dying* through *sing*. And if *gathering* bodes the time when no birds sing, the sound of *swallows* flies off from the funereal shadow of *sallows* (willows). In the letter-text, Keats ended with a long dash after *Skies*, prolonging it all.

"It is a flaw / In happiness to see beyond our bourn — " Keats reflected to Reynolds in March 1818 (*K* 120), knowing that to sight any bourn is already a flaw. By autumn 1819, the flaw is an entailment of happiness. "Think not" cannot but think (not bee-think), and in Keats's thoughts is the mortal bourn of Wordsworth's *Ode: Intimations of Immortality*:

> The Clouds that gather round the setting sun
> Do take a sober colouring from an eye
> That hath kept watch o'er man's mortality.

On such watch, Keats could endorse Wordsworth's elegy in stanza 10, with his own postscript:

> 'Nothing can bring back the hour
> Of splendour in the grass and glory in the flower'
> I once thought this a Melancholist's dream——
>
> (31 May 1819, *K* 256)

On this correction of thought, Keats writes out a declarative couplet that forgets Wordsworth's subordinate syntax ("Though nothing can bring back..."), keyed in the Intimations *Ode* to the discipline of "We will grieve not, rather find / Strength in what remains behind" (179–89). As usual in Wordsworth's most strenuous philosophy, the disciplinary syntax doesn't erase its impetus. Wordsworth keeps his watch on mortality, Keats wrote to Bailey back in 1817, by having "philantrophy enough to overcome the disposition [to] an indolent enjoyment of intellect...brave enough to volunteer for uncomfortable hours." I'm tempted to read *philantrophy* as Keats's deliberate punning coinage.[12] Keats knows on his pulses the anatomy of melancholy and the love of its trophies, and, contrarily, the disposition of indolence; he knows the uncomfortable hours and the luxury of hours and hours that seem otherwise. Poised between the mind of winter and the songs of spring, *To Autumn* writes up the wistfully complicated interval between.

CHAPTER 10

Late poems & lasting Keats

Late poems

Keats lived what he called a "posthumous existence" – not just in his sad last days in Rome but under such a shadow from early years on that even first poems come across as late-minded. A sonnet from January 1817, beginning "AFTER dark vapors have oppress'd our plains / For a long dreary season, comes a day / Born of the gentle SOUTH," concludes its sweet catalogue of vernal promise with "a Poet's death."[1] In another untitled sonnet, written as he was finishing *Endymion* (31 January 1818), Keats renders that peculiar genre of pre-posthumous epitaph:

> When I have fears that I may cease to be
>   Before my pen has glean'd my teeming brain,
> Before high piled Books, in charactery,
>   Hold like rich garners the full ripened grain——
> When I behold upon the night's starr'd face,
>   Huge cloudy symbols of a high romance,
> And think that I may never live to trace
>   Their shadows with the magic hand of chance:
> And when I feel, fair creature of an hour,
>   That I shall never look upon thee more,
> Never have relish in the fairy power
>   Of unreflecting Love: then on the Shore
>   Of the wide world I stand alone and think
>   Till Love and Fame to Nothingness do sink. ——
>
> *(K 97)*

The sonnet is imprinted with the temporal urgencies of Shakespeare's Sonnet XII ("When I do count the clock that tells the time") and the echo in Milton's Sonnet XVI ("When I consider how my light is spent"), both fated for a reckoning volta (turn). But Shakespeare turns the count outward ("Then of thy beauty do I question make"), and Milton's *When* cues "patience to prevent / That murmur" (but not before seven lines).

Keats delays his volta until the caesura of line 12, then springs it open to no saving clause: "then on the Shore." *Shore* fronts a blank page, prefiguring the "Nothingness" into which Keats sinks his one-sentence pile-up of thinkings. Just a few weeks before, he had written of nothingness as a muse: "The feel of not to feel it / Was never said in rhyme" (*P* 221). He needed the negative for this oxymoron; and for the claim of rhyme, he needed *versed* (compressed by the magic hand of chance) in "n*ever said*."

And what a change in mood from *On First Looking into Chapman's Homer* to another sonnet of response, written scarcely a half year on: *On Seeing the Elgin Marbles*. Looking at these magnificent fragments of the glory that was Greece, Keats is prompted to no intimations of immortality – quite the opposite:

> My spirit is too weak—Mortality
>   Weighs heavily on me like unwilling sleep,
>   And each imagined pinnacle and steep
> Of godlike hardship, tells me I must die
>
>   (1–4)

The very syntax tells this in the way line 3 seems to be part of Mortality's weight. The sensation is of sublimely impossible aspiration:

> Such dim-conceived glories of the brain
>   Bring round the heart an undescribable feud;
> So do these wonders a most dizzy pain,
>   That mingles Grecian grandeur with the rude
> Wasting of old time—with a billowy main—
> A sun—a shadow of a magnitude.   (9–14)

The volta at 9 works as accelerant: the sculptor's conceiving brain (long gone) relays into the poet's brain of astonished despair, time's wasting felt on the cerebral pulse, and a heart-sense of what is, *undescribable*, beyond the pen of mortal scribe. Keats's pen recovers just enough to dash the sentence into expressive fragments. Sea and sun persist, and wonders of magnitude are ravished by shadowy thought.

Love, Fame, time's wasting, the heart's feuds, and the call to poetry all return in poems involved with Fanny Brawne, the fair creature next door whom Keats met in the summer of 1818, pledged himself to in December, and hoped to marry when financially eligible. These late writings include three sonnets, two odes, and a mysterious fragment, "This living hand." Passionately, painfully in love, frustrated by fame, struggling with finances, and in failing health, and with no aim of publishing, Keats turned to poetry to grapple with the turmoils. Other than the sonnet "Bright Star" and "This living hand," these are not much known, and usually regarded as a sad decline. Yet their turmoil verges on unexpected discoveries, no less critical than disjunctive.

It matters mightily that Keats in love vexes Keats the poet, and that being in love conjures those old gordian complications:

> Full many a lady
> I have ey'd with best regard; and many a time
> The harmony of their tongues hath into bondage
> Brought my too diligent ear: for several virtues
> Have I lik'd several women; never any
> With so full soul, but some defect in her
> Did quarrel with the noblest grace she ow'd,
> And put it to the foil . . .
>
> (*Tempest* 3.1; *Dramatic Works*, 1:37)

Keats underlined this, Ferdinand's prologue to his declaration of Miranda's "peerless" perfection. But the other line from *The Tempest* that plays in mind is Caliban's, on waking from his enchanted dreaming, "I cried to dream again" (3.2), words that Keats also underlined, and wrote, in quotation to "My sweet Fanny" absent from her company in October 1819.[2] Feeding deep, deep on the lover's quarrel between bondage and defects, and sensing no easy remedy, Keats scoured Burton's *Anatomy* for choice items of preemptive defense as he worked on *Lamia*. So pleased was he with one stretch of misogyny (in the same Part/Section as the story of Lycius) that he copied it out for George and Georgiana. It's a blazon of "such errors or imperfections of boddy or mind" an admiring Lover will overlook in his Mistress.[3] "There's a dose for you—fine!!," Keats cheers; "I would give my favourite leg to have written this as a speech in a Play" (*L* 2:191–92). He's willing to play his own anatomy, placed or wittily displaced, into the bargain. He knew "that the man who rediicules romance is the most romantic of Men—that he who abuses women and slights them—loves them the most" (19 February 1819; *L* 2:67).

"This moment I have set myself to copy some verses out fair. I cannot proceed with any degree of content. I must write you a line or two and see if that will assist in dismissing you from my Mind," he writes his "dearest Girl" in October 1819 (*K* 276). What happens to fair verses in the throes of such passion? One discipline of self-possession would seem the sonnet. Yet when Keats writes "I cry your mercy," the form presses discipline to a crisis. Another one of his single-sentence sonnets, this one propels its syntax into fragments, contracts and frays grammar, loses the pace of meter, and makes rhyme compete with urgent repetition:

I CRY your mercy—pity—love! —aye, love!
  Merciful love that tantalises not,
One-thoughted, never wand'ring, guileless love,
  Unmask'd, and being seen—without a blot!
O, let me have thee whole, —all, —all—be mine!
  That shape, that fairness, that sweet minor zest
Of love, your kiss, those hands, those eyes divine,
  That warm, white, lucent, million-pleasured breast,—
Yourself—your soul—in pity give me all,
  Withhold no atom's atom or I die,
Or living on perhaps, your wretched thrall,
  Forget, in the mist of idle misery,
Life's purposes,—the palate of my mind
Losing its gust, and my ambition blind.   (*K* 285)

"I cry your mercy" can't even manage the sarcasm of Othello's unhinged slam to Desdemona's protest of never-wand'ring love: "I cry you mercy, then, / I took you for that cunning whore of Venice" (*Othello* 4.2.90–91). Keats can't even get to taking; it's all pleading anguish. With its object, a thrice cried *all*, absorbed (in sound and sense) into *thrall*, Keats joins what he had ironized for his Knight: "death pale were they all / They cried – La belle dame sans merci / Thee hath in thrall" (*K* 248). The strong chain links *I cry / Aye love / I die / idle misery*. And what of *love*? It gets no partner in the mist of idle misery, just a crying repetition of itself. The sonnet is a swirl of desire, of anguished agent and elusive object, a mist forever midst.

When Keats sighed to his "dear Girl" in August 1819, "it seems to me that a few more moments thought of you would uncrystallize and dissolve me," he knew the antidote: "I must not give way to it—but turn to my writing again—if I fail I shall die hard" (*L* 2:142). It was worse a year on. "My dearest Girl," he writes in August 1820, "I wish you could invent some means to make me at all happy without you. Every hour I am more and more concentrated in you." She is an impossible muse, charged with an invention against her force. For Keats, the extremes are so merciless – "I cannot bear flashes of light and return into my glooms again" – that he can sign off only, "I wish I was either in your arms full of faith or that a Thunder bolt would strike me." In this syntax, "full of faith" has to modify her arms and "I" at once. Keats was by this time bound for Italy, and this may have been his last letter to her.

Before this farewell, he tendered a rueful pun (one he used before, to double a mood into a vocation): "For all this I am averse to seeing you." "I am a verse" sounds the glooms: "If my health would bear it, I could write a Poem which I have in my head, which would be a consolation for people in such a situation as mine. I would show some one in Love as I am, with a person living in such Liberty as you do." The *with* in this prologue is doubly damning: in Love with her; in Love, with her in Liberty. Hence a bitter summons: "Shakspeare always sums up matters in the most sovereign manner. Hamlet's heart was full of such Misery as mine is when he said to Ophelia 'Go to a Nunnery, go, go!'" (*Hamlet* 3.1; *K* 423–24). Trying for Shakespeare's "sovereign manner," Keats revises a sonnet on his way to Italy, knowing he'll die there.[4]

It begins "Bright Star, would I were stedfast as thou art" and works toward a Shakespearean couplet. But the couplet binds the romance to a sweet unrest a breath away from death. Even the keynote, Caesar's declaration, "I am constant as the northern star" (*Julius Caesar* 3.1.58) is said on his way to dire death, in Italy even. Keats's sonnet no sooner expresses its wish than qualifies it: "Not in lone splendour hung aloft the night" (2). And *stedfast* turns more infantine than heroic, with the chimes of *still* ringing changes from insistence, to arrest, to quiet, to for ever:

> No—yet still stedfast, still unchangeable,
>   Pillow'd upon my fair love's ripening breast,
> To feel for ever its soft swell and fall,
>   Awake for ever in a sweet unrest,
> Still, still to hear her tender-taken breath,
> And so live ever—or else swoon to death.
>   (9–14)

An arrest of sweet unrest is what Keats wanted to imagine, yearn for, as he was being separated for ever (he knew on his pulses) from his fair love, on course to uneaseful death. "I have two luxuries to brood over in my walk, your Loveliness and the hour of my death," he sighed to his love in July 1819; "O that I could have possession of them both in the same minute" (*K* 263). The sonnet is this possession, for a minute.

The crises of love and self-possession have pressed Keatsian aesthetics into critical deformations, or by another measure, exploratory formal extremes. The nineteenth century liked to call "Bright Star" Keats's *Last Sonnet*.[5] A rival for *last* is a fragment that sets its stakes, vampirically, on the unsweetest of unrest:

> This living hand, now warm and capable
> Of earnest grasping, would, if it were cold
> and in the icy silence of the tomb,
> So haunt thy days and chill thy dreaming nights
>   heat
> That thou would wish thine ʌ own dry of blood
> So in my veins red life might stream again,

Fig. 9 Joseph Severn's sketch of John Keats, January 1821. Keats–Shelley House, Rome.
Joseph Severn writes below, "28 January, 1821, 3 o'clock in the morning, drawn to keep me
awake. A deadly sweat was on him all this night." Keats seems suspended between life and
death, mysteriously dreaming. "The source of light in the cell-like bedroom is of course a
candle off to the left, leaving the artist in shadow, like a witness. The peace on Keats's face
is both fatal exhaustion and acceptance . . . Severn creates a large black sun to relieve the
face against . . . massive in its animation, dramatic in its contrast" (Stanley Plumly,
Posthumous Keats [New York: W. W. Norton, 2008], 35–36). Keats died on the evening of
23 February 1821.

> and thou be conscience-calm'd – see here it is ‡
> I hold it towards you—
>
> (*K* 286)

The hand is both somatic and scriptive. How can we know the hand writing from the handwriting? A warm living hand becomes a cold dead hand, then handwriting coolly handed to us. The single sentence dilates its subjunctive ("would, if it were") to absorb its addressee ("that thou would"), with a double-thrust "So" (intensely, in consequence). Working a relentlessly elaborated proposition into stark immediacy ("see here it is"), stagey eloquence into colloquial intimacy, accretive syntax into spare monosyllables, Keats's lines conjure the present of writing into the future of reading: "here it is / I hold it towards you." Twice-told, this *it* grabs all the referents in the poetic field: living hand, cold hand, writing hand, handwriting. Keats's lines revive to survive as the gothic version of the legal burden, *mort-main*.

    Held ever towards a live reader, these lines rival Keats's sadly self-sentenced epitaph on his deathbed, "Here lies one whose name was writ in Water," his final echo of Shakespeare: "Men's evil manners live in brass, their virtues / We write in water" (*Henry VIII* 4.2).[6] You might, in either case, expect *on water*, the surface, but it's crueler to have the very ink so transparent, so ephemeral – and so mistaken, unless Keats's last hope was that *was* might be revised forward and into a medium that would last, as long as writing lasts.[7] Red life might stream again as a read life.

Lasting Keats

Keats really suffered two deaths: one from consumption in Rome in February 1821 and another, later in the year, in Shelley's elegy, *Adonais*. Shelley meant to honor Keats's genius, to vindicate his fame in eternity, and to rail against the temporal reviewers that (Shelley had heard) so wounded the vulnerable poet that he died of the anguish. But *Adonais* overplayed its hand, making Keats too frail by half. Byron was one of the first to turn Shelley's fable to farce, in *Don Juan* Canto XI (1823), amidst a litany of poets in the vagaries of fame:

> John Keats—who was kill'd off by one critique,
>   Just as he really promised something great,
>   . . .
> Poor fellow! His was an untoward fate:
> 'T is strange the mind, that very fiery particle,
> Should let itself be snuff'd out by an article.
>
> (XI.60)

Byron's couplet marked Keats far more indelibly than Shelley's fifty-five Spenserian stanzas, launching a riot of iterations that relentlessly across the nineteenth century recalled the poor fellow to snuff him out again. As late as the 1870s, *Cornhill* was wielding Byron's phrasing to smirk that *Adonais* advanced "the theory that poetry and manliness are incompatible."[8] On this score, R. M. Milnes's *Life, Letters, and Literary Remains of John Keats* (1848) was a dubious success. Although Milnes meant to uproot Shelley's frail flower and blunt Byron's barb with a story "to make prominent the brave front" that Keats "opposed to poverty and pain" and his devotion to "higher aspirations," such argument could not but expose the spur. Reviewing Milnes's Keats, *The Edinburgh Review* anatomized a poet in whom the "passive part of intellect, the powers of susceptibility and appreciation" defined "a feminine mould," in which "masculine energy" seems to have "existed deficiently, or had not time for its full development."[9] To a friend who confessed interest in Milnes's *Keats*, Thomas Carlyle "retorted, 'That shows you to be a soft-horn!'"[10] Keats was the differential by which men assured themselves, and others, of their own hard horns.

Even so, whatever the reception of Milnes's muscled-up Keats, what was materially consequential was Milnes's assembly of a raft of new or freshly set writing by Keats: in addition to the work in Keats's lifetime volumes, there were forty more poems (twenty-six from scattered periodicals, the others from manuscripts) and eighty letters, most here for the first time (Hunt's memoir of 1828 had a few). Keats's three lifetime volumes, in print-runs of 500 or less, were out of circulation; later editions failed or were unavailable in England.[11] Milnes's mid-century Keats was not only a poet of substantially wider achievement than had been known but also a freshly presented, most appealing epistolary personality: ironic, sentimental, thoughtful, funny, passionate, and issuing brilliant, compelling formulations about poetic style and poetic method. This Keats was a craftsman and a philosopher, an aesthete and a reflective reader, an acute social observer and a practicing poet. With Milnes's production reviewed everywhere, Keats was reborn to a new generation. Whatever story was told about the historical John Keats (battered boy, effeminate gusher, avatar of beauty, martyr to art) appreciation for Keats's verbal craft and vibrant pictorial imaging was emerging and growing, shaping not only his fame but also the reading of poetry in a Keatsian vein, as an artistry of an intense conception and verbal skill.

Twentieth-century Keats brings composites or new combinations. Reworking his essay on "The English Renaissance," Wilde elevated Keats as the champion of beauty: "Byron was a rebel and Shelley a dreamer; but in the calmness and clearness of his vision, his perfect self-control,

his unerring sense of beauty and his recognition of a separate realm for
the imagination, Keats was the pure and serene artist . . . It is in Keats that
the artistic spirit of this century first found its absolute incarnation."[12] In
acclaiming the aesthete and romancing the martyr, Wilde also brought forward a Keats for love among an elite coterie of male artists. Virginia Woolf,
thinking of Coleridge's surmise that "a great mind must be androgynous,"
then put Keats in a canon of male writers responsive to "the woman part
of the brain."[13] Half a century later, Keats was earning distinct feminist
honors. In 1983 Elaine Showalter described women's theories of women's
writing (in distinction from men writing on the subject) as "theories proved
on our own pulses" – echoing Keats's view that "axioms in philosophy"
have no value unless "proved upon our pulses."[14] The pulse could be
sociological, too. Margaret Homans thought Keats's class origins and lack
of classical education reflected "certain aspects of women's experience as
outsiders relative to the major literary tradition" of "masculine" practices,
and she allied this with Adrienne Rich's designation of negative capability
as a female aesthetic. Rich was thinking of Nancy Chodorow's comment
about woman's "so-called 'weak ego boundaries'" and wanted to upgrade
this "negative way of describing the fact that women have tremendous
powers of intuitive identification and sympathy with other people." She
used the term "Negative capability" and generalized it: "Any artist has to
have it."[15] Not long after, Erica Jong, writing on Rich, made the sensi-
bility into a feminist badge: "feminism *means* empathy. And empathy is
akin to the quality Keats called 'negative capability' – that unique gift for
projecting oneself into other states of consciousness."[16] Keats winds up "an
honorary woman," in Homans's phrase.[17] Forgotten, it seems, was Keats's
own marking of these qualities for a "man of achievement" and his taking
Shakespeare as the model (*K* 78), in no small part to deflect a cultural
disposition to judge such sensibilities as unmanly, even effeminate. It was
"Adam's Dream," not Eve's, that supplied Keats with a comparison to
"Imagination" in its ideal power (*K* 69). And quite sarcastic about "literary
women" (*K* 59), he was never interested in meeting any in the London
world: Joanna Baillie, Charlotte Smith, Mary Shelley, Mary Lamb, the
Misses Porter.

   This is not to indict Keats's male bonding, literary and social. It's to note
how "Keats," from first reviews to latest literary theory, lends a language for
various identifications, invested ways of thinking and writing. Charges of
effeminacy, defenses of manliness, praise for "feminine" qualities, briefs for
liberal gender values, speculations on mental androgyny: these are not just
Keats-causes but cultural markers.[18] Who is reading? in what circumstance?

with what sort of culturally shaped habits and expectations? While Keats's words are the same, the history of reading Keats is activated by different systems of meaning, new configurations of information and evaluation, depending on who is reading and how reading is done.

None of this would matter at all were it not for the extraordinary poetry. Reading Keats is the durable pleasure, intellectual and sensuous, complex and complicating, as it takes the pulse of the conflicts and uncertainties of its historical moment, the rich diversity of literary traditions, and its own alert and variable practices. When I sit down to read *Ode on a Grecian Urn* once again, I find that even if I'm not forever young, the poem is still to be enjoy'd – not only for its smart aesthetic play, but also for its uncertain vibrations with cultures of art and uses of gender. When old age shall my generation waste, Keats's poetry will survive, and no doubt focus new ways of knowing. Critic David Harlan has nicely captured this effect:

> Canonical texts . . . generate new ways of seeing old things and new things we have never seen before. No matter how subtly or radically we change our approach to them, they always respond with something new; no matter how many times we reinterpret them, they always have something illuminating to tell us. Their very indeterminacy means that they can never be exhausted . . . Canonical works are multi-dimensional, omni-significant, inexhaustible, perpetually new.[19]

Although Keats was not determined to be indeterminate, this resistance to exhaustion is of a piece with a temper of unrest.

Shuttling in September 1819 between another round with *Hyperion* and enjoying the unexpected, easeful inspiration of *To Autumn*, Keats writes to Reynolds, "It strikes me to night that I have led a very odd sort of life for the two or three last years – Here & there – No anchor – I am glad of it – ." Then, in a heartbeat, he parodies his habitual turns: "I shall beg leave to have a third opinion in the first discussion you have with Woodhouse – just half way – between you both" (*L* 2:167–68). And so our conversations on Keats: open to new opinions, never settled, because Keats provokes rereading, and rereading happens with fresh contexts of interest, ever new angles of attention. I've written *Reading John Keats* just about 200 years after Keats's first efforts at writing poetry. It won't be the last time that anyone writes about reading Keats, glad for his ever evolving place among the English Poets.

A few famous formulations

As with phrasings in the poetry, some formulations in Keats's letters are so widely known as to install Keats not just among the English poets, but in the English language. This brief list is redacted from my fuller one in *The Cambridge Companion to John Keats* (xl–xliii). Ellipses are mine.

"Not begun at all 'till half done" [to Benjamin R. Haydon, 10 May 1817]

"we shall enjoy ourselves here after by having what we called happiness on Earth repeated in a finer tone" [to Benjamin Bailey, 22 November 1817]

"*Negative Capability*, that is when man is capable of being in uncertainties, Mysteries, doubts, without any irritable reaching after fact & reason" [to his brothers, December 1817]

"We hate poetry that has a palpable design upon us" [to J. H. Reynolds about Wordsworth, 3 February 1818]

"Poetry should surprise by a fine excess . . . if Poetry comes not as naturally as the leaves to a tree it had better not come at all" [to John Taylor, 27 February 1818, while proofreading *Endymion*]

"every mental pursuit takes its reality and worth from the ardour of the pursuer" [to Bailey, 13 March 1818]

"The innumerable compositions and decompositions which take place between the intellect and its thousand materials before it arrives at that trembling delicate and snail-horn perception of Beauty" [to Haydon, 8 April 1818]

"the most unhappy hours in our lives are those in which we recollect times past to our own blushing—If we are immortal that must be the Hell" [to Reynolds, 27 April 1818]

"As to the poetical Character itself, (I mean that sort of which, if I am any thing, I am a Member; that sort distinguished from the wordsworthian or egotistical sublime; which is a thing per se and stands alone) it is not itself—it has no self—it is every thing and nothing—It has no character—it enjoys light and shade, it lives in gusto, be it foul or fair . . . What shocks the virtuous philosopher, delights the camelion Poet . . . A Poet is the most unpoetical of any thing in existence because he has no Identity—he is continually in for—and filling some other Body" [to Richard Woodhouse, 27 October 1818]

"the history of [Jesus] was written and revised by Men interested in the pious frauds of Religion. Yet through all this I see his splendour."

"Though a quarrel in the streets is a thing to be hated, the energies displayed in it are fine; the commonest Man shows a grace in his quarrel—By a superior being our reasoning[s] may take the same tone—though erroneous they may be fine—This is the very thing in which consists poetry; and if so it is not so fine a thing as philosophy— For the same reason that an eagle is not so fine a thing as a truth." [to his brother and sister-in-law, 19 March 1819]

"I have but lately stood on my guard against Milton. Life to him would be death to me." [to the same, 24 September 1819]

"I am leading a posthumous existence" [to Charles Brown, 30 November 1820]

At a glance: Keats in context
(*fuller chronology in* CCK)

K: John Keats   GK: George Keats   TK: Tom Keats

1795   John Keats born, 31 October, at the Swan and Hoop Livery Stables, to Frances Jennings Keats (daughter of the proprietor) and Thomas Keats, chief ostler. High food prices and famine in England; legislation against mass assemblies. Napoleon invades Italy.

1796   Mary Robinson, *Sappho and Phaon*. Death of Robert Burns.

1797   George Keats born 28 February.

1798   Napoleon defeated at the Battle of the Nile; Irish Rebellion; *Lyrical Ballads* (Wordsworth and Coleridge), including *Tintern Abbey*.

1799   Thomas (Tom) Keats born 18 November. Napoleon becomes first consul in a coup d'état. Parliament outlaws political societies and labor unions.

1800   New edition of *Lyrical Ballads* (with Wordsworth's Preface); first collected edition of Burns. Union of England and Ireland; Alessandro Volta produces electricity from a cell.

1801   Edward Keats born (dies before February 1805). First census.

1802   Founded: Cobbett's *Weekly Political Register*; *Edinburgh Review*; Society for the Suppression of Vice. The Peace of Amiens between England and France briefly opens the Continent; France invades Switzerland. Walter Scott, *Minstrelsy of the Scottish Border*.

1803   Fanny Keats born; GK and K at Enfield Academy.
        War with France resumes. British capture Delhi, India. Lord Elgin takes fragments from the Athenian Parthenon to England.

1804   April: K's father dies in a riding accident; his mother remarries in June; the children are sent to live with her parents.

Napoleon becomes Emperor, prepares to invade England; Beethoven's *Eroica* celebrates him as a liberator; Britain declares war on Spain. Corn Laws enacted (taxation of imported grains to protect high prices for English crops).

1805 March: K's grandfather Jennings dies. Scott, *Lay of the Last Minstrel*. William Hazlitt's *Essay on the Principles of Human Action*. Admiral Nelson, British naval hero, dies in the battle with France at Trafalgar; French victory over Austria and Russia.

1806 Scott's *Ballads and Lyrical Pieces*; William Bowles's edition of Alexander Pope. Napoleon's victories across Europe.

1807 Wordsworth, *Poems, in Two Volumes*; Moore, *Irish Melodies*. Britain supports the Iberian resistance against Napoleon; slave trade abolished, but not colonial slavery.

1808 *Edinburgh Review* ridicules Byron's *Hours of Idleness* (1807). Leigh Hunt edits *The Examiner*. Charles Lamb, *Specimens of English Dramatic Poets*. Spanish uprising in May is betrayed by Britain's treaty to guarantee the French (with booty) safe passage out.

1809 Byron's satire, *English Bards and Scotch Reviewers*. William Gifford edits *The Quarterly Review*. Napoleon defeated in Austria.

1810 K's mother dies of tuberculosis.

1811 Guardian Richard Abbey removes K, age sixteen, from Enfield and apprentices him to a surgeon; GK clerks at Abbey's counting-house.

George III deemed incompetent; Prince of Wales becomes Regent. Luddite riots smash weaving frames in despair of unemployment. National Society for the Education of the Poor founded. Elgin's proposal to sell the Parthenon fragments to the British government provokes controversy about the cost, ethics, and aesthetic worth. Shelley is expelled from Oxford for *The Necessity of Atheism* (a pamphlet indicting the corruption of the Church). Mary Tighe, *Psyche; or the Legend of Love*; Hunt, *The Feast of the Poets*.

1812 Byron's "maiden" speech in the House of Lords opposes the death penalty for frame-breaking; *Childe Harold's Pilgrimage* an overnight sensation; Canto II calls Elgin a thief and pirate. Britain declares war on the US; Napoleon's catastrophic retreat from Russia.

1813 Byron's *The Giaour* and *The Bride of Abydos*. Coleridge's play *Remorse* is a success. Southey publishes *Life of Nelson* and becomes Poet Laureate; Wordsworth gets a government patronage position; Hunt imprisoned for libel for publishing *The Prince of Wales v. The Examiner*. Shelley's *Queen Mab* excoriates Kingcraft and Priestcraft.

Austria joins the Alliance against France; Napoleon defeated at Leipzig.

1814   K's first poems: *Imitation of Spenser*, sonnets *On Peace* (hoped for), and *To Lord Byron*. December: Grandmother Jennings dies; Fanny Keats goes to the Abbeys' home.

Byron's *Corsair* sells 10,000 on the day of publication. Also out: Henry Cary's translation of Dante's *Divine Comedy*, Wordsworth's *Excursion*; Reynolds's *Safie, An Eastern Tale* and *The Eden of Imagination*; Hunt's new *Feast of the Poets*; Shelley's *A Refutation of Deism*. Edmund Kean's celebrated debut at Covent Garden theater; Charles Brown's play *Narensky* succeeds at Drury Lane.

The Allies invade France; Napoleon abdicates and is exiled to Elba; the monarchy is restored. Shelley elopes to the Continent with Mary Wollstonecraft Godwin.

1815   2 February: K's sonnet, *Written on the Day that Mr. Leigh Hunt left Prison*; writes *Ode to Apollo*. October: K begins study at Guy's Hospital in London.

Byron's four-volume *Poems*; Wordsworth's *Poems*, including a fully titled *Ode, Intimations of Immortality from Recollections of Early Childhood*. Hunt's *The Descent of Liberty, a Mask*. Napoleon escapes Elba; Louis XVIII flees to England as Napoleon advances to Paris and then Waterloo, where he is vanquished (June), then exiled to an Atlantic island. French monarchy restored; new repressions. In England: new Corn Laws; widespread misery and starvation.

1816   K now a surgeon's assistant. 5 May: sonnet, *O Solitude* in *The Examiner*. July: K passes apothecaries exam (eligible to practice medicine), vacations with TK at Margate; writes verse-epistles to GK and C. C. Clarke. September: the brothers live together. Fall: K meets painters Haydon and Severn, poet Reynolds, and Leigh Hunt. November: visits Haydon's studio and writes "Great Spirits" (Haydon sends it to Wordsworth); works on *Sleep and Poetry* and "I stood tip-toe." December: Hunt's "Young Poets" (*The Examiner*) includes *On First Looking into Chapman's Homer*; K meets Shelley.

March: Haydon defends the Elgin Marbles in *The Examiner*; a May issue has Hazlitt's essay *On Gusto*, important for K's aesthetics. Hunt's *Story of Rimini* outrages conservative reviews. Also out: Shelley's quest-romance *Alastor*, Reynolds's *The Naiad*, Coleridge's *Christabel, Kubla Khan, The Pains of Sleep*. May: Byron leaves England forever; *The Prisoner of Chillon* and *Childe Harold's Pilgrimage* Canto III (year-end) are huge successes. Elgin Marbles are purchased and displayed in the British Museum. Political unrest, riots, and trials of activist publishers.

1817   Hunt shows K's poetry to Shelley and Hazlitt, publishes sonnets *To Kosciusko* and "After dark vapors" in *The Examiner*. March: K and TK move to Hampstead, north of London; Haydon takes K to see the Marbles, inspiring two sonnets, which Reynolds puts in *The Champion* and Hunt in *The Examiner*. K's *Poems* is published, hailed by Reynolds in *The Champion*. K meets publisher John Taylor and his adviser Richard Woodhouse, also Charles Brown and Benjamin Bailey; starts *Endymion*; writes a sonnet *On the Sea*, which appears in *The Champion*. In the summer Hunt praises *Poems* in *The Examiner*. September: K's sonnet, "The poetry of the earth is never dead" in *The Examiner*; with Bailey at Oxford, K works on Book III; takes mercury for venereal disease. November: K reads Coleridge's poems, *Sibylline Leaves*, finishes *Endymion*. December: K sees Kean in Shakespeare's *Richard III* and hails his return to the stage in *The Champion*; sees Benjamin West's painting of *Death on a Pale Horse* and formulates "negative capability"; at Haydon's "immortal dinner" (Wordsworth attends), K and Lamb drink a toast against Newton.

Byron's *Manfred*; Hazlitt's *Characters of Shakespear's Plays*. *Blackwood's Edinburgh Magazine* founded; in October is Z.'s first "Cockney School" paper, attacking Hunt, and targeting K. Habeas Corpus suspended; legislation against "Seditious Meetings." William Hone tried for blasphemous parodies of the liturgy. Princess Charlotte dies after delivering a dead child; death of Polish patriot Kosciusko, one of K's heroes, who also fought in the US Revolutionary War.

1818   January: K visits Wordsworth in London and recites "Hymn to Pan" from *Endymion*; attends theater, writes a sonnet about rereading *King Lear*, attends Hazlitt's lectures on English poetry. While proofreading *Endymion*, he writes a playful, philosophical

verse-epistle to Reynolds, and soon begins *Isabella*. Amid
socializing in Hunt's circle (meeting the Shelleys' friends, T. J.
Hogg, Claire Claremont, and T. L. Peacock), K reads histories
by Voltaire and Gibbon, writes sonnets and a self-castigating
Preface to *Endymion* (his publishers reject it); takes TK to seaside
Teignmouth. Haydon reprints the sonnets on the Elgin Marbles
in *Annals of the Fine Arts*. *Endymion* is published late April; K
finishes *Isabella*. GK and new bride Georgiana Wylie emigrate
to America. *Poems* panned in *The British Critic*. With Brown, K
takes a summer walking tour of the Lake District, Scotland, and
Ireland, visiting Wordsworth's home and Burns's tomb, hiking
up Ben Nevis, reading Cary's translation of *Divine Comedy*. Sore
throat and chills force a return to London in August. TK very
ill; K meets Fanny Brawne, her family the summer tenants of
Brown's quarters at Wentworth Place (in Hampstead, now the
Keats House museum). *The Quarterly* and *Blackwood's* skewer
Poems and *Endymion*. K begins *Hyperion* while nursing Tom,
who dies 1 December; accepts Brown's offer to move in with
him. By December, he and Fanny Brawne are in love.

  Byron, *Childe Harold's Pilgrimage* Canto IV; Shelley, *The
Revolt of Islam*; Hunt, *Foliage, or Poems Original and Translated*;
Hazlitt, *Lectures on the English Poets* and a brisk rebuke, in *The
Examiner*, of *The Quarterly's* attack-dog, *A Letter to William
Gifford, Esq.* which K greatly enjoys. Radical atheist publisher
Richard Carlile imprisoned. Habeas Corpus restored.

1819 K contends with financial problems as Haydon pesters him for
loans. January: *The Eve of St. Agnes*; February: *The Eve of St.
Mark*; March: Severn's miniature of K exhibited at the Royal
Academy; April: the Brawnes rent Dilke's half of Wentworth
Place; K meets Coleridge and they talk of nightingales. K sets
aside *Hyperion* and writes *La belle dame sans merci/mercy*, "If by
dull rhymes," and *Ode to Psyche*. May: K describes the world as
a vale Soul-making and in the spring writes more odes (*Grecian
Urn, Indolence, Melancholy*, and *Nightingale*). July: *Ode to a
Nightingale* published in *Annals of the Fine Arts*. Summer: writes
Lamia. K with Brown on Isle of Wight to work on *Otho the
Great* (hoping for Kean to star); it's accepted by Drury Lane but
Kean is unavailable. K burns his letters, returns his books, and
decides to publish no more. Worsening sore throat. September:
works on *The Fall of Hyperion*, writes *To Autumn*; later fall:

poems about Fanny Brawne, to whom he becomes engaged in December.

Outraged reviews of Shelley's *The Revolt of Islam* (*The Quarterly*) and everywhere of *The Cenci*; Hazlitt's *Lectures on the English Comic Writers*; Byron's *Don Juan* I–II (mixed reviews) and *Childe Harold's Pilgrimage* I–IV collected; K's review of Reynolds's satire, *Peter Bell, A Lyrical Ballad* (published before Wordsworth's *Peter Bell*). Hunt founds *The Indicator*. August: "Peterloo Massacre": a militia charge on a peaceful workers' demonstration in Manchester. Its star, Henry Hunt (no relation to Leigh Hunt), arrested at Manchester, makes "a triumphal entry" in London for his trial, K among a cheering crowd of 200,000. December: Parliament passes acts restricting freedom of assembly, speech, and print. William Parry's Arctic expedition.

1820   January: GK comes to London, seeking funds from TK's estate and compromising K's claim; this is the last time K sees GK, and he stops writing to him. Haydon publishes *Ode on a Grecian Urn* in *Annals of the Fine Arts*; K and Brown send *Otho* to Covent Garden theater. K suffers heart trouble and pulmonary hemorrhaging; severe episode in February. March: K revises *Lamia &c*. In London and Edinburgh, Haydon exhibits *Christ's Entry into Jerusalem*, with K in the crowd. April: *London Magazine* praises *Endymion*. May: Brown rents out his half of Wentworth Place and K has to move; Hunt publishes *La belle dame sans mercy* in *The Indicator*, and in June, *A Dream, After Reading Dante's Episode of Paulo and Francesca*. K corrects proofs for *Lamia &c*; coughs blood, goes to Hunt's home for care. July: *Lamia, Isabella, The Eve of St. Agnes, and Other Poems* published; K inscribes a copy for Fanny Brawne. July: Lamb praises *Lamia &c* in *The New Times*; Hunt reprints this in *The Indicator*, and his own praises in *The Examiner*. *Ode to a Nightingale, To Autumn*, and other poems in *The Literary Gazette*; *To Autumn* in *The London Chronicle*. August: influential critic Francis Jeffrey praises *Endymion* and *Lamia &c* in *The Edinburgh Review*. K returns to Wentworth Place, where the Brawnes care for him. Shelley invites him to Italy, and K declines, but his doctor and friends convince him to winter in Italy and they raise the funds. K writes his will and for £200 assigns copyright to Taylor & Hessey. September: *Lamia*

&c praised in *The Monthly Magazine*, *The New Monthly Magazine*, *The British Critic* and Baldwin's *London Magazine*. K sails for Italy with Severn (Hunt publishes a farewell in *The Indicator*); after a rough voyage, they reach Naples harbor late October; early November, they lodge in Rome's English district; K's last known letters, to Brown. December: severe relapse.

Murray publishes Byron's poems in eight volumes (1818–20). Taylor & Hessey found *The London Magazine*. Shelley publishes *Prometheus Unbound*.

1821   23 February: K dies in Severn's arms; 26 February: buried in Rome's Protestant Cemetery. The news reaches London, 17 March.

* * *

1821   In Pisa, Shelley publishes *Adonais*, an elegy for K, well meant but fixing the fable of fatal reviews; *Blackwood's* ridicules it. Fanny Brawne pays a call to Fanny Keats, the beginning of a close friendship.

1822   July: Shelley drowns in a storm at sea.

1823   *Don Juan* XI describes K "snuff'd out by an article" – a phrase oft reiterated. Fanny Keats, now of age, goes to live with the Brawnes.

1824   April: Byron dies of malaria in Greece, while supporting the War of Independence.

1826   Fanny Keats marries Spanish novelist Valentin Llanos, born the same year as K, whom he may have visited in Rome.

1828   *Adonais* published in England. Hunt recounts a witty, resilient, and poetically powerful K in *Lord Byron and Some of His Contemporaries* (2 vols.; London: Henry Colburn).

1829   *The Poetical Works of Coleridge, Shelley and Keats* (Paris: A. and W. Galignani) includes K's lifetime publications and some new pieces: "In drear-nighted December," "Four seasons," *On a Leander Gem*, and *To Ailsa Rock*, along with a memoir based on Hunt's. Poet Thomas Hood (married to Reynolds's sister), edits the gift-book annual, *The Gem*, where K's *Leander Gem* is first published.

1833   Fanny Brawne, having mourned for Keats for half a decade and now living in France, meets and marries Louis Lindo (later Lindon).

1834   Woodhouse dies after a five-year bout with tuberculosis. Coleridge dies.

1835	Hunt writes about K in *Leigh Hunt's London Journal*.

1835 Hunt writes about K in *Leigh Hunt's London Journal*.
1836 Brown gives a public lecture on K, and plans a biography.
1840 *The Poetical Works of John Keats* is published in London; Matthew Arnold had a copy.
1841 Brown gives his Keats manuscripts to R. M. Milnes. GK dies Christmas Eve.
1842 Brown dies in New Zealand; Tennyson's fame emerges with *Poems*.
1843 Georgiana Keats marries John Jeffrey.
1844 The first chapter of Hunt's *Imagination and Fancy* is on Keats.
1845 Taylor sells his rights to K's poems and letters to Edward Moxon, Milnes's publisher. Jeffrey sends Milnes transcriptions of the poems and letters K sent to George and Georgiana Keats.
1846 Haydon commits suicide. Moxon publishes *The Poetical Works of John Keats. A New Edition* – the one Tennyson carried around in his pocket.
1848 Milnes's *Life, Letters, and Literary Remains of John Keats* is widely reviewed, with decisive influence.
1850 Wordsworth dies; Tennyson publishes *In Memoriam* and is appointed Poet Laureate.
1851 Bailey dies.
1852 Reynolds dies.
1854 Milnes's *Poetical Works of John Keats*. Poet Algernon Charles Swinburne gives this to his sister in 1861; Amy Lowell, poet and devoted biographer of K, also owns this edition.
1857 *Another Version of Keats's "Hyperion"* is published (thought to be the original).
1863 Severn's "On the Vicissitudes of Keats's Fame," *Atlantic Monthly* (April).
1865 December: Fanny Brawne dies, entrusting to her children Keats's letters to her.
1867 Milnes's new edition of *Life, Letters, and Literary Remains*.
1874 Charles Cowden Clarke's "Recollections of John Keats" in *Gentleman's Magazine* provides a view of K's school days.
1876 Milnes (now Lord Houghton) publishes a new *Poetical Works of John Keats*.
1877 Oscar Wilde's "The Tomb of Keats" published in *The Irish Monthly* (July).
1878 H. Buxton Forman edits and introduces *Letters of John Keats to Fanny Brawne*, to much controversy and widespread disdain,

notably from Arnold and Swinburne. Keats-in-love is lamented and ridiculed. Fanny Brawne is despised as girlishly heartless and unworthy.

1882   Wilde praises Keats's genius in his American lectures and is presented the manuscript of the sonnet "Blue!" by K's niece in Kentucky.

1883   Forman's scholarly four-volume *The Poetic Works and Other Writing of John Keats* confirms K's place "among the English poets." Pre-Raphaelite poet, designer, and socialist William Morris gives this edition as gift to his daughter Jenny. Poet Laureate Alfred Lord Tennyson's praises of K are published in his son's *Memoir*.

1885   Keats's letters to Fanny Brawne are sold for a little more than £543.

1887   Sidney Colvin's literary biography of K in "The English Men of Letters" series.

1889   December: Fanny Keats dies in Madrid (age eighty-six).

Notes

PREFACE

1 *On the Grasshopper and Cricket* (*K* 31).

2 14 October 1818; HK1.39.146 (*L* 1:394).

3 *Poems by Oscar Wilde and his Lecture on the English Renaissance*, Seaside Library VIII.1183 (New York: George Munro, 1882), 30.

4 To Rev. Matthew Russell, S. J., editor of *The Irish Monthly* (*Selected Letters of Oscar Wilde*, ed. Rupert Hart-Davis [Oxford University Press, 1962], 40). Wilde published *Heu Miserande Puer* (Latin: *Alas Poor Boy*), later titled *The Grave of Keats* ("Rid of the world's injustice") in *Irish Monthly*, July 1877.

5 Matthew Arnold, "Preface," *Poems* (London: Longman &c, 1853), xxi–xxii (spelling *sic*).

6 William T. Arnold (*The Poetical Works of John Keats* [London: Kegan Paul, Trench, 1884], ix). He is quoting his brother-in-law Thomas Humphry Ward, *The English Poets: Wordsworth to Tennyson* (1880) and John Ruskin, *Modern Painters* (1860).

7 Hallam Tennyson, *Alfred Lord Tennyson: A Memoir* (London: Macmillan, 1897), 2:286, 504.

8 *Blackwood's Edinburgh Magazine* (1818), and *Quarterly Review* (1818).

9 Byron's comments to Murray and friends; some were published (posthumously for both Keats and Byron) in *The Works of Lord Byron* (London: John Murray, 1833), 15:92n.

10 *Sleep and Poetry* (1817), 97–99.

11 Oscar Wilde, *Pall Mall Gazette*, 12 July 1889.

1 LIFE AND TIMES

1 *Sleep and Poetry*, 53–55, drafted October 1816.

2 "Great Spirits" (11–14); HK.1.4.15; see also *1817* Sonnet XIV.

3 *The Letters of William and Dorothy Wordsworth, II: The Middle Years*, ed. Ernest de Selincourt, Mary Moorman, and Alan G. Hill (Oxford: Clarendon Press, 1970), 2:360–61. Hereafter *MY*.

4 Hazlitt, "On Mr. Wordsworth's Excursion," *Examiner* (28 August 1814) 556.

5 For Haydon's report (1845) despising Wordsworth, see *KC* 2:143–44. Having championed Keats to Wordsworth, Haydon may have been sore that Wordsworth never acknowledged receiving Keats's warmly inscribed debut volume to him (Fig. 2, p. 25).

6 Wordsworth, *MY* 2:578. This painting is reproduced, along with a detail of Keats and Wordsworth, in Stephen Hebron's sumptuously illustrated *John Keats* (Oxford University Press, 2008), 52–53.

7 See Murray to Byron, 3 February 1814; Byron to John Hunt, 29 April 1823 (*BLJ* 10:161).

8 Hazlitt, *Lectures on the English Poets* (London: Taylor & Hessey, 1818), 2, quoting Romeo's father comparing his lovesick son to a flower thwarted of such blooming (*Romeo and Juliet* 1.1.148–49). With the line just previous, "A bud bit by an envious worm, / Ere he spread . . . " (etc.), Hazlitt would summon this verse to describe Keats's abuse by critics ("On Living to One's-Self,", in *Table Talk* [London: John Warren, 1821], 230).

9 To Haydon, 10 January 1818; HK1.18.62.

10 Hazlitt, *Lectures*, 318–20.

11 *Edinburgh Magazine and Literary Miscellany* 2nd series 1 (October 1817) 256, though with regret for the "licentious" style of the Cockney School.

12 For example, see Francis Jeffrey, *Edinburgh Review* 1 (1802) especially 63–72.

13 *To Solitude*, *Examiner* (5 May 1816) 82.

14 Leigh Hunt, "Young Poets," *Examiner* (1 December 1816) 761–62.

15 The articles were unsigned, the custom signifying corporate opinion. *Blackwood's* reviewer "Z" was J. G. Lockhart; *The Quarterly's* was notoriously nasty J. W. Croker.

16 9 May 1818, a few weeks after *Endymion* appeared. For the politics of paganism, see Nicholas Roe, *John Keats and the Culture of Dissent* (Oxford: Clarendon Press, 1997), 82–83.

17 Z, "On the Cockney School of Poetry. No. 1," *Blackwood's Edinburgh Magazine* 2 (October 1817) 38.

18 Z, "Cockney School IV" (*Blackwood's* 2:40–41).

19 *K* 212; HK1.39.157. For Keats's sonnet "on Fame" see HK1.5.266 and *K* 252–53.

20 HK1.13.42–43 (see also *K* 61–62).

21 *Quarterly* 19 (1818) 204–08 (see also *K* 203–05).

22 Hebron, *John Keats*, 70. Clare would soon be on Taylor's list.

23 C. C. Clarke, *Recollections of Writers* (London: Sampson Low, 1878), 122–23, 126.

24 Clarke, quoted in Sidney Colvin, *John Keats* (New York: Harper and Brothers, 1887), 13.

25 For the details on the will and its frustrations to the children, see W. J. Bate, *John Keats* (Cambridge, MA: Harvard University Press, 1963), 709. George's comment is reported by Keats, HK1.7.21–3 (see also *K* 52–54).

26 Leigh Hunt, review of Keats's *1817*, *Examiner* (13 July 1817) 443; Haydon, in *L* 1:125.

27 Z, "Cockney School IV," 520; Reynolds to Keats, 14 October 1818 (in *L* 1:376).

28 Keats to Haydon, 10–11 May 1817; HK1.7.21–23 (see also *K* 52–54).
29 Keats to Haydon, 28 September 1817; HK1.12.38.
30 Keats to Bailey, 22 November 1817; HK1.16.56 (see also *K* 70).
31 P. B. Shelley, quoted in *Shelley Memorials*, ed. Lady Shelley (Boston, MA: Ticknor and Fields, 1859), 170.
32 See HK1.16.55 and *K* 70.
33 Dreaming of "the Garden of bliss," Adam "waked and found / Before mine eyes all real, as the dream / Had lively shadow'd" (*PL* 8.309–11), lines Keats marked (*1808* 2:61–62; Lau 147).
34 *Lyrical Ballads* (2 vols.; London: Longman and Rees, 1800), 1:xvii, xiv, xxxiii, xv.
35 *The Excursion* (London: Longman &c, 1814), xi–xii; Wordsworth's italics.
36 "Essay, Supplementary to the Preface," *Poems* (2 vols.; London: Longman &c, 1815), 1:343.
37 Hazlitt, *Lectures on the English Poets*, 2, 309.
38 The line that impressed Keats is "Blows them traverse ten thousand leagues away" (3:488); *1808* 1:74 (Lau 104; *K* 234).
39 Harvard's Keats-copy of Hazlitt, *Characters* (London: R. Hunter and C. & J. Ollier), 54, 182.
40 Keats to Woodhouse, 27 October 1818; HK1.38.139 (see also *K* 214).
41 Keats to Reynolds, 21 September 1819; HK1.64.315 (see also *K* 267–68); *quiz* means *jest at*.
42 I use "Keats" to indicate (as contexts require) the historical author or his poetic agent – both in distinction from the self-allusion that Wordsworth solicits and Byron displays. "Lord Byron cuts a figure – but he is not figurative," said Keats, citing Shakespeare's mode as the latter (*K* 240). For a smart survey of author, "author," and "author-function," see Jack Stillinger, *Multiple Authorship and the Myth of Solitary Genius* (Oxford University Press, 1991), chapter 1.
43 To Woodhouse, 27 October 1818; HK1.38.139; *K* 214.
44 *PL* 9:179–91; *1808* 2:80 (Lau 153); also *K* 237. Keats coined "prosiable."
45 *1808* 1:5 (Lau 74); also *K* 226–27.

2 CONCEIVING EARLY POEMS, AND *POEMS*

1 The account and texts are from C. C. Clarke, *Recollections of Writers* (London: Sampson Low, 1878), 129–30.
2 Byron, *Childe Harold's Pilgrimage* (London: John Murray, 1812), Canto II:LXIX (later LXX).
3 Tennyson's smug advice, "History requires here *Balbóa*" (*The Golden Treasury* [London: Macmillan, 1861], 320), was for a long time, well into the 1990s even, cited for Keats's "error." But there is a logic for Cortez – *his* first view, not *the* first view. First argued by Charles C. Walcutt (*Explicator* 5.8 [1947]) then C. V. Wicker (*College English* 17 [1956]), Keats's choice has been endorsed by me and others – and Keats, too: he left it "uncorrected" in all his drafts and publications. It's not the event of an historical "first" that Keats signifies

but rather anyone's "first look." For a smartly theorized review of the chorus on Keats's "error," see Charles J. Rzepka, "'Cortez: Or Balboa, or Somebody like That': Form, Fact, and Forgetting in Keats's 'Chapman's Homer' Sonnet," *Keats–Shelley Journal* 51 (2002) 35–75.

4 Bonnycastle, Letter XXII (*Introduction* [London: Joseph Johnson, 1787], 403–4); Robertson, *The History of America* (2 vols., London: W. Strahan, T. Cadell, 1777), 1:203–04.

5 William Sharp, *The Life and Letters of Joseph Severn* (London: Sampson Low, Marston, 1892), 20, 21.

6 *The Story of Rimini* (London: John Murray / Edinburgh: W. Blackwood, 1816), p. 78; Keats's epigraph, p. 68. The imprint reflects Byron's pull; Hunt warmly dedicated *Rimini* to him, a pretention that outraged *Blackwood's* Z.

7 For the complicated politics, see William Keach, "Keats's Cockney Couplets," *SiR* 25 (1986) 182–96.

8 Marjorie Levinson reads a class stance in this strain: who "stands tip-toe? Children, short grown-ups, and people struggling to penetrate a defended view or to seize a remote one. Keats, from a political standpoint, was in 1817 all of those things" (*Keats's Life of Allegory: The Origins of a Style* [New York and Oxford: Basil Blackwell, 1988], 239).

9 Morris Dickstein, *Keats and His Poetry* (University of Chicago Press, 1971), 49.

10 Note in his copy of *1817*, opposite p. 106 (Stuart Sperry, "Richard Woodhouse's Interleaved and Annotated Copy of Keats's *Poems*," *Literary Monographs* 1 [Madison: University of Wisconsin Press, 1967], 154).

11 Z, *Blackwood's Edinburgh Magazine* 3 (August 1818) 520, 522; Amy Lowell, *John Keats* (2 vols., Boston, MA, and New York: Houghton Mifflin Co., 1925; Cambridge, MA: The Riverside Press, 1925), 1:222–23.

12 I may be the only editor to have noticed this. Stillinger (*P* 75) and Jeffrey N. Cox (*Keats's Poetry and Prose*, A Critical Edition, ed. Cox [New York and London: W. W. Norton & Co., 2009], 65) and others attach 269 to the previous paragraph, without comment. But it's clear from *Poems*, 113–14, that 269 is its own stanza, at the top of 114. It could easily have been set on the bottom of 113 as part of the previous verse paragraph, where there is a blank inter-stanza page-line.

3 FALLING IN AND OUT OF LOVE WITH *ENDYMION: A POETIC ROMANCE*; REREADING *KING LEAR*

1 Copied in a letter to Bailey, 8 October 1817; HK1.13.42–43; *K* 61–62 (ellipses mine).

2 Stuart M. Sperry, *Keats the Poet* (Princeton University Press, 1973), 97. I'm exploiting the confusions to which Sperry's allegory (Endymion's education into sympathy and humanitarian service) is ever alert. The favorite allegory is to see *Endymion's* sensuous eroticism answering the Platonic dualism of Shelley's *Alastor*.

3 Karen Swann brilliantly interprets *Endymion* as a meta-poetic luxuriating in an array of "beautiful dreamers" (*CCK*).

4 *Blackwood's* 3 (August 1818) 524; *British Critic* 9 (June 1818) 652.

5 The "outstretched poesy of this miserable Self-polluter," said Byron of Keats (*BLJ* 7:217).

6 First published in 1867 (Milnes's new edition of *1848*). The first draft, held by the Pierpont Morgan Library, is transcribed in *K* 116–17. For Keats's letter to Reynolds, 9 April 1818, about the need for a new draft, see *L* 1:266–68, and Reynolds, *KC* 2:178.

7 Keats to Haydon, 10–11 May 1817; HK1.7.21–22 (see also *K* 52–53; *L* 1:142–43).

8 Clarke, *Recollections*, 126 (*FQ* II.XII.23).

9 Letter to his publisher, John Taylor, 30 January 1818 (*K* 93–94).

10 *The British Critic* was so beside itself that it censured the first line, italicizing *dress* without reading on to discover that this was hair-styling, not voyeurism (new series 9 [1918] 650). Even so, as Christopher Ricks remarks, the mistake is solicited by Keats's coy linear poetics (*Keats and Embarrassment* [Oxford University Press, 1976], 87).

11 *Encyclopedia Britannica* 8th edn. (Edinburgh: Adam and Charles Black, 1857), 13:56. Karen Swann suggests that a deeper embarrassment is the overt solicitation of the entire scene.

12 Dickstein, *Keats and His Poetry*, 109; see also Sperry, *Keats the Poet*, 107–08.

13 *1808* 1:125 (Lau 126).

14 17 September 1819; *L* 2:187–88

15 Ricks, *Keats and Embarrassment*, 58–59.

16 Sperry, *Keats the Poet*, 115.

17 *FQ* II.VII.28. Spenser and Keats know Jesus' caution that one cannot serve both God and Mammon (Matthew 6:24).

18 *The Trembling of the Veil* (London: private printing, 1922), 189.

19 Keats to Bailey, 8 October 1817; HK1.13.42–43 (see also *K* 61–62).

20 I quote the letter-text (based on John Jeffrey's copy) in *1848* 1:96–97; but I interpolate the sonnet from an autograph MS, dated "Jany 22–1818," on a blank page opposite the start of *King Lear* in his facsimile of Shakespeare's first folio (Keats House, Hampstead).

21 Samuel Johnson, *The Plays of William Shakespeare* 1765 (10 vols., London, 1778), 9:566.

22 For Keats's attention, see Caroline Spurgeon, *Keats's Shakespeare* (Oxford University Press, 1928), 151.

4 VENTURING "NEW ROMANCE": *ISABELLA; OR, THE POT OF BASIL*. A STORY FROM BOCCACCIO

1 For this argument, see Jack Stillinger, *"The Hoodwinking of Madeline" and Other Essays on Keats's Poems* (Urbana: University of Illinois Press, 1971), 36–45.

2 Keats read a 1684 edition of the first English translation, by John Florio (1620).

3 Keats to Bailey, 10 June 1818; HK1.30.110 (*L* 1.294).

4 Dallas, *Poetics: An Essay on Poetry* (London: Smith, Elder, 1852), 9; *British Critic* 14 (September 1820) 264.

5 Ricks, *Keats and Embarrassment*, 98.

6 Shaw, "Keats," in *John Keats Memorial Volume*, ed. G. C. Williamson (London: John Lane, 1921), 175–76.

7 Keats to Woodhouse, 21 September 1819; HK1.64.315; *K* 267; *L* 2:174.

8 Hazlitt, *Lectures on the English Poets* (London: Taylor & Hessey, 1818), 162.

9 *P* 608. The sarcasm was Croker's, in *The Quarterly* 19 (April/September 1818) 207.

10 Keats had Fairfax's translation of Tasso's *Gerusalemme Liberata* (1600), usually cited as the cue for his *ottava rima*. By the time *Isabella* was published, 1820, Byron's *Don Juan* (Cantos I–II, 1819) had made *ottava rima* the signature of his satire.

11 Keats to George and Georgiana Keats, 14–31 October 1818, HK1.39.146 (see also *K* 208–09).

12 Keats to Woodhouse, 21 September 1819; HK1.64.315 (see also *K* 267); *smokeable* is archaic slang (OED, citing Keats *L* 2:19).

5 FALLING WITH *HYPERION*

1 Coleridge, *The Statesman's Manual; or The Bible the Best Guide to Political Skill and Foresight* (London: several printers, 1816), Appendix C:ix–x.

2 To George and Georgiana Keats, 14 October 1818; HK1.39.150–51; *L* 1:396–97.

3 *1808* I:119–20 (Lau 84). Charles II's Licenser for the Press took note of this verse.

4 *Endymion: A Facsimile of Woodhouse's Annotated Copy*, ed. Jack Stillinger (New York and London: Garland Publishing, 1985), 220.

5 Shelley, *The Revolt of Islam; A Poem* (London: C. & J. Ollier, 1818), ix–xi.

6 For a smart account of political despair in 1818, see John Barnard, *John Keats* (Cambridge University Press, 1987), 40–43.

7 Hunt, *Autobiography* (2 vols., New York: Harper and Brothers, 1850), 2:36. Hunt would have seen the term in the title of Kant's "Idea of a Universal History on a Cosmo-Political Plan," namely a grand perspective, a "cosmopolitan station for the survey of history" and a sort of prototype for a United Nations to prevent further wars: "the formation of a great primary state-body, or cosmopolitic Areopagus"; *London Magazine* 10 (October 1824) 385–93; I quote from 391–92.

8 27 October 1818 (HK1.38.139; *K* 214). On the relay of ease and disease, see Geoffrey Hartman, "Spectral Symbolism and Authorial Self in Keats's *Hyperion*," in *The Fate of Reading* (University of Chicago Press), 60–62.

9 Keats to C. W. Dilke, 20–21 September 1818 (*K* 200), quoting *PL* 9.121–22. *1808* 2:78l (Lau 150).

10 Hartman, "Spectral Symbolism," 60.

11 W. M. Rossetti, "Memoir," in *The Poetical Works of Shelley* (London: Edward Moxon, 1870), cxxxiii–cxxxiv.

12 To George and Georgiana Keats, 16–18 December 1818; HK1.45.177 and 180; *L* 2:4, 14.

13 *PL* 12.41; *1808* 2:171 (Lau 175).

14 OED lists only one *utterless* before Keats's, in Milton's *Divorce* tracts. Google books turns up just one more (*The Wedding Day*, a poem "By a Citizen of London" [1762], p. 35).

15 For example, this scorecard on Belial: "his thoughts were low; / To vice industrious, but to Nobler deeds / Timorous and slothful" (2.115–17). For the debate-markings see Lau 80–90.

16 "I never can feel certain of any truth but from a clear perception of its Beauty," he wrote on 31 December 1818, calling himself "very young minded even in that perceptive power" (*L* 2:19).

17 *PL* 1.535–65; *1808* 1:18–19 (Lau 82–83); *K* 227–29.

18 *1808* 1:19 (Lau 84); *K* 229.

19 Hunt, *Indicator* 14 (9 August 1820) 350, and *Lord Byron and Some of His Contemporaries* (London, 1828), 219.

20 *1820* 199. The draft is Woodhouse's copy, HK3.2.201; see also *P* 356.

21 *Richard II* (2.1.40–51ff); John of Gaunt's son Henry Bolingbroke, the future Henry IV, deposed and then arranged the murder of his cousin Richard II. *PL* 1.243–45.

22 *PL* 9.158–59, 179–91; *1808* 2:79–80 (Lau 152–53).

23 To Murray, November 1821, about eight months after Keats's death. "He is a loss to our literature; and the more so," Byron added, noting that he "was re-forming his style upon the more classical models of the language." This is a late footnote in a lengthy essay that Byron wanted to publish in 1820 or soon after. It was first published in volume XVII of *The Works of Lord Byron* (London: John Murray, 1833); the footnote is on p. 92.

24 Annotated copy of *Endymion*, April 1819 (Berg Collection, New York Public Library); see H. B. Forman, *The Poetical Works of John Keats* (New York: Crowell, 1895), 314.

25 Bate, *Keats*, 388.

6 STILL ROMANCING: *THE EVE OF ST. AGNES*; A DREAM-SONNET; *LA BELLE DAME*

1 In February 1818 *Monthly Magazine* reported 4,000 copies "bespoken" before publication (45:68); at 12 shillings, this was £2,400, nearly a tenth of the sale; total sales would reach 10,000.

2 See Jack Stillinger, *Reading The Eve of St. Agnes* (Oxford University Press, 1999), Appendix C, for a census. Setting the poem with two stanzas to the page, *1820* gives the effect of a proto-picture gallery.

3 Wasserman, *The Finer Tone* (Baltimore: Johns Hopkins University Press, 1953), 101–37. Stillinger, *"Hoodwinking,"* 82; the essay first appeared in 1961. Stuart Sperry mediates the extremes by describing a mode of "wish-fulfillment," a conscious fiction seasoned with a sophisticated pleasure in blatant conventions

and extravagant artifice (*Keats the Poet,* chapter 8). See also my *Questioning Presence: Wordsworth, Keats, and the Interrogative Modes of Romantic Poetry* (Ithaca: Cornell University Press, 1986) on the "pro and con" of romance poetics (288–96). When Stillinger gave an entire book to the poem, the subtitle he chose was *The Multiples of Complex Literary Transaction.*

4 HK.2.21.5. Subsequent MS citations are to page only. Keats completed a draft in January; he revised in September, and a further revision, canceling some of the September work and recovering some of January's, was the basis for *1820.* For a careful, expert account, see Stillinger, *Reading,* 17–32, and *P* 626–29.

5 In the 1790s, Ann Radcliffe earned unheard of advances, £500 plus, for her gothic novels.

6 *The Tempest* Act 3, scene 3 (Shakespeare's *Dramatic Works,* 1:45), and Keats's manuscript, pp. 13–14.

7 [Scott], Baldwin's *London Magazine* 2 (September 1820) 318–19.

8 OED gives Keats this credit. The comparative degree here becomes a superlative in *To Sleep* ("O soothest sleep"); HK1.53.266 (see also *K* 253).

9 "Twinkle, twinkle, little star" begins Jane Taylor's rhyme, *The Star* (*Poems for the Nursery,* 1806, 100 editions following). An author on Taylor & Hessey's list, she was known to Keats, who gave her *Essays in Rhyme* to his sister in September 1817 (*L* 1:155).

10 From Woodhouse's copy of Keats's now lost first version, HK3.2.225–26.

11 Keats to Woodhouse, 18 December 1818; HK1.41.163; *L* 1:410, 412.

12 Taylor to Woodhouse, 25 September 1819; *KC* 1:96–97.

13 *PL* 2.587–89, 10.697–98; *1808* 1:45, 2:130 (Lau 93, 166).

14 Wasserman writes nicely about the way Keats's shift from verbs into adjectival "quality of being" moves the lovers "outside of time and activity" (*Finer Tone,* 125).

15 Woodhouse to Taylor, 31 August 1819 (*KC* 1:91). Keats read *Don Juan* when it first came out, in the summer of 1819.

16 Keats's sonnet first appeared in Leigh Hunt's new weekly journal *The Indicator* 38 (28 June 1820) 304). This weekly was launched as a sociable miscellany, in contrast to the news-driven *Examiner.* I use Keats's 1819 letter-text (HK1.53.247), for its proximity to his drafts of *La belle dame,* and the completion of *The Eve of St. Agnes.*

17 *PL* 11.130–33; *1808* 2:149 (Lau 168).

18 I use the letter-text (HK1.53.253–55) for its compositional proximity to the *Dream-sonnet* and *The Eve of St. Agnes.* The one published in *The Indicator* (10 May 1820 [31:246–48]) has variants, the most compelling one barbed for satire: "wretched wight" for "Knight at arms." The version in *1848* (2:268–70), based on the letter-draft, was long the standard.

19 See Karen Swann, "Harassing the Muse," in *Romanticism and Feminism,* ed. Anne Mellor (Bloomington and Indianapolis: Indiana University Press, 1988). For the aura of this back-story, see my *Questioning Presence* and my essay in *Approaches to Teaching Keats's Poetry,* ed. Walter H. Evart and Jack W. Rhodes (New York: MLA, 1991).

20 Part.1.Sec. 3.Mem.2.Subs.4: *Symptomes of Women's Melancholy*, 10th edition (London: Vernor and Hood &c, 1804), 302.

21 Sidney Colvin, *John Keats* (New York: Harper and Brothers, 1887), 164.

7 REFORMING THE SONNET AND FORMING THE *ODES* OF SPRING 1819: *PSYCHE; NIGHTINGALE; GRECIAN URN; MELANCHOLY; INDOLENCE*

1 HK1.52.270–71 (see also *K* 254–5).

2 See John Hollander on loosening "rhyming's chains without actually breaking them or having them slip off" (*Melodious Guile: Fictive Pattern in Poetic Language* [New Haven: Yale University Press, 1988], 94). *Poesy* is set into the *d*-chord (*be* and the triple rhyme *be free*) but is weak at best.

3 This form is noted by Bate (*Keats*, 495–97), with credit to H. W. Garrod and M. R. Ridley. I build on this work in "Keats's Thinking in Sonnets," *Front Porch Journal* (2012).

4 13 March 1818; HK1.23.81 (see also *K* 114).

5 Coleridge, *Biographia Literaria* (1817), 2:16. Foundational work on Keats's odes at this pitch of poetic density and cognitive intensity includes Cleanth Brooks (*The Well Wrought Urn* [San Diego: Harcourt Brace Jovanovich, 1947]), Jack Stillinger, "Imagination and Reality in the Odes" (in *"Hoodwinking"*), David Perkins (*The Quest for Permanence: The Symbolism of Wordsworth, Shelley, and Keats* [Cambridge, MA: Harvard University Press), and Stuart Sperry ("Romantic Irony and the Great Odes," in *Keats the Poet*).

6 Keats's *Paradise Lost* (*1808* 2:4; *K* 235).

7 The odes in *1820* follow the title-romances not as a distinct unit but as a frame in "Other Poems": *Nightingale, Grecian Urn*, and *Psyche* leading off, *Autumn* and *Melancholy* at the end, before the fragment of *Hyperion. Ode on Indolence* was first published in *1848*.

8 HK1:53.270, 267 (all spelling *sic*); *The Metamorphosis, or Golden Ass of Apuleius* was first translated into English in 1566 (Books V–VI). Keats knew this well, and also a six-canto romance in Spenserian stanzas based on it, Mary Tighe's *Psyche* (1805/16).

9 Keats would know the entry in Lemprière's *Classical Dictionary*: "Psyche: The word signifies *the soul*... Psyche is generally represented with the wings of a butterfly, to imitate the lightness of the soul, of which the butterfly is a symbol."

10 *PL* 4.325–26, 4.736–91. Keats underlined 4.325–26 (*1808* 1:94; Lau 113).

11 See HK1.53.268; *P* 365.

12 Letter, 3 May 1818, *K* 127–28; *Hamlet* 3.1.62–63.

13 The first four listings in the OED (1756–1818) are medical diagnoses of "home-sickness."

14 Hazlitt, "Character of Mr. Wordsworth's New Poem, *The Excursion*," *Examiner* (21 August 1814) 541.

15 "Mr Kean," *Champion*, 21 December 1817 (*K* 74–75). I think Hazlitt read this review and remembered it in the lecture attended by Keats a few weeks on,

when he said of Shakespeare, "His language is hieroglyphical. It translates thoughts into visible images" (*Lectures on the English Poets* [London: Taylor & Hessey, 1818], 107). And I think Shelley remembered both when he wrote in *A Defence of Poetry* that poets are the only artists to use "language as the hieroglyphic of their thoughts" (*Essays* [London: Edward Moxon, 1841], 1:9).

16 *1808* 1:23 (Lau 87).

17 HK1.8.26. See also *L* 1:146 (Rollins hyphenates "over-wrought"; Keats does not). This playfully abject letter to his publishers begins in a riot of puns and parodies.

18 Vol. IV, No. 15 (January 1820), 639. Charles Brown's copy, probably made from Keats's (lost) original, is close to the *Annals* text in the capital Bs and Ts, and no quotation marks.

19 I don't accept Rollins's routinely credited sober emendation to {hie}*rogue*glyphics (*L* 2:247).

20 William Empson, *Seven Types of Ambiguity* (1927; 2nd rev. edition, Cleveland: World Publishing, 1964), 243.

21 *K* 369, citing the autograph MS in the R. H. Taylor Collection, Princeton University Library.

22 Sperry, *Keats the Poet*, 282–83.

23 The manuscript in Keats's hand at Princeton Library has "Mistress" in stanza 2, kin to capital-M Melancholy.

24 This nice audit is Garrett Stewart's, *CCK* 145, with a nod to Herbert F. Tucker (*Modern Language Quarterly* 1997).

25 Autograph manuscript, Albert A. Berg Collection, New York Public Library; see *P* 375n.

26 HK1.53.230–31 (see also *K* 241–42); "is grows" slips a present-tense verb in place of *it*.

27 19 February 1818; signed autograph letter, Taylor Collection, Princeton University (*K* 105–12).

28 Jesus's advice about trusting in God's providence (KJB: Matthew 6:26–29). My text for the *Ode* is the first publication, *1848* 2:276–78.

29 "spinning-machine . . . having a continuous action, the processes of drawing, twisting, and winding being carried on simultaneously." OED's earliest listing of this sense is 1825 – close enough, I think, for Keats to have picked up in his reading about weaver-politics.

8 WRITHING, WREATHING, WRITING *LAMIA*

1 *PL* 9.516–17; *1808* 2:89 (Lau 156).

2 *1808* 1:95 (Lau 113). W. T. Arnold is only the first to note Keats's "fondness for the word 'Gordian'" (*Poetical Works of John Keats* [London: Kegan Paul, Trench, 1884], xxxiii).

3 I quote from *1848* 1:175–76. See also *L* 2:341–42, *K* 191–92; there are no verbal variants.

4 Ariadne gave Theseus the clue for escaping Crete's labyrinth, where he was imprisoned, to be devoured by its minotaur. Expecting his pledge of love, she was soon abandoned.

5 Sperry, *Keats the Poet*, 296–300.

6 On the optics, see David Perkins's smart census (*Quest for Permanence*, 272–74); on labyrinths, optic implications, and the interpretive maze, see Gene Bernstein, "Keats's 'Lamia': The Sense of a Non-Ending," *Papers on Language and Literature* 15 (1979) 175–92. On all this, in subtlest verbal weavings, see Stewart's Lamian tour de force: "*Lamia* and the Language of Metamorphosis," *SiR* 15 (1976) 3–41.

7 For this unusual transitive verb, meaning *hide* (as if behind blinds), the OED cites this very text.

8 *Centaine* is an obsolete word for "a company of one hundred." "Of bad lines a Centaine dose / Is sure enough," Keats self-mockingly winds up his verse-letter to Reynolds (*K* 121).

9 Hazlitt, about the passage in *Excursion* Book IV that Keats loved; *Examiner* (28 August 1814) 556.

10 Lemprière's *Dictionary* describes Apollonius as "well skilled in the secret arts of magic," especially over "the populace."

11 Colvin, *Keats*, 408; Sperry, *Keats the Poet*, 292; Bate, *Keats*, 547; Bernstein, "Keats's 'Lamia'"; Stewart, "*Lamia* and the Language of Metamorphosis," 4.

12 *1820* 45–46. Partition 3 (*Love-Melancholy*), Section 2, Member 1, Substratum 1: *Heroical Love causing Melancholy. His Pedigree, Power and Extent* (9th edn. [London, 1800] 2: 196–97).

9 FALLING IN FALL 1819: *THE FALL OF HYPERION* AND *TO AUTUMN*

1 This title derives from Woodhouse's transcript. Charles Brown's *Life of Keats* describes Keats "remodelling... 'Hyperion' into a Vision" (*KC* 2:72), and Milnes relied on this chronology for *1848* (1:244). But with *Another Version*, he put "priority" in question (3–4), even as he remembered enough from Brown to supply an internal title, *A Vision*. W. M. Rossetti's edition (London: Edward Moxon, 1871) recast *Another* into *An Earlier* (274) and other editors followed: William T. Arnold (1884, p. 312); H. Buxton Forman (1884), confidently presenting "The First Version" (315) set right after *Hyperion*, as if its deep archaeology. After Colvin's *Keats* (1887) painstakingly corrected the error (183, 226–27), Forman amended his subtitling in his five-volume *Complete Works* of 1901 to "An Attempt made at the end of 1819 to reconstruct the Poem" and to give (with a nod to Woodhouse) the title we now use, *The Fall of Hyperion, A Dream* (3:167).

2 Woodhouse's manuscript has a note that Keats "seems to have intended" to cancel a redundant 184–210. Milnes' *Version* uses this advice but later editors keep it all.

3 "On Poetry in General," in *Lectures on the English Poets* (London: Taylor & Hessey, 1818), 34–36.
4 *Ibid.*, 34–35.
5 HK1.64.11, the only autograph of 2.1–6. Keats, having phrased *Though it blows*, wrote *though the trees*. Editors always say this must be *through* (e.g., *L* 2:171); but Keats's liking of fine sound let his ear guide his hand to this repetition.
6 *Purgatorio* 9:86–87; Henry Cary's translation, which Keats owned.
7 *K* 225; see Lau 72 for the page-image.
8 Keats underscored the lines at the end of *Paradise Lost*, in which the angel-squad sent to torch Eden glide "as evening mist / Risen from a river o'er the marish glides, / And gathers ground fast at the labourer's heel" (12.629–31); see *1808* 2:182 (Lau 175). In the Keatsian archive of mists are the dark passages, after the Chamber of Maiden-Thought falls away, that leave us "in a Mist . . . We feel the 'burden of the Mystery'" (*K* 130), and the mist that invades Hyperion's lucent empire.
9 Geoffrey Hartman, "Poem and Ideology: Keats's 'To Autumn'" (1973), in *The Fate of Reading* (University of Chicago Press, 1975), 130.
10 Sperry, *Keats the Poet*, 284.
11 Keats's early draft HK2.27.2 (see *P* 477). For the springtime cues, see Hartman, "Poem and Ideology," 128.
12 29 October 1817; HK1.14.47 (see also *L* 1:173). Chris Rovee alerted me to the coining.

10 LATE POEMS & LASTING KEATS

1 Keats, "SONNET," *Examiner* (23 February 1817) 124, col. 2, about a month before *Poems* appeared.
2 19 October 1819, HK1.67.325 (*K* 277). Keats underlined all of the lovely report that ends in these lines (*Dramatic Works* 1:42–43), a sympathy with lovelorn dreamers from Endymion on.
3 3.2.Member 3: "*Symptoms or signs of Love-Melancholy, in Body, Mind, good, bad &c.*" Just two Members on from the one on which *Lamia* draws, this passage suggests the proximity in Keats's range of attention of a fable of fatal enchantment and a pleasures in misogynist satire. 9th edn., 2:314.
4 I follow *P*, the text of Keats's fair copy.
5 Milnes first used this title in *1848* (2:306), with some editorial changes to the manuscript text.
6 Keats's companion Joseph Severn relayed this to their friend Haslam, *KC* 1: 273 (1 June 1823). Leigh Hunt tells this deathbed story of Keats's dictated epitaph (a story he too received from Severn) in *Lord Byron* (268).
7 Stanley Plumly nicely meditates on the contingency of *was*, potentially transformable in the future (153).
8 "Thoughts on Criticism, by a Critic," *Cornhill Magazine* 34 (1876) 558.
9 *Edinburgh Review* 90 Article III (October 1849) 428.
10 *William Allingham: A Diary, 1824–1889* (London: Macmillan, 1907), 205.

11 A. & W. Galignani's Paris edition was hard to come by in England. In 1840 William Smith put out a *Poetical Works* in London; 1846 saw a New York edition from Wiley & Putnam.

12 *Miscellanies*, ed. Robert Baldwin Ross (London: Methuen, 1908), 249.

13 *A Room of One's Own* (1929; Harcourt, Brace, 1957), 102, 107, citing Coleridge's *Table Talk* for 1 September 1832.

14 "Critical Cross-Dressing: Male Feminists and the Woman of the Year," *Raritan* 3.2 (1983) 147, and *K* 129.

15 Homans, *Women Writers and Poetic Identity* (Princeton University Press, 1980) 240n25, 251n15; Rich, "Three Conversations," in *Adrienne Rich's Poetry*, ed. Barbara Charlesworth Gelpi and Albert Gelpi (New York and London: W. W. Norton & Co., 1975), 115, citing Chodorow's *Family Structure and Feminine Personality*. Anne Mellor described the "anti-masculine conception of identity" evolving in this conversation (*Romanticism and Gender* [New York and London: Routledge, 1993], 174).

16 "Visionary Anger," *Ms.* 11 (July 1973), 171–72.

17 Homans, "Keats Reading Women, Women Reading Keats," *SiR* 29 (1990) 343.

18 In *Victorian Keats: Manliness, Sexuality, and Desire* (Houndmills and New York: Palgrave, 2002), especially his great chapter on "Keats's 'Posthumous Life'" (11–51), James Najarian gives a fresh review, from the angle of homoerotic reception, to my first foray into Keats and gender criticism ("Feminizing Keats," in *Critical Essays on John Keats*, ed. Hermione de Almeida [Boston, MA: G. K. Hall and Company, 1990]).

19 "Intellectual History and the Return of Literature," *American Historical Review* 94 (1989) 598. I thank Jack Stillinger for pointing me to this essay.

Further reading

EDITIONS

Poems (London: C. & J. Ollier, 1817), *Endymion* (London: Taylor & Hessey, 1818), and *Lamia, Isabella, The Eve of St. Agnes, and Other Poems* (London: Taylor & Hessey, 1820) are available on google books.

The Poems of John Keats, ed. Jack Stillinger. Cambridge, MA: Harvard University Press, 1978; concordance, ed. Noah Comet: www.rc.umd.edu/reference/keatsconcordance/.

The Letters of John Keats, 1814–1821, ed. Hyder E. Rollins. 2 vols. Cambridge, MA: Harvard University Press, 1958; David Pollard, *A KWIC Concordance to the Letters of John Keats*. Hove: Geraldson Imprints, 1989.

The Letters of John Keats, ed. Robert Gittings, rev. John Mee. Oxford University Press, 2002.

John Keats: A Longman Cultural Edition, ed. Susan J. Wolfson. London: Longman, 2006.

CHIEF BIOGRAPHIES (CHRONOLOGICAL)

Hunt, Leigh. "Mr. Keats," in *Lord Byron and Some of His Contemporaries*. 2 vols. London: Henry Colburn, 1828.

Milnes, Richard M. *Life, Letters, and Literary Remains, of John Keats*. London: Edward Moxon, 1848.

Colvin, Sidney. *John Keats: His Life and Poetry, his Friends, Critics, and After-Fame*. London: Macmillan, 1917.

Lowell, Amy. *John Keats*. 2 vols. Boston, MA, and New York: Houghton Mifflin Co., 1925.

Bate, Walter Jackson. *John Keats*. Cambridge, MA: Harvard University Press, 1963.

Hirst, Wolf Z. *John Keats*. Boston, MA: Twayne, 1981.

Clark, Tom. *Junkets on a Sad Planet*. Santa Rosa: Black Sparrow Press, 1994. A biography in poems.

Motion, Andrew. *Keats*. New York: Farrar, Straus and Giroux, 1997.

Plumly, Stanley. *Posthumous Keats*. New York: W. W. Norton, 2008.

    The Immortal Evening. New York: W. W. Norton, 2014.

Roe, Nicholas. *John Keats: A New Life*. New Haven: Yale University Press, 2012.

LIFETIME REVIEWS, EARLY RECEPTION, POSTHUMOUS FAME

Ford, George H. *Keats and the Victorians ... 1821–1895*. New Haven: Yale University Press, 1944.

Marquess, William H. *Lives of the Poet: The First Century of Keats Biography*. University Park and London: Pennsylvania State University Press, 1985.

Matthews, G. M., ed. *Keats: The Critical Heritage*. New York: Barnes & Noble, 1971.

REFERENCES AND BIBLIOGRAPHIES (CHRONOLOGICAL)

The Keats Circle: Letters and Papers, ed. Hyder E. Rollins. 2 vols. Cambridge, MA: Harvard University Press, 1965.

The Romantics and Their Contemporaries, ed. Susan J. Wolfson and Peter J. Manning, vol. 2a of *Longman Anthology of British Literature*, 5th edition. London: Longman, 2012.

SOME CRITICAL STUDIES

Books

Barnard, John. *John Keats*. Cambridge University Press, 1987.

Bennett, Andrew. *Keats, Narrative and Audience: The Posthumous Life of Writing*. Cambridge University Press, 1994.

Blades, John. *John Keats: The Poems*. Houndmills and New York: Palgrave, 2002.

Cox, Jeffrey. *Poetry and Politics in the Cockney School*. Cambridge University Press, 1998.

Dickstein, Morris. *Keats and His Poetry*. University of Chicago Press, 1971.

Ende, Stuart. *Keats and the Sublime*. New Haven: Yale University Press, 1976.

Jones, John. *John Keats's Dream of Truth*. London: Chatto and Windus, 1969.

Lau, Beth. *Keats's Paradise Lost*. Gainesville: University Press of Florida, 1998.

Levinson, Marjorie. *Keats's Life of Allegory: The Origins of a Style*. New York and Oxford: Basil Blackwell, 1988.

Najarian, James. *Victorian Keats: Manliness, Sexuality, and Desire*. Houndmills and New York: Palgrave, 2002.

Ricks, Christopher. *Keats and Embarrassment*. Oxford University Press, 1976.

Roe, Nicholas. *John Keats and the Culture of Dissent*. Oxford: Clarendon Press, 1997.

Scott, Grant F. *The Sculpted Word: Keats, Ekphrasis, and the Visual Arts*. Hanover: University Press of New England, 1999.

Sperry, Stuart M. *Keats the Poet*. Princeton University Press, 1973.

Stillinger, Jack. *"The Hoodwinking of Madeline" and Other Essays on Keats's Poems*. Urbana: University of Illinois Press, 1971.

  Reading The Eve of St. Agnes. Oxford University Press, 1999.

Vendler, Helen. *The Odes of John Keats*. Cambridge, MA: Harvard University Press, 1983.

Waldoff, Leon. *Keats and the Silent Work of Imagination*. Urbana: University of
Illinois Press, 1985.

Walker, Carol Kyros. *Walking North With Keats*. New Haven: Yale University
Press, 1992.

Watkins, Daniel. *Keats's Poetry and the Politics of the Imagination*. Rutherford, NJ:
Farleigh Dickinson University Press, 1989.

ARTICLES, CHAPTERS, BOOKS WITH RELEVANT CHAPTERS

KSJ: *Keats–Shelley Journal* / *SiR*: *Studies in Romanticism*

Barnard, John. "Keats's Letters," in *CCK*.

Bernstein, Gene. "Keats's 'Lamia': The Sense of a Non-Ending," *Papers on Language and Literature* 15 (1979) 175–92 – the title playing off of Frank Kermode's
The Sense of an Ending.

Bewell, Alan. "The Political Implication of Keats's Classicist Aesthetics," *SiR* 25
(1986) 221–30.

Bloom, Harold. "Keats and the Embarrassments of Poetic Tradition," in *The
Ringers in the Tower*. University of Chicago Press, 1971.

Bostetter, Edward E. "Keats," in *The Romantic Ventriloquists*. 1963; rev. edition
Seattle: University of Washington Press, 1975.

Bromwich, David. "Keats," in *Hazlitt: The Mind of a Critic*. Oxford University
Press, 1983.

"Keats's Radicalism," *SiR* 25 (1986) 197–210.

Brooks, Cleanth. "Keats's Sylvan Historian: History without Footnotes" (1944),
in *The Well Wrought Urn*. San Diego: Harcourt Brace Jovanovich, 1947.

Burke, Kenneth. "Symbolic Action in a Poem by Keats," *Accent* 4 (1943); rpt. *A
Grammar of Motives*. Cleveland: World, 1962, 447–63.

Curran, Stuart. *Poetic Form and British Romanticism*. Oxford University Press,
1986.

Dickstein, Morris. "Keats and Politics," *SiR* 25 (1986) 175–81.

Fry, Paul. "History, Existence, and 'To Autumn,'" *SiR* 25 (1986) 211–19.

Hartman, Geoffrey. "Poem and Ideology: Keats's 'To Autumn'" (1973) and "Spectral Symbolism and Authorial Self in Keats's *Hyperion*" (1974), in *The Fate of
Reading*. University of Chicago Press, 1975.

"Reading Aright: Keats's *Ode to Psyche*," in *Centre and Labyrinth*, ed. Eleanor
Cook &c. University of Toronto Press, 1983, 210–26.

Homans, Margaret. "Keats Reading Women, Women Reading Keats," *SiR* 29
(1990) 341–70.

Kandl, John. "Leigh Hunt's *Examiner* and the Construction of a Public 'John
Keats,'" *KSJ* 44 (1995) 84–101.

"The Politics of Keats's Early Poetry," in *CCK*.

Keach, William. "Byron Reads Keats," in *CCK*.

"The Politics of Rhyme," in *Arbitrary Power*. Princeton University Press, 2004
(based on "Cockney Couplets," *SiR* 25 [1986]182–96).

Kelley, Theresa M. "Keats and 'Ekphrasis'," in *CCK*.

Kern, Robert. "Keats and the Problem of Romance," *Philological Quarterly* 58 (1979) 171–91.

Kucich, Greg. *Keats, Shelley, and Romantic Spenserianism*. University Park and London: Pennsylvania State University Press, 1991.
  "Keats and English Poetry," in *CCK*.

Levinson, Marjorie. "The Dependent Fragment: 'Hyperion' and 'The Fall of Hyperion,'" in *The Romantic Fragment Poem*. Chapel Hill: University of North Carolina Press, 1986.

Luke, David. "Keats's Letters: Fragments of an Aesthetic of Fragments," *Genre* 2 (1978) 209–26.

Manning, Peter J. "Reading and Ravishing: The 'Ode on a Grecian Urn,'" in *Approaches to Teaching Keats's Poetry*, ed. Walter H. Evert and Jack W. Rhodes. New York: Modern Language Association, 1991, 131–36.

McGann, Jerome J. "Keats and the Historical Method in Literary Criticism" (1979), in *The Beauty of Inflections*, 1985; Oxford: Clarendon Press, 1988.

Mellor, Anne. "Keats and the Complexities of Gender," in *CCK*. See also *Romanticism and Gender*. New York and London: Routledge, 1993.

Newey, Vincent. "*Hyperion, The Fall of Hyperion*, and Keats's Epic Ambitions," in *CCK*.

Perkins, David. "Keats: The Uncertainties of Vision," in *The Quest for Permanence: The Symbolism of Wordsworth, Shelley, and Keats*. Cambridge, MA: Harvard University Press, 1959. 217–57.

Rajan, Tilottama. *Dark Interpreter: The Discourse of Romanticism*. Ithaca: Cornell University Press, 1980.

Richardson, Alan. "Keats and Romantic Science," in *CCK*.

Ricks, Christopher. "Keats's Sources, Keats's Allusions," in *CCK*.

Rovee, Christopher. "Trashing Keats," *ELH* 75 (2008) 993–1022.

Rzepka, Charles J. "Keats: Watcher and Witness," in *The Self as Mind*. Cambridge, MA: Harvard University Press, 1986.

Sheats, Paul. "Stylistic Discipline in The Fall of Hyperion," *KSJ* 17 (1968) 75–88.
  "Keats and the Ode," in *CCK*.

Stewart, Garrett. "*Lamia* and the Language of Metamorphosis," *SiR* 15 (1976) 3–40. "Keats and Language," in *CCK*.

Stillinger, Jack. "The 'Story' of Keats," in *CCK*.

Swann, Karen. "*Endymion*'s Beautiful Dreamers," in *CCK*.
  "Harassing the Muse," in *Romanticism and Feminism*, ed. Anne Mellor. Bloomington and Indianapolis: Indiana University Press, 1988; on *La belle dame*.
  "The Strange Time of Reading," *European Romantic Review* 9 (1998) 275–82.

Vendler, Helen. "John Keats: Perfecting the Sonnet," in *Coming of Age as a Poet*. Cambridge, MA: Harvard University Press, 2003.

Vogler, Thomas. *Preludes to Vision: The Epic Venture*. Berkeley and Los Angeles: University of California Press, 1971.

Wu, Duncan. "Keats and the 'Cockney School,'" in *CCK*.

Several of my books are involved with Keats: *The Questioning Presence: Wordsworth, Keats, and the Interrogative Modes of Romantic Poetry* (Ithaca: Cornell University Press, 1986), *Formal Charges: The Shaping of Poetry in British Romanticism* (Palo Alto: Stanford University Press, 1997; with a chapter on Keats's last poems), and *Borderlines: The Shiftings of Gender in British Romanticism* (Palo Alto: Stanford University Press, 2006), with two chapters on Keats's gendered writing; on "gendering Keats" (manly, unmanly, feminine, effeminate, androgynist, feminist). I've also edited *The Cambridge Companion to John Keats* (Cambridge University Press, 2001), which has my chapter on the late lyrics. I have chapters in *The Cambridge Companion to English Poets* (Cambridge University Press, 2011), *Keats and History* (Cambridge University Press, 2000; on Shelley's Adonais on Keats's reputation), and "The New Poetries," in *The Cambridge History of English Romantic Literature* (Cambridge University Press, 2009). My other essays include "Keats the Letter-Writer: Epistolary Poetics," *Romanticism Past and Present* 6 (1982); "What's Wrong with Formalist Criticism?," *Studies in Romanticism* 37 (1998); "The Know of Not to Know It: Teaching Keats's *Ode on a Grecian Urn*", *Praxis* (October 2003), www.rc.umd.edu/praxis; "Keats's Thinking in Sonnets," *Front Porch Journal* (2012); "Yeats's Latent Keats / Keats Latent Yeats" (forthcoming).

My work as textual and interpretive editor, and as teacher, is reflected in *John Keats: A Longman Cultural Edition* (New York: Pearson, 2007) and the unit on Keats in *The Longman Anthology of British Literature: The Romantics and Their Contemporaries* (New York: Pearson, 1998–2012).

Index

Keats's poetical works are indexed under *title* or "well-known first words."

Not indexed: page runs synonymous with chapters on a major work; Keats in Context; Further Reading; incidental information in the Notes.

Printed in the United States
By Bookmasters